PRAISE FOR JOHN ROSSMAN
AND *THINK LIKE AMAZON*

In today's landscape, you're either competing with Amazon or figuring out how to leverage it. Either way, you'd better understand its mindset, which drives how it operates. Having worked at Amazon in its early years, I can attest that this book definitely captures the essence and unwavering principles that make Amazon like no other company.

> —Kirk Beardsley, EVP of Digital at Nordstrom and former
> Director of Business Development at Amazon

Use the tools in this book to solve the seemingly impossible challenges your business faces today, and your customers will thank you with their loyalty and wallets.

> —James Thomson, partner at Buy Box Experts and former
> head of Amazon Services

This book provides innovators with a powerful framework to lead in today's age of digital disruption and transformation. Whether your organization is a single-person startup or a member of the Fortune 500, John Rossman's 50½ ideas will empower executives and their teams to rethink their business, obsess over customers, and win in the digital era.

> —Mark Bertolini, former Chairman and CEO of Aetna Inc.

Reading *Think Like Amazon* is like having Jeff Bezos advise me. This is the best strategy and tactics book I have read in a long time.

> —Eric Martinez, Founder and CEO of Modjoul and
> former EVP at AIG

Rossman shares the deep insights only an Amazon insider with a front-row seat to Jeff Bezos could uncover. From culture, strategy, business, and technology, this is a bible for transforming any organization for the digital era. *Think Like Amazon* is a must-read for board members, executives, and the entire organization.

> —R "Ray" Wang, Founder and Chairman of Constellation
> Research, Inc., and author of *Disrupting Digital Business*

John Rossman has once again made complex business topics approachable. In *Think Like Amazon*, he reveals an insider's perspective of the core operating principles of one of the world's most iconic and highly valued companies and translated them into 50 clear lessons that any business leader can use and immediately apply. Perhaps the most useful is the ½ idea with which he challenges the reader. Relevant, timely, and easy to consume.

> —Gregg Garrett, CEO of CGS Advisors, former Chief
> Strategy Officer of Volkswagen North America, and
> author of *Competing in the Connecting World*

Think Like Amazon offers insights for companies faced with the challenge of crossing the innovation chasm. It offers a concrete and proven methodology that has been employed by Amazon to innovate in an effective way to overcome the rising antibodies in corporations that resist change. Highly recommended for anyone trying to understand disruptive technology and how it can change innovation with the right processes and strategy.

> —Michael J.T. Steep, Executive Director of the Digital
> Cities Program at Stanford Global Projects and
> former SVP at Xerox PARC

An inspiring and thought-provoking book that provides a window into one of the great companies and one of the great leaders of our time. The 50½ ideas are precious insights into the relentless pursuit of a frictionless customer experience that is fundamental to becoming a digital leader—and to be the disrupter instead of the disrupted!

> —Dick Hyatt, Founder and CEO of Decisiv

John Rossman has demonstrated his deep understanding of how Jeff Bezos and the Amazon team have curated a repeatable and methodical approach to becoming the preeminent customer-obsessed company to win in the digital era. In *Think Like Amazon*, John successfully outlines what business leaders can learn from Amazon's industry-leading model and how they can apply these learnings to digitally transform their own companies. First and foremost is a reluctance to rely on old business models and past successes to define the future road map. It also emphasizes how important a passion for embracing new ways of thinking is to succeed in today's highly disruptive and turbulent global economy. Necessary reading for all technology and business executives who are looking to propel their businesses forward in the next era of the digital economy.

—Hunter Muller, President and CEO of HMG Strategy

John Rossman's ability to take Amazon's extraordinary processes and translate them into strategies we can use is an extraordinary feat. Packed with actionable, clear ideas, chapter after chapter had me scribbling notes on habits I need to "test adopt" immediately.

—Brendan McSheffrey, Chief Strategist at BMNT Partners

Think Like Amazon provides digestible and actionable ideas that are essential for operating, thriving, and winning customers in the digital economy. More important, these have been proven at Amazon and are applicable to all.

—Beth Devin, head of Innovation Network and
Emerging Technology at Citi Ventures

Packed with razor-sharp insights and simple but profound ideas. John blends experience, expertise, and wisdom to create a practical playbook for those of us who are obsessed, relentless, and couldn't care less about joining a country club.

—Nathan Robinson, CEO of The Leadership Network

In *Think Like Amazon*, John tells a compelling story of strong leadership with the benefit of an insider's perspective. CEOs and Boards can learn so much about how vital the digital tone at the top is to the future of business.

—Bob Zukis, CEO of Digital Directors Network

John Rossman continues to explore fresh new ways and approaches to evolve businesses and whole industries as we plunge forward into the next decade. *Think Like Amazon* is a must-read.

—Bill Roberti, former CEO of Brooks Brothers and
Managing Director of Alvarez and Marsal

Think Like Amazon should be on the must-read list of every entrepreneur and, frankly, anyone working for a business interested in staying relevant. John simply and eloquently highlights fundamental principles necessary to grow a digital business in today's rapidly evolving environment.

—Scott Drucker, DMD, MS, Cofounder and
President of SupplyClinic

John Rossman presents a vital read for today's corporate leadership. This is especially true for those who wish to be relevant tomorrow. Commercial enterprises are subject to strong winds of change, and only those operating with a clear mission and vision will survive. Rossman doesn't give the reader pat answers about how to do things. Rather, he leads the reader to think differently. He guides the reader into adopting a customer-obsessed culture, advocating responsibility and ownership to solve problems.

—Major General (Ret.) Charles R. Henry, Founder and
former (first) Commander of the Defense Contract
Management Agency

think like
amazon

50½ IDEAS TO BECOME A
DIGITAL LEADER

John Rossman

Mc
Graw
Hill

NEW YORK   CHICAGO   SAN FRANCISCO
ATHENS   LONDON   MADRID
MEXICO CITY   MILAN   NEW DELHI
SINGAPORE   SYDNEY   TORONTO

1 2 3 4 5 6 7 8 9   LCR   24 23 22 21 20 19

ISBN 978-1-260-45549-6
MHID   1-260-45549-1

e-ISBN 978-1-260-45550-2
e-MHID   1-260-45550-5

McGraw-Hill Education books are available at special quantity discounts to use as premiums and sales promotions or for use in corporate training programs. To contact a representative, please visit the Contact Us pages at www.mhprofessional.com.

CONTENTS

Part II
Strategy

Part III
Business and Technology

Part IV
Approach and Execution

INTRODUCTION:
WHAT WOULD JEFF DO?

In the 1990s, the acronym WWJD?—"What would Jesus do?"—began appearing on bumper stickers and T-shirts around the United States. The variations weren't far behind. Scientists asked, "What would Darwin do?" Deadheads asked, "What would Jerry do?" The whole concept went so far afield that I once saw a sticker that read, "What would Atticus Finch do?" Anyway, you get the picture.

For the last five years, my clients and the readers of my two previous books have asked repeatedly their own version of this question: "What would Jeff do?" Of course, when people ask me, "WWJD?" they're really asking questions like these: "What does 'being digital' mean?" "How do I avoid disruption?" "Will Amazon enter this business or geography?" "How does Amazon get these types of results?" "Would Amazon be interested in partnering with me?" "Would Amazon be interested in acquiring our company?" "How do I make my function as easy as shopping at Amazon?" There are hundreds of questions in this vein, but they can all be boiled down to "What would Jeff do?"

What makes me think I can answer any of those questions? Come to think of it, what makes me think I can write a book outlining 50½ ideas to help you compete in the digital era? Since leaving Amazon in late 2005, I've spent much of my time answering these types of questions for clients in many industries, with different objectives, in a host of scenarios. But the real secret to answering "What would Jeff do?" is recognizing that Jeff Bezos and Amazon have a remarkably consistent way of approaching and meeting challenges, operating their business and technology, and thinking about new ideas, markets, and growth.

In other words, there is a playbook or system of beliefs and approaches for how they get results and think about their business. If you've been paying attention, you too can figure out how to think like Amazon. The wide set of scenarios and examples in *Think Like Amazon* may not directly answer your specific question, but by understanding Jeff's general world view, you can better apply his insights and principles to your circumstances.

THE BEST OFFENSE IS MORE OFFENSE

Why will 80 percent of the Fortune 1000 be replaced over the next 10 years? Why is "disruption" a real threat? At the risk of answering a complex question with an overly simple answer, here is my answer. First, companies fall in love with their prior thinking, models, and approaches; and second, change is really hard. The concept of "transformation" sounds great, but in reality, it is incredibly elusive. More often than not, this grand idea of organizational and business revitalization tends to materialize as short-term projects and energy, not the creation of lasting change or long-term value creation.

"Companies have short life spans, and Amazon will be disrupted one day," Bezos said in a 2013 interview. "I don't worry about it because I know it is inevitable. Companies come and go. Companies that are the shiniest and most important of any era, and you just wait a couple of decades and they are gone. I would love for it [Amazon's disruption] to be after I'm dead."[1]

Companies that don't let old models and past successes define who they are retain the potential to remain leaders and define the next era, and they are able to transition and grow through these turbulent times. Fostering and maintaining that potential requires world-class mental agility. So instead of resting on the momentum of its existing businesses, which are still growing, and trying to drive to improved profitability, Amazon is investing today in initiatives that might not pay back for years, if ever.

The acquisition of PillPack by Amazon in June 2018 is an example of "more offense." PillPack sorts a customer's prescribed medications by the dose and delivers them to the customer's door, implenting a customer-centric approach to both packaging and delivery. If you have many medications and either don't want to or are limited in your ability to physically get to a pharmacy, PillPack is a vast improvement on how every other pharmacy operates. Amazon doesn't need to enter the healthcare market now, but the company has taken this relatively small step and will figure out the business and how to leverage PillPack's capabilities and the state licenses to deliver pharmaceutical items (potential Whole Foods pharmacies?) as part of an overall strategy, with many angles and business models.

WHY SHOULD I THINK LIKE AMAZON?

Amazon Web Services (AWS) is the biggest of the "on-demand" cloud computing companies. It was also the first. However, this business did not originate from a disruptive strategy when it upended the traditional hardware and software industry procurement, licensing, and management model. That strategy came later. Instead, the business sprang from Amazon the retailer's need to scale its computing infrastructure.

Here's how it happened. During the holiday season of 2003, we had challenges with website reliability during the busiest and most crucial time of the year. No bueno. Immediately after we wobbled through that holiday season, a task force was formed to address website scaling and reliability. This team decided to centralize computing infrastructure management. We were going to serve internal customers. Internal customers, it was discovered, are not demanding customers—only external customers are truly demanding customers. Hence, the edict to invert the infrastructure and offer it to external developers. We learned in a hurry that developers loved the on-demand capabilities. Just like that, the strategy of AWS was developed.

Think of all the businesses Amazon is in today: retail in almost every conceivable category; marketplace; cloud computing; movie and TV production; book publishing; smart speakers; devices such as Echo, Kindle, and Ring doorbells; logistics and supply chains; groceries; over 80 private label brands; and healthcare. Amazon is a conglomerate business that prides itself on being entrepreneurial, customer centric, and low bureaucracy. Each of these businesses has external clients and could, conceptually, be an independent company serving other Amazon units, as well as other companies and customers. Amazon manages this without drowning in countless layers of bureaucracy largely because of its leadership principles . . . and many of the ideas we will explore in this book.

Of course, to think like Amazon is not solely about innovation. All of this is supported by fanatical world-class operations. Relentless.com was the name registered by Bezos for his startup venture, and the web address still goes to Amazon.com. Relentless is Amazon's attitude about operational excellence. Amazon is one of five companies that Gartner lists as "master" in supply chain operations. Gartner has described Amazon as a "bimodal" supply chain organization, unique in both its ability to operate at scale and innovate. In 2016, Amazon had 80 patents in supply chain technology alone![2]

The ability to both operate in a world-class manner and be a systematic innovator that is passionate about its customers—isn't that what every CEO wants? This is why "thinking like Amazon" is vital.

HOW TO READ *THINK LIKE AMAZON*

I've loaded this book with 50½ ideas. I'm not a big believer in massive transformation programs. The digital journey is about both company change and individual change. You must develop your own journey, be deliberate about the changes, and build new habits. You must simultaneously have patience and a sense of urgency. You must be poised to derive the best from yourself and your organization.

There are diverse ways to approach *Think Like Amazon*. Read it from start to finish. Jump around the book. Read it as a leader, and seed your team with its ideas as needed. Better yet, build team cohesiveness by reading this book as a unit and discussing one idea a week for a year. Or read the whole book together in one shot and discuss which ideas might be applied.

Ultimately, I want to hear that dog-eared copies of *Think Like Amazon* have spawned deep conversations and ideas key to helping you and your team compete in a new way and that you had fun doing it. Bear in mind, this is a book of ideas, not a master plan for strategy or change. That is up to *you* to develop, using the unique ingredients of your situation, its constraints and opportunities, and your own talents and ideas.

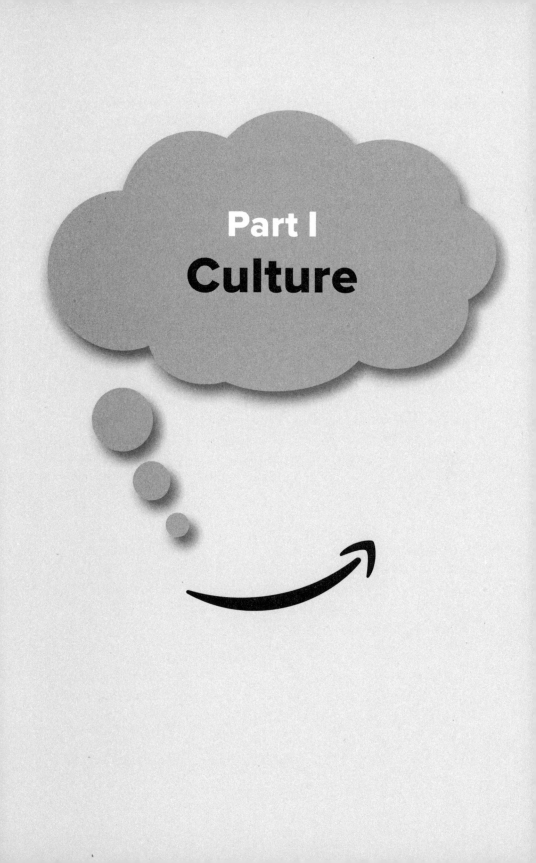

Part I
Culture

RESET YOUR CLOCKS

Your Journey Will Not Be
Short or a Straight Line

Not all who wander are lost.
—J.R.R. Tolkien

Other than being a wildly popular publicity opportunity dominating the headlines the world over, what was Amazon's "contest" for its second headquarters city about? This initiative, dubbed "HQ2," was one of the most unique proposals in the history of business.

I was part of a CNBC broadcast panel interview debating the attributes of different cities in the running for HQ2. While the other two panelists argued which location would be more appealing to the selfie generation, my point was that this was all about the long-term risk for Amazon of being able to hire and retain world-class technology talent.

Companies moving headquarters locations has precedent. Boeing moved its HQ from Seattle to Chicago in 2001. More recently, GE moved its HQ from Fairfield, Connecticut, to Boston, Massachusetts. And, yes, companies have solicited bids from cities and states for tax incentives tied to building a new location and creating jobs, but never has the combination of potential jobs and the transparent bidding process hit such a media-fueled crescendo.

Think of it this way. The city that won the Amazon contest would be acquiring a prize far more valuable than what Chicago received when Boeing moved from Seattle. HQ2 promises a $5 billion investment, as many as 50,000 high-paying jobs, an expectation of igniting more growth, and the immediate prestige of digital technology leadership.

> **idea 1:** If you can strategize and evaluate your plans over a long period of time, you will be able to make investments and "bets" that other businesses cannot. Identify the long-term risks and constraints in your business. You might be able to find strategic leverage by addressing them early.

So what problem was Amazon trying to solve? Was it about the growing resentment of some factions in Seattle regarding Amazon's local impact? Was it about the tension with the city of Seattle and state of Washington? Was Amazon growing weary of the Puget Sound gloom? Why go through this exercise?

Answering the question "What was Amazon's real motivation for HQ2?" requires first asking a deeper question: "What is the long-term throttle or constraint to Amazon's growth?" I believe Amazon asked itself this question, and the top answer centered on being able to recruit and retain talent, especially world-class technology talent, to the Seattle area. Seattle is a beautiful place, but it's not for everyone. It is a long way from many places in the world, there is a 10-hour time difference between Seattle and most of Europe, and it is not central to the rest of the United States. The price of living in Seattle has skyrocketed. As of a March 2017 report from the *NWREporter*, the median price for a home in Seattle had jumped to $777,000.[1] In short, the typical house in Seattle costs about $100,000 more than it did just a year earlier.

Between 2015 and 2017, the Amazon headcount grew from a little more than 200,000 to 541,000.[2] In Washington State, Amazon estimates the number to be at 40,000, with 25,000 of those employees being located in its Seattle headquarters.[3] And Amazon expects to continue this torrid growth or even (gasp!) to accelerate.[4] How will the company recruit and retain employees while keeping their standard of living high?

What would most leaders and companies do under these circumstances? Some would not even recognize the long-term risk facing them, looming like an iceberg in the night many miles ahead of their personal *Titanic*. Many would recognize it but fall silent, rein in their actions, and utilize short-term thinking. Why not kick the can down the road to the next generation of company leadership? Why take the expense, bad publicity, and management attention now if they're only going to be at the helm for 5 to 10 years? It's a common question in the C suite and boardroom.

Amazon's second leadership principle is "Ownership," by which leaders at Amazon strive to never sacrifice long-term value for short-term results. HQ2 was about long-term thinking and tackling a topic using an approach that derived many other benefits, instead of waiting until the potential leverage diminished to zero. Amazon's leaders were not kicking the can down the road on this long-term business constraint.

Amazon's Leadership Principles

Amazon has 14 leadership principles. When I was at Amazon, they were not formalized, but we talked about them every day and used them to make decisions. At some point after I left in late 2005, the leadership principles were codified. The LPs, as they are called at Amazon, play a key role in scaling Amazon by keeping a balance of speed, accountability, risk taking, and getting the right results. You need to be careful not to lean too heavily on one LP in relation to the others, and they need to be used with wisdom.

1. Customer Obsession
2. Ownership
3. Invent and Simplify
4. Are Right, a Lot
5. Learn and Be Curious
6. Hire and Develop the Best
7. Insist on the Highest Standards
8. Think Big
9. Bias for Action
10. Frugality
11. Earn Trust
12. Dive Deep
13. Have Backbone; Disagree and Commit
14. Deliver Results

Source: Amazon Jobs, https://www.amazon.jobs/en/principles.

Jeff Bezos evaluates things on a time frame that allows him to invest for the long term. Really long term in some cases. It is common knowledge that

Bezos is closely associated with the Long Now Foundation, whose members are concerned with society's ever-shortening focus. On a Bezos-owned West Texas property, the organization has built a clock that ticks once a year. The century hand advances once every 100 years, and the cuckoo will emerge once every millennium for the next 10,000 years.

Needless to say, Jeff is big on symbols. The 10,000-Year Clock is symbolic of his desire to always be thinking big and looking long term—as a company, as a culture, and as a world:

> If everything you do needs to work on a three-year time horizon, then you're competing against a lot of people. But if you're willing to invest on a seven-year time horizon, you're now competing against a fraction of those people because very few companies are willing to do that. Just by lengthening the time horizon, you can engage in endeavors that you could never otherwise pursue. At Amazon we like things to work in five to seven years. We're willing to plant seeds, let them grow—and we're very stubborn.[5]

BECOMING DIGITAL

So how does this apply to your digital strategy and competing in the digital era? Well, first let's ask ourselves, "What is digital?"

Most organization are under pressure to innovate and be digital. As a result, it's a question that launches a lot of my keynotes. But what does "being digital" mean? A lot of companies believe it means investing in your mobile experience and handheld devices and e-commerce. Others think it's about cloud computing, on-demand capabilities, and application programming interfaces (APIs). While these are all important enablers, they are *not* what being digital is.

Digging down, digital is about two things: speed and agility—externally to your customers and market and internally within your organization. More specifically, it is about speed and agility wrapped in new business models, innovation, and the collection and use of an immense amount of data. *Speed* is a very precise repetitive motion. It's about moving in one direction very efficiently, very precisely. Operational excellence at scale is the business equivalent to speed. *Agility*, on the other hand, is the attribute or skill to sense key facts, indicators, and market shifts and to quickly make changes and adjustments. Innovation in your business is driven by agility—that is, the ability to make both big and small change happen.

Amazon's DNA is defined by these two traits: speed and agility. But how does Amazon simultaneously operate and scale world-class operations quickly and innovate on a systematic basis, year over year? It doesn't happen just once, or by accident. For most organizations, this is like juggling chainsaws on ice skates. Yet Amazon has created their world-beating system of speed and agility using many of the ideas presented in this book and articulated in their leadership principles. Becoming digital is about your business building these traits and competing differently.

THE LONG VIEW

Developing these traits in your own organization is not a single project. It will be difficult to develop a business case and to forecast results. Predictability will be hard to find. But you must believe in the transformational powers of data, technology, innovation, and the pursuit of perfection—applied to all disciplines.

To succeed, it is vital to take the long view. Constant knee-jerk reactions to the quarter-to-quarter mentality that drives most American business is not only inefficient. It's also toxic to your culture. Liberate your thinking. If you consider digital a short-term initiative or if you think you're going to see the benefits and results in a really brief time, you don't understand the journey you're starting, and you won't have the patience or the support to see it to fruition.

Let's start the development of speed and agility by talking about customer obsession. After all, that is where Amazon started.

QUESTIONS TO CONSIDER

1. What are the long-term risks facing your industry and company?

2. What does "being digital" mean to you?

3. Is this definition shared and used to drive strategy by the C suite?

MERCENARY OR MISSION DRIVEN?

Be Strategic and Honest in Your Obsession, and Then Obsess to Win

> *Man is so made that when anything fires his soul, impossibilities vanish.*
> —Jean de La Fontaine

In the first grade, I had a friend who knew he wanted to be a surgeon. Not just a doctor, mind you, a surgeon. And he became one. I was always jealous of his certainty and the clarity of his mission.

How do you create passion and develop a mission if the path is not innately clear? It's a question I posed to myself, and it's a question I pose to leaders. Perhaps, I tell them, the art of leadership is the ability to uncover the passions of each individual and find ways to align and build value from each person's strengths to accomplish the mission of the organization.

> **idea 2:** You will stick through the hard times if you are passionate about the cause and the customer. Consistent messaging regarding the mission will take the "mildly interested" majority of employees in most organizations and make them fanatics for your business, for winning, and for the mission.

There is nothing wrong with being motivated by other priorities, such as the ability to pursue personal passions, garner influence, or achieve financial stability. In fact, for many business models, careers, and personal lives, these are probably requisite for success. Looking back over my own career, it's clear my intrinsic interest has been to improve business performance through three approaches: (1) efficiency, or creating processes that yield better quality with lower costs; (2) integration across disparate processes, data, systems, and eco-systems to create seamless capabilities; and (3) the development of new business models and capabilities allowing a business to compete differently.

I once had a colleague who defined *mercenary* as someone who was "coin operated." By that, he meant that the only thing mercenaries care about is making money. The term carries some negative connotations. If you're out to build a strong culture, you probably won't be calling for a bunch of mercenaries.

Ultimately, financial returns and sales are output metrics. As a leader, you don't have direct control over them. They are the result of many other things you do. What you can control are the inputs. To win in digital, you must be deeply connected to your customers and users because that's where the insights are.

In all fairness, success is primarily measured by financial results. Shareholders frequently like mercenaries because a team of mercenaries can drive a burst of short-term revenue. As a result, to have employees with a mercenary streak in them is not necessarily the worst thing in the world. A hybrid can be created. The key is making sure that your mercenary is a patriot. What's a patriot?

BUILDING A PATRIOT

Jeff talks a lot about how mission-driven teams build better products. That's great, but what does it mean to be mission driven?

It's said that wars are won by patriots, not mercenaries. We fight and care differently if we have a stake in the outcome of the war, if the commitment is cemented by something personal. And while it is great if the cement is mixed with a deep passion for the customer, a cement mixed with other ingredients can be just as strong and beneficial to the cause.

Here's the deal. Most employees don't start off as patriots. Usually, they're grateful for the job, but they are only mildly interested in the mission, and they are generally unclear on it. If they can't be inspired, they usually shrug their shoulders and start focusing on doing a good enough job to continue collecting paychecks every two weeks.

As a leader, it's your responsibility to transform these people from self-centered mercenaries to dyed-in-the-wool patriots. So how do you convert these mildly interested employees into the passionate ambassadors you need for your company to be able to compete successfully in the digital era? You must find a way to clearly define the mission, inject it with a sense of legacy and importance, and then figure out how to connect that mission to each and every one of them.

I joined Amazon in early 2002 to lead the launch of the Amazon Marketplace business. Today, that business accounts for over 50 percent of all units sold at Amazon, and there are over 3 million sellers on the platform. However, when I came aboard, two earlier attempts at a "third-party" business had failed and eBay had what felt like an unassailable position. A different strategy was needed, and the entire Amazon leadership team was hoping that the third time was going to be the charm. Of course, when I arrived, I was met with skeptics. Yes, "customer obsession" was alive and well, but I discovered a profound internal apathy for the vendors. I sensed that the organization viewed sellers as third-class citizens. Of course, these were the people we were counting on to populate the very business we were building. They had to be the lifeblood.

Amazon needed to convince these merchants to invest in building their businesses to serve Amazon customers. We had to sell them on these great tools and capabilities that we had built for them to succeed. We had to enable them with everything we could to help them deliver to demanding standards. In short, we needed to build, almost from scratch, an obsession for merchants.

I started by writing out this vision and understanding, holding several town hall meetings, and making the connection that "merchant obsession" was key to winning in this business. And, boy, did we need this business to work for us. The pressure was immense.

As I built the merchant organization, I needed a wide variety of technical, project management, and business skills. Yes, I could have (perhaps "should have") insisted that everyone have an incredible passion for customers and sellers, but I was not going to let "perfect be the enemy of good enough." If I hired motivated, excited, and talented people, I felt I could harness them to the mission. It was vital to develop a personal relationship with the employees as individuals. I had to learn their personal passions, strengths, and motivations. Finding their individual unique connections to the mission and guiding their passion to its legacy were keys to success. And the process never ended. It required that I continuously wave the seller-obsessed mission banner before them as a constant reminder and inspiration that we were doing something revolutionary, something world changing.

BEZOS'S POINT OF VIEW

Jeff talks about the need for a committed, customer-obsessed team. Quite frankly, it's one of his greatest hits, and he plays it often:

> I strongly believe that missionaries make better products. They care more. For a missionary, it's not just about the business. There has to be a business, and the business has to make sense, but that's not why you do it. You do it because you have something meaningful that motivates you.[1]

Jeff's point is clear and hard to debate. But it is also incomplete. It's incomplete because it doesn't explain that the business or team mission has to be aligned with every individual's mission. Furthermore, if the opinion is that people can't develop this mission if they don't have it when entering a business, then hiring or transitioning a team gets tricky. Define the mission, figure out how it connects to passions, interests, and personal missions, and consistently integrate the mission in communications and meetings. You will be able to bring much more of the team along.

If you can continue to build excitement and purpose for yourself and your team, you will build a better product, a better experience, and a better business serving customers. And you will be setting the stage to be a Day 1 business.

QUESTIONS TO CONSIDER

1. What is the obsession for your business?

2. Is this obsession defined and consistently communicated?

3. Are there enough patriots in the organization?

MOVE FORWARD TO GET BACK TO DAY 1

Change the Culture of the Status Quo

Pain is temporary. Quitting lasts forever.
—Lance Armstrong

I am a cycling fan. For years, I enjoyed grinding up and down hills and mountains on a road bike in the Pacific Northwest. My wife and I became fans of Lance Armstrong when he donned the rainbow jersey after winning the cycling World Championships in Oslo, Norway, in 1993. This was well before he won his first Tour de France in 1999. Our oldest son was born in 1998, and we almost named him after Lance—thank goodness, we didn't. I shudder to think of poor "Lance Rossman." What a dark and complex legacy to carry around just because your parents liked to watch people race bicycles.

Lance Armstrong won the Tour de France a record seven consecutive times from 1999 to 2005. However, in 2012 he was banned from sanctioned Olympic sports for life and stripped of his Tour de France victories because of long-term doping offenses. As a result, all his wins dating back to 1998 were voided.

idea 3: If your business has become stagnant or is at risk of commoditization or standing still, admit the situation, change the questions you are asking, and be purposeful in your communication.

I now live in Southern California and spend too much time driving in a car. I enjoy listening to podcasts, and I am always in search of great content and learning. When a friend recommended Lance Armstrong's podcast *The Forward*, to me, I reluctantly gave it a listen, and guess what, I loved it. *The Forward* is about owning your past and deciding to, well, move forward. No matter your history, you decide how to live with it and how you want to write your going-forward history. If you are at risk of having your best days behind you, you decide whether to resign yourself to slow, painful acceptance and erosion, or you figure out a way to reinvent yourself and move forward. That's the long and short of it, anyway. Obviously, it's a theme with which Armstrong is familiar.

Armstrong does an excellent job interviewing his podcast guests. He delves into their pasts and examines their stories and how they are moving forward. Meanwhile, he is honest and self-effacing about his own complex past. The podcast is clearly therapy for him.

When assessing personal mistakes, the first step toward a correction is honest self-appraisal. Big, successful companies are no different. No matter the past, no matter the level of achievement, you make decisions that define how you move forward. These decisions can be either conscious or unconscious, but they are made nonetheless.

Bezos has outlined his perspective that there are basically two types of companies—Day 1 or Day 2 companies. In the 2016 Amazon letter to shareholders, he wrote:

> Jeff, what does Day 2 look like? That's a question I just got at our most recent all-hands meeting. I've been reminding people that it's Day 1 for a couple of decades. I work in an Amazon building named Day 1, and when I moved buildings, I took the name with me. I spend time thinking about this topic.
>
> Day 2 is stasis. Followed by irrelevance. Followed by excruciating, painful decline. Followed by death. And that is why it is always Day 1. To be sure, this kind of decline would happen in extreme slow motion. An established company might harvest Day 2 for decades, but the final result would still come.
>
> I'm interested in the question, how do you fend off Day 2? What are the techniques and tactics? How do you keep the vitality of Day 1, even inside a large organization? Such a question can't have a simple answer. There will be many elements, multiple paths,

and many traps. I don't know the whole answer, but I may know bits of it. Here's a starter pack of essentials for Day 1 defense: customer obsession, a skeptical view of proxies, the eager adoption of external trends, and high-velocity decision making.[1]

Here's what's interesting to me about Jeff's starter pack of essentials—they are all elements of culture. They define our priorities and how we work together. They are neither financial goals nor market goals. They are *fully* within the leaders' control, not the market's or competitors'.

While Jeff is focused on fending off Day 2, I'm interested in the questions, "What do you do if you are already a Day 2 company? How do you change course? Do you just accept your fate? If so, isn't this a form of quitting? Or do you accept the risk and pain, and figure out how to move forward?"

MOVING FORWARD

If you are a Day 2 company, this book is written for you! Apply these ideas with purpose and patience. Thomas Wolfe was wrong. You can go home again. Here's how to return to Day 1.

Commit to a Path

Although innovation and renewal can and should come from anywhere inside or outside your organization, only the leadership team and board can be purposeful and specific. You likely know some of the painful moves you need to make to get going; you've just been reluctant to do so.

Commit to a path, take the medicine you need to early, and then start innovating. Perhaps it means selling a business, parting with a leader, or admitting the reality of an eroding channel of business.

Recognize and Feature the Bad News

The bad news does not get better with age. What are the signs of being Day 2? Often it is slowing growth, services and products becoming commoditized, increasing loss percentages on new opportunities, or what you are hearing from your customers.

You need to not only admit the situation but take accountability. You must understand what you believe in and what you are willing to do. What you are willing to personally commit to will, in large part, define the options available to you. By featuring the bad news, you are declaring it as the past. You are saying, "The current situation is no longer acceptable. We have a new mission, and we need to do better."

Amazon's Leadership Principle 11 is "Earn Trust," which means being "vocally self-critical even when doing so is awkward and embarrassing. Leaders do not believe their or their team's body odor smells of perfume. They benchmark themselves and their teams against the best."[2] Start business or operations reviews with perspectives like "Here's how my team/business/operation sucked," and then list the metrics and root causes. Discuss how you are going to fix them and what you need from others. If you start "featuring the bad news," the stigma goes away, but it takes bold leadership.

Change the Questions You Are Asking

Ask questions that impose constraints ("How would we make our product/service/capability completely 'self-service'"?). Ask questions that create more customer empathy ("What is our customer's worst day?"). Ask questions that pose a different reality ("How would our product or service be completely 'software defined'"?).

Be purposeful and deliberate in fleshing out scenarios and potential answers to these questions. Use narratives (Idea 44) or future press releases (Idea 45).

Be on Target with Communication Always

To your team, to your investors, to your board, to your customers—everyone in a leadership role needs to commit and be on point in their communications. Change does not happen with a memo or one meeting and declaration. Your priorities, your actions, and your communications need to always line up with your plan. Communications need to be both scheduled and planned, as well as spontaneous.

Equip yourself and your leaders with message points to incorporate in everything you and they do. Repeat.

.   .   .

All that said, the history of companies changing the tide and reinventing themselves is dominated by failure. Two examples of companies that have been hugely successful at changing the fortunes of their business are Apple and, more recently, Microsoft. These have not been just product transitions, but cultural transitions. Change is hard, and it's risky. Maybe it's easier to simply let the next generation of management deal with it. You might be able to ride this out for years. But can you live with the knowledge you preside over a Day 2 company?

Even Amazon is dealing with this. Of the companies on the Fortune 1000 list, only Walmart is over $400 billion in annual revenue. Walmart is growing at a five-year average of less than 2 percent. Meanwhile, Amazon's forecasted 2018 revenue is $240 billion, with an annual growth rate of 38 percent. In a few years, likely less than three, Amazon will be over $400 billion in annual revenue. Amazon's leaders are asking questions about how to manage a business like this, because not many leadership teams have done it, especially with these growth dynamics. Regardless, they remain committed to the long haul and staying a Day 1 company.

Outside of Amazon, in his emerging philanthropic endeavors, Bezos is applying many of the same beliefs and values to create a big vision and reinvent on behalf of the customer. Announced in September 2018, the Bezos Day One Fund will focus on the homelessness epidemic and preschool education. "We'll use the same set of principles that have driven Amazon. Most important among those will be genuine, intense customer obsession," he tweeted. "The child will be the customer."[3]

Staying a Day 1 company is going to be difficult. You're going to have good days and bad days. You're going to lose some people along the way. You are going to have to be obsessed. Fortunately, we will talk about that in the next chapter.

QUESTIONS TO CONSIDER

1. What bad news are you not being honest about?

2. What personnel matter are you not dealing with directly and honestly?

3. Are you a Day 2 company and more interested in keeping the status quo?

idea 4

OBSESSED IS DIFFERENT

Create Customer Obsession in Your Business

Obsession is the wellspring of genius and madness.
—Michel de Montaigne

Captain Ahab, the monomaniacal character at the heart of Herman Melville's *Moby-Dick*, was obsessed with the white whale. Not just interested. Not fascinated. He was totally obsessed by the beast that had taken his leg. When Ahab set out to harpoon his obsession, did he delegate the job of finding the white whale? Absolutely not. The crew of the *Pequod* thought they were hunting sperm whales, not traveling to the ends of the earth to destroy their captain's obsession.

Ahab probably isn't the best example of a leader. The mad captain's obsession was a deadly one that concluded with a one-way trip to the bottom of the ocean, tethered to the whale. Yet when it comes to obsession—true obsession—it can sometimes be difficult to discern between genius and madness.

> **idea 4:** It's everyone's job to know and have empathy and passion for the customer. Make sure everyone knows it's their job. Find many ways to deliberately practice and build this expectation. Dive deep into the issues experienced by customers (or other key stakeholders), and don't delegate figuring out the root causes. Know the details of the customer experience and what causes friction for customers.

Surely, you have dealt with people who are obsessed with something. Perhaps with some pursuit like sports. The word *fan*, after all, is short for "fanatic." What was your reaction to their obsession? Did they come across as weird, distracted, odd, excited, or hard to understand? Did anything else really matter to them? Perhaps their obsession even created some conflict between the two of you.

Although there are 14 leadership principles at Amazon, Leadership Principle 1 is "Customer Obsession," and it is the first among equals of Amazon's leadership principles. Isn't "being customer focused" or "hearing your customer" good enough? To go from good to great, to "see around the corner" for your customer,[1] or to change an internal culture, obsession will deliver different insights.

CHIEF CUSTOMER OFFICER—BLECCH!

"Wanted: Seasoned executive to become a champion of the customer. Must be adept at breaking down organizational silos to create a persistent customer-first mentality across physical and digital channels. Requirements include diplomacy skills, an innovative spirit, customer service excellence, and a data-driven mindset."[2]

In the eternal spirit of *Mad Magazine*, I say "blecch" whenever I hear the title of the latest management trend: chief customer officer (CCO). Don't get me wrong. The description and skills needed are great. But wouldn't it be better if *everyone* in the organization acted as the chief customer officer?

I appreciate that having a CCO might be a way to help start and accelerate customer obsession in your organization, but my concern is that having the role sends the exact opposite message to the rest of the organization. If everyone thinks it's someone else's job to be obsessed with the customer, the vast majority of your team is not doing it. If you are going to have a CCO, make sure this position's first priority is to create a culture of customer obsession, so that being a customer advocate is everyone's job. If successful, the role of CCO becomes pointless. Why? Because everyone's doing it.

MAKE IT HAPPEN

What are the different methods of systematically creating and practicing customer obsession? Here's a smattering of approaches:

1. **Use metrics that measure the customer experience.** We will talk more about metrics in Idea 31, but create metrics that measure *all* phases of the customer experience. Find a way to measure it rather than just surveying it. This will lead to innovation. Be creative in measuring as much of the customer experience as possible, even in nondigital experiences. You *can* measure the waiting time customers are experiencing in a real-time manner. Don't use "We are not a digital business or product" as an excuse.

2. **Create a voice of the customer program.** Create a voice of the customer program that not only highlights a customer issue but also assigns prioritized action items and work for any teams needed to fix the root cause.

3. **Everything starts with describing "customer delight."** In your narratives, your results, your shareholder letters, your plans, your strategies, your documentation, start with describing what delights your customer about this topic. If you can't identify the customer impact, should you be spending time on it?

4. **Manage by walking around.** Spend considerable time as a customer, with your sales and service team, and interview the front line of your partners. Don't rely too much on surveys because they don't deliver many deep insights. Also, don't rely solely on common proxies such as market reports or other summarized material—because they typically work only to confirm our opinion. Instead, you want to disconfirm your beliefs and opinions, and you want to understand the specific moments when you are disappointing a customer, gathering as many details of the situation as you can. *Management by walking around* (MBWA) is the practice of managers getting out of their ivory towers and spending time with customers and in the field so that they can gain better insight and empathy for what is really happening.

THE RESULTS ARE NOT JUST CUSTOMER SATISFACTION

By making customer obsession everyone's job, you hope that customer satisfaction will improve. That would be great, but in baseball parlance, I consider this a "single." Customer obsession leads to operational excellence, which we will discuss more in Idea 22. However, the "home run," nay the "grand slam," of customer obsession is to build on customer satisfaction and operational excellence. The grand slam is innovation and business model evolution—becoming inspired to develop and expand beyond your current products, services, and business model.

Amazon's sophisticated logistics expertise did not come from wanting to be a supply chain company. It came from understanding that the customer experience was greatly affected by flexibility, speed, and quality of delivery. Amazon Web Services (AWS) did not come from wanting to be a cloud technology company but from needing to provide a scalable infrastructure to provide a great online customer experience.

Where could customer obsession lead you? Here's a hint: it's not to the bottom of the ocean, tethered to a whale. However, as we will discover in the next chapter, it's not bad to have people on board with a little Ahab in them. As we'll discuss, being "nice" all the time can be a liability for your team.

QUESTIONS TO CONSIDER

1. If customer obsession were a shared value across your organization, what would be different?

2. Do you have deep metrics measuring all aspects of the customer experience, even in the nondigital parts of your business?

3. Do you rely too much on surveys, competitive intelligence, and other proxies for customer experience?

DON'T GO ALONG TO GET ALONG

The Risk Social Cohesion Poses to Achieving Hard Results

Management is doing things right.
Leadership is doing the right things.
—Peter Drucker

Amazon is known as a demanding place to work. It's not for everyone. You could say the company is "aggressive." Aggressive for results—that is, the right types of results. Aggressive for people to produce and have mastery of their domain. Aggressive for teams and leaders to achieve the impossible: perfection.

Think about how most large companies operate. Big-company politics tend to rule the day. Discussions are not forthright. Meetings are layered in so much posturing and subtle deception, they are downright Shakespearean. Seniority and titles matter more than having the right data or insight. People speak out of both sides of their mouths. They smile and nod their heads yes without agreeing. In this world, civility is more important than being right. Results suffer for the sake of harmony.

But, alas, that is the way it is. Jeff recognized this unfortunate condition early, however, and decided he'd rather form a company that didn't just look good but also innovated, operated extremely well, and evolved over time.

idea 5: Make being right the most important thing. Set the tone from the top that we will win by doing the right thing, having honest conversations leading with customer obsession and data, seeking perfection through data, and ignoring job titles, while still treating each other with respect. Many of the ideas in this book will help reinforce this principle.

Of all Jeff's management notions, perhaps the most distinctive is his belief that harmony is often overvalued in the workplace, that it can stifle honest critique and encourage polite praise for flawed ideas and execution. Instead, Amazonians are instructed to "Disagree and Commit" (Leadership Principle 13)—to vigorously debate colleagues' ideas with feedback that can be painfully blunt before lining up behind a decision.

"We always want to arrive at the right answer," said Tony Galbato, Amazon's vice president for human resources, in an e-mail statement. "It would certainly be much easier and socially cohesive to just compromise and not debate, but that may lead to the wrong decision."[1]

Amazon has a name for the approach of getting at intellectual honesty and being self-critical. It's called "truth seeking," the goal of which is to avoid consensus-based social cohesion where nobody has to be wrong and to get to the right answer or insight. Bezos's belief is that if you are a truth-seeking company competing against a compromise company, you will win. Don't fall into being a compromise company when it is possible to measure and define the truth. This is "featuring the bad news."

However, it's important not to twist this notion to mean that being a great colleague or respectful to others is not important. It's just that it's not enough, and it's not the top priority. Being nice and getting along are necessary and valued. You can't achieve the right results if you leave nothing but burned bridges behind you. But getting along is simply not *the most* important thing. Think about your organization's priorities and social norms. If getting along is more valued than being right, the business will become more about getting along than about doing the right thing over time. This value seeps in slowly, but definitively.

Author Brad Stone has collected some of Bezos's greatest in-meeting quips, as recalled by Amazon veterans:

"Are you lazy or just incompetent?"

"I'm sorry, did I take my stupid pills today?"

"Do I need to go down and get the certificate that says I'm CEO of the company to get you to stop challenging me on this?"

"If I hear that idea again, I'm gonna have to kill myself."

After an engineer's presentation: "Why are you wasting my life?"

Source: Brad Stone, *The Everything Store: Jeff Bezos and the Age of Amazon*, Little, Brown, New York, 2013.

Bezos abhors what he calls "social cohesion"—that is, the natural impulse to seek consensus.[2] He'd rather his employees battle it out with numerical swords and customer passion. He has codified this approach in one of Amazon's 14 leadership principles, the company's highly prized values that are inculcated into new hires and discussed throughout each employee's life cycle in the organization.

Consensus poses two dangers for the business trying to be innovative. The first danger is that hard, honest, forthright conversations are not being had. The second danger is that ideas that are truly innovative tend to be counterintuitive, and they often seem stupid, impossible, counterproductive, or all three.

WHAT TO DO?

1. **Test it through practice.** Try to catch moments when honest conversations are not taking place. Be purposeful in communicating that both parties demand rigorous thought and execution. And while both parties must be respectful of others, the business needs *both* demanding conversations and respect.

2. *Slow down* **certain conversations and meetings.** Debate the issue, and review the type of conversation you are having and the principles or approach you are taking in making decisions. This helps the team get better at understanding why we are making a decision in a certain manner.

3. **Use metrics and service-level agreements (SLAs).** Hold each other accountable with metrics, service-level agreements (SLAs), and deep root-cause conversations. Root-cause conversations often take considerable effort, and you must be disciplined to understand the multiple improvements that might be needed. Exercises like asking "the five whys" where you ask "Why did this happen" or "Why did I allow this to affect my business" five times help to get past superficial answers and get to the real root cause.

Many of the ideas in this book force better conversations and, hopefully, better decisions and better operations. Ideas such as writing narratives (Idea 44) and continuously building metrics (Idea 31) are key ideas to fighting social cohesion. They are forcing functions for healthy conflict.

As a leader, you may be hesitant to create internal conflict. That's understandable. Yet any coach will tell you that winning solves all problems when it comes to locker room culture. Everyone's getting along when a team is winning, and getting along is a by-product of getting it right, which requires healthy conflict. If you can tilt the bias to doing the right thing through more honest conversations, you'll quickly incorporate the notion of getting the right results into how you work. Let's explore that next.

QUESTIONS TO CONSIDER

1. How does your company culture prioritize being right and communicating clarity?

2. Does your company culture allow for everyday hard discussions and candor?

3. Is getting along more important than being right?

DELIVER RESULTS

Own Your Dependencies to Overcome and Succeed

When a team takes ownership of its problem,
the problem gets solved. It is true on the battlefield,
it is true in business, and it is true in life.
—Jocko Willink

Amazon is both a world-class operator and a systematic innovator. For such a gargantuan company, it empowers people to be decision-makers in an environment that's surprisingly free of bureaucracy. For this to work, the culture allows and enables leaders to be accountable for getting the right results.

But it's one thing to say, "You're accountable." It's another to actually create a systematic method allowing leaders to better manage and influence key risks so they can deliver hard results and be accountable. What is Amazon's method?

idea 6: Set the expectation that leaders cannot point the finger at others if they don't achieve the right results. Demonstrate how to better manage dependencies so they can better deliver outstanding results in distributed organizations.

THE BUCK STOPS HERE

Jocko Willink was the commander of Task Unit Bruiser, the most decorated special operations unit of the Iraq War. He's also coauthor of the *New York Times* bestseller *Extreme Ownership*.

As you might imagine from a Navy SEAL, the book's messaging is heavy on personal discipline and responsibility. "War is hell," Willink says. "It is a brutal teacher."[1] While business will never be war—and Willink makes this very, very clear—there is no reason why you cannot transpose that intensity, those types of brick-wall dependencies, to your organization. Willink's book reminds me of an Adam Lashinsky story regarding Steve Jobs and Apple's vice presidents and janitors, which I will paraphrase here.

According to Lashinksy, Steve Jobs told employees a short story when they were promoted to vice president at Apple. Jobs would tell the VP that if the garbage in his office was not being emptied, Jobs would naturally demand an explanation from the janitor. "Well, the lock on the door was changed," the janitor could reasonably respond. "And I couldn't get a key." It's an irritation for Jobs, but the janitor's response is reasonable. It's an understandable excuse. The janitor can't do his job without the key. As a janitor, he's allowed to have excuses. "When you're the janitor, reasons matter," Jobs told his newly minted VPs. "Somewhere between the janitor and the CEO, reasons stop mattering." In other words, the Rubicon of accountability is "crossed when the employee becomes a vice president. He or she must vacate all excuses for failure. A vice president is responsible for any mistakes that happen, and it doesn't matter what you say."[2]

YOU OWN YOUR DEPENDENCIES

If you've crossed that Rubicon of accountability and there are no excuses, you are acting like an owner. Everyone in business depends on others for success. Those around you—colleagues, team members, outside suppliers and partners, those in other departments who touch your work—contribute essential elements that make you effective. This means that when they let you down, they can also cause you to fail, sometimes miserably.

At Amazon, one of your primary directives is to identify and tenaciously manage every potential business-derailing dependency you have. It is not OK to fail because of a breakdown of dependencies. That's a failure of leadership.

When called to account for a problem caused in part or in whole by a dependency breakdown, you must be able to say, "I did these things to manage my dependencies. I went above and beyond the reasonable in my efforts to manage them." That means having rock-solid contracts, service-level agreements, and penalties in place as well as continual, active management of communications. You can assume nothing.

In a 2003 S Team meeting, Jeff broke the process of managing dependencies into three easy steps:

1. Whenever possible, take over the dependencies so you don't have to rely on someone else.

2. If that is impossible, negotiate and manage unambiguous and clear commitments from others.

3. Create hedges wherever possible. For every dependency, devise a fallback plan—a redundancy in a supply chain, for example.

Taking absolute responsibility for every possible dependency under your purview is no small task. This is one reason that very few have the rigor, determination, and tenacity to make it in a leadership role at Amazon. It is a company of control freaks run by control freaks and lorded over by the king of control freaks. As one ex-Amazon engineer famously said, Jeff Bezos is such a control freak that he "makes ordinary control freaks look like stoned hippies."[3]

And since your own team is one of the most important dependencies under your authority, your ability to mentor those around you is a key metric during your annual evaluation. That means your success is intrinsically linked to the success your people have achieved over the course of their careers at Amazon.

This concept of managing dependencies in a proactive manner, far beyond a normal expectation, will resonate with motivated leaders. They often ask how it's accomplished. While there are many ways, start by asking more questions than you normally do with your colleagues. These questions help minimize the assumptions and surprises. Second, don't just trust. Instead, trust and verify.

Consider Jocko Willink. He will tell you that even when leaders are not directly responsible for all outcomes, it is their method of communication and guidance, or lack thereof, that leads to the results. When this becomes the norm in a company, asking for details is no longer seen as a challenge to someone's competence. It becomes part of the culture.

DELIVER RESULTS

Amazon is synonymous with delivering results. Using roughly 120 million square feet of fulfillment centers across the United States, Amazon ships an average of 608 million packages each year.[4] That's about 1,600,000 packages a day. While its delivery times are some of the best in the world, they are experimenting with launching their own delivery service to bypass FedEx and UPS, lower costs, and improve delivery results.

Meanwhile, AWS will have generated an estimated $24 billion in net sales in 2018. That was up from $17.5 billion in 2017. It ranks as one of the most popular public cloud infrastructure and platform services running applications worldwide.[5] AWS includes a service-level agreement with its users to maintain a monthly uptime percentage of at least 99.99 percent.[6]

You don't get these types of results unless you manage dependencies aggressively. And every other Amazon leadership principle simply supports and facilitates this final, crucial principle: deliver results.

Of course, if you're a leader who does get these types of results, eventually the conversation must turn to rewards and compensation.

QUESTIONS TO CONSIDER

1. Does your team routinely deliver hard results?

2. Does your team point at others when results are not delivered?

3. Do you manage dependencies in a forthright manner to improve the odds of success?

OWNERSHIP FOR EVERYONE

Compensation Strategy to Drive Enterprise Optimization

We must, indeed, all hang together,
or most assuredly, we shall all hang separately.
—Benjamin Franklin

Much has been written about Amazon's compensation structure. The commonly held belief is that the top salary in the organization is $165,000 per year. The only other compensation is stock grants. While that is not universally consistent across Amazon anymore, Amazon does avoid individual or team-based bonus structures and keeps salaries low relative to market. Why is that?

People game the system. It's human nature to optimize those functions for which we are measured and rewarded. It's just human nature.

It was a biological necessity back when we lived in prehistoric hunter-gatherer clans. And today it's especially true for upper and middle management. Oh, you might think you can avoid this "coin-operated" mentality in

> **idea 7:** Craft a compensation structure incenting long-term enterprise value creation. Communicate the strategy and value of your compensation structure often to build alignment. When dramatic shifts are needed in a business, dramatic shifts in compensation structure become necessary.

your own organization. But over the long run, consciously or subconsciously, human nature overrides your Pollyannaish hopes. Teams become oriented to hitting targets that optimize for variable compensation. They can't help themselves.

So what drives Amazon's compensation strategy? Ownership. Otherwise known as Amazon's Leadership Principle 2. It reads, "Leaders are owners. They think long term and don't sacrifice long-term value for short-term results. They act on behalf of the entire company, beyond just their own team. They never say, 'That's not my job'":

> "We pay very low cash compensation relative to most companies," says Bezos. "We also have no incentive compensation of any kind. And the reason we don't is because it is detrimental to teamwork."[1]

If you want to create commitment, and commitment to hard change, you likely need to align your compensation structure. Make it clear that we will all win, and we will only win when we have accomplished our enterprise objectives. If you lose some people over this, you're likely better off having it happen early.

GAIN ALIGNMENT WITH YOUR LIEUTENANTS

Amazon presents an interesting and radical example of compensation structure, and it's worked for them. Especially since 2008, the stock has seen a meteoric increase going from $41 to over $2,000 a share in 2018. It may not be the right recipe for any other enterprise. But if a CEO or team leader needs to make a quick and decisive change, when "business as usual" will not cut it anymore, the CEO should rethink the compensation structure of the executive team and make sure that (a) we win only if dramatic changes are made, and (b) we win only with enterprise improvements. Team or individual achievements will not be rewarded.

As W. Edwards Deming said, "Sub-optimization is when everyone is for himself. Optimization is when everyone is working to help the company."[2] Guess what else a poor compensation strategy can buy you? A country club. Find out what I mean by that in the next chapter.

QUESTIONS TO CONSIDER

1. Is compensation optimizing for enterprise results?

2. Do you see suboptimization happening due to goals and compensation?

3. Is everyone aligned to increasing enterprise value?

AVOID COUNTRY CLUBS

Stay Hungry Even When You're Successful

> *Ironically, in a changing world, playing it safe*
> *is one of the riskiest things you can do.*
> —Reid Hoffman

I was lucky to be a leader at Amazon during a period of great inflection for the company. I was equally fortunate to follow that experience with 12 years as a managing director at Alvarez and Marsal, or A&M as it is known. A&M is a crisis and restructuring professional services firm. It is brought in when fast and dramatic business change is needed, often as interim leadership. I worked with restructuring clients, private equity clients, and healthy corporate clients.

Guess at which client organizations it is easiest to make meaningful, impactful improvements and change? The ones that are in crisis and restructuring. Why? Because they have nothing to lose. Healthy corporations say they want to change, but they resist the true essence of becoming digital and parting with many of their prior practices and beliefs.

Why is it harder for healthy companies and their leadership teams to change the traditions that digital businesses demand? Think of it this way. Why do musicians typically release terrible second albums? Why do athletes

> **idea 8:** Companies that have had success and that have benefited from a rise in equity appreciation are at risk of playing it safe. Find ways to keep tension in the wire for growth, innovation, and long-term enterprise goals.

struggle to perform signing a large contract? Well, they spent years creating or training to become successful. When they actually *achieve* success, something intrinsic happens. They are no longer quite as hungry. Suddenly, they want to protect what they have, play it safe, and not get injured. The sense of urgency and desperation that enabled the "go for it" mindset may switch to a "don't lose it" or "let's enjoy it" mindset.

Like newly successful rock bands or athletes, these healthy client organizations have all options open to them. They can make long-term investments, and they have the luxury of positive momentum. They recognize the opportunities, saying they want to change. But in reality, they have lost their underdog attitude. They start playing it safe, and they get comfortable. In short, they have created a country club culture. Without even being conscious of it, an attitude of "don't risk it" subconsciously influences how the business is approached.

Urban lore has it that in the 1990s at Microsoft, employees could be seen wearing T-shirts with "FYIFV" on them, which stood for "F*&? You, I'm Fully Vested."[1] This notion was well known in Seattle, and it was an early reference point for Bezos. I was quoted in the *New York Times* article in 2015 on the subject:

> Mr. Rossman, the former executive, said that Mr. Bezos was addressing a meeting in 2003 when he turned in the direction of Microsoft, across the water from Seattle, and said he didn't want Amazon to become "a country club." If Amazon becomes like Microsoft, "we would die," Mr. Bezos added.[2]

In the same article, the author writes this:

> According to early executives and employees, Mr. Bezos was determined almost from the moment he founded Amazon in 1994 to resist the forces he thought sapped businesses over time— bureaucracy, profligate spending, lack of rigor. As the company grew, he wanted to codify his ideas about the workplace, some of them proudly counterintuitive, into instructions simple enough for a new worker to understand, general enough to apply to the nearly limitless number of businesses he wanted to enter, and stringent enough to stave off the mediocrity he feared.[3]

Warren Buffett refers to this disease as the "ABCs of corporate decay—Arrogance, Bureaucracy, and Complacency."[4]

There are many ways to avoid or recover from country club disease. The cure starts with recognition. How do you recognize the onset of country club-itis? A bit too much self-congratulation; too much stock price watching and managing to Wall Street; more focus on internal affairs than on customers. Other symptoms include slowing growth expectations, reducing risks, and starting to optimize for short-term financial results instead of aggressively investing in new businesses. Basically, playing it safe and playing "not to lose."

What do you do? Here's a specific exercise. With both internal leaders and external advisors such as a startup leader or venture capital operator, have the group develop specific plans answering questions such as, "How would you pitch to an investor or competitor a business to compete and disrupt our existing business?" I prefer to do this as part of a retreat so that mindsets are away from the daily operations.

Essentially, build business plans to disrupt your own business. After development, review these plans with additional external leaders (internal thinking will be limited and biased). Then conduct a board and leadership team retreat to thoroughly discuss these ideas. Use narratives (Idea 44) and future press releases (Idea 45). Go on the offense!

As the beer brand Dos Equis's "most interesting man in the world" advises, "Stay hungry, my friends." And if you can create hunger inside big enterprises, then you're ready for the next step—moving quickly to make changes in innovations—even in enterprises the size of elephants.

QUESTIONS TO CONSIDER

1. Is past success, especially equity appreciation, creating risk aversion in senior leadership and the board?

2. Do you sense that the organization is playing it safe?

3. Is there any aspect of a country club culture at your company?

MAKE THE ELEPHANT DANCE

Portfolio Strategy and Governance for Innovation

It isn't a question of whether elephants can prevail over ants. It's a question of whether a particular elephant can dance. If it can, the ants must leave the dance floor.
—Louis V. Gerstner, Jr.

How does a company the size of Amazon consistently innovate? How do you get an elephant to dance? If you study Amazon as I have, you'll realize that there are a few tricks and approaches that can help an elephant—or any other company—innovate.

The most important decisions executive management makes is where to put its resources. The essence of strategy is deciding what to say yes to and what to say no to. As in any investment portfolio, there are likely low-risk, low-reward investments, and higher-risk, higher-reward investments. Here are a few tips.

> **idea 9:** Innovating requires a different investment and governance mindset than what most companies typically have. If you define, manage, staff, and evaluate innovation investments the same way you do less risky investments, the system will not lead to the outcomes you've intended. You need a different governance framework.

INVEST LIKE A VENTURE CAPITAL FIRM AND CREATE AN INNOVATION PORTFOLIO

Many companies squash innovation and invention because they want predictable results—a predictable time frame, predictable investment, predictable financial returns with moderate risk. This is how a private equity company invests. There are times when this is the right mentality.

For example, you should understand the returns and risks when improving and automating an internal process, building a new distribution center, or implementing a marketing system. These should have a clear business case and understanding as to what is needed for success to happen. But when you're creating new, innovative customer features or developing new business lines, your investments, risks, and returns will be harder to predict. In this case, the job of a successful innovator is to act like a venture capital firm.

The key is maintaining a balanced investment portfolio and understanding the differences among its segments (Figure 9.1). High-risk investments need to be small experiments to prove key aspects before scaling. Think big, but act small.

CONSIDER AUTONOMY AND SEPARATION

To create significant departure and disruption from current business practices, the teams within your company that are dedicated to creating innovation need to be separated from the teams representing the status quo. In Amazon's case, the company has a special team called Lab126 that is focused only on creating innovation in their devices. Tellingly, that team is based in California, far from the company's Seattle base.

While physical separation can be important, it's more about independence from the legacy business and having unfiltered communication and collaboration with a company's CEO or senior leader. Jeff Bezos is often referred to as "chief product officer" for projects. It is his job to keep that team insulated while maintaining detailed collaboration and visibility with senior leadership. The separation can be physical or just organizational. But remember how difficult it is to ask a team to both run a business and invent ways to do it completely differently.

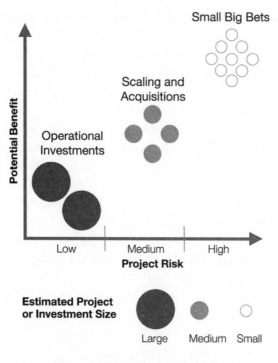

Figure 9.1 Digital Project Portfolio

DEDICATE A SENIOR, CAPABLE LEADER TO THE INITIATIVE

At many companies, you can identify a leader's cachet by the headcount and expense budget he or she manages. Not so at Amazon, where senior people are often dedicated to leading new big bets. Take, for example, Steve Kessel, the longtime executive who launched the first Kindle. Kessel's latest project is Amazon's nascent retail store initiative, which launched in Seattle.[1] Steve started with a very small team, but a critical mission. Now, some years later, Kessel once again runs a large organization.

Jeff and Amazon believe there's added power in opening up key teams and leaders to focus on something new. The critical word used at Amazon is "obsession"—let a top leader obsess about his or her objectives. If the initiative is just one of the teams and objectives that leader manages, it can't possibly benefit from the level of obsession that complete dedication brings.

CRAFT THE RIGHT METRICS AND GOALS

Hint: They're not typically about profit. Long before a new project launched at Amazon, the team behind it would outline its goals—whether growth, operational performance, customer experience, or costs—and create a set of metrics to measure those goals over time.

The idea was that if the goals and metrics were right, the team could succeed with more independence and less governance. That independence would also lead to more creativity, as team members found new ways to meet those goals.

BUILD SMALL, INTEGRATED, MULTIDISCIPLINARY TEAMS

Amazon has two rules of thumb for building teams that think and act innovatively. The first is to create a team composed of people with a variety of disciplines and backgrounds. Unique ideas and the ability to execute on them usually stem from teams that can think broadly.

The second rule of thumb is to focus on small teams. Amazon often quantifies this as a "Two-Pizza Team." In other words, you should be able to feed your whole team with two pizzas. That means no more than 8 to 10 people. Two-Pizza Teams not only own a capability. They're also responsible for everything from the market definition and product road map to the building and operations. (See Idea 20, "Pizza for All!")

CREATE AN INSANELY BETTER PRODUCT OR SERVICE

In the end, the above ingredients cannot yield a merely good product or service. It must be *insanely* good. Like jaws-to-the-floor good. This is not about marginal improvement. This is not a "completely new, but still average" product. Successful innovation results in an incredible experience—at the right price point. It surprises users, and it very quickly becomes indispensable to your customers.

. . .

Those are a few ideas to help get the big animal moving. The success of the strategies depends on strong leadership—the right approaches enabled by weak leadership will fail. Leaders must be deeply involved, have great instincts, and be willing to stick with it when the going is difficult.

QUESTIONS TO CONSIDER

1. Do you have a defined process for innovation, including a portfolio of investments best characterized as bets?

2. Are bets managed differently from normal projects and in a way that supports hypothesis testing and an agile process?

3. Are teams focused on bets composed of primarily full-time employees who obsess on the success of initiatives?

YOU ARE THE CHIEF PRODUCT OFFICER

The New Management Science of Being a Builder

*Building product is not about having a large
team to manage. It is about having a small team
with the right people on it.*
—Fred Wilson

A friend of mine told me a story about how, after earning his undergraduate degree in 1994, he took a job at a small engineering firm in Los Gatos, California, that developed ultracapacitors. When his new boss showed him to his work space, he found it littered with maps of the greater San Francisco Bay Area.

"Sorry about the clutter," his manager said, sweeping the maps into a recycling bin.

"What are the maps for?"

"We had to fire the last guy because he wouldn't stop working on his personal projects here at work," the manager said. "These were his." As my friend settled into his new work space, he removed the fired employee's nameplate and replaced it with his own. Years later, of course, MapQuest, Tesla, and SpaceX would make it a household name. But at the time it was just a memorable name.

"Elon Musk," my friend said. "Weird name. Weird guy."

Even today, decades later, Musk reportedly spends 80 percent of his time on engineering and design.[1] Think about that. One of the most powerful leaders in global business spends only 20 percent of his time managing people. That's how important the product is to Musk.

idea 10: Leaders who can design product, define architectures, and deeply understand and articulate what exactly needs to be delivered are powerful in a digital enterprise. This is a change from the traditional approach of overseeing and staying out of the details. You need to have the skills, the interest, and the insights into where to dive deep, and you need to be the designer.

Amazon Leadership Principle 4 is "Leaders Are Right, a Lot." To be right a lot at Amazon, leaders must have expertise and acute attention to detail. The traditional (read "outdated") model of management is about managing budgets, people, and locations. The greater the managerial load, the greater the leader. The "coin of the realm" was typically the number of people or budget in your charge. Historically, these types of leaders would tell subordinates and consultants to "just get it done." While initially easy, this type of command-and-control leadership demands a whole lot of trust in those handed the task. Sometimes it goes right, sometimes it doesn't. Either way, these types of leaders rarely understand *why* something did or didn't work.

At Amazon, senior leaders are often put in charge of a "big idea" from the beginning, usually with little headcount and a small budget. These senior leaders get to be personally and intimately involved in the details, evaluating and inventing every aspect of the project from the beginning. They are the "chief product officers" for the idea.

Being the chief product officers requires certain skills, some of which may have atrophied over the years as people have advanced through the Byzantine ranks of an organization. The younger versions of ourselves may have been acutely talented chief product officers. Yet as we migrated away from the real work and into the nebulous world of management, we may have lost our edge. Suddenly, as chief product officer, you are expected to write the idea (see Idea 44 on narratives), conduct the interviews, design the user experience, figure out the technical requirements, and rationalize the market fit requirements and target cost to produce. You need to be "the builder."

There are many benefits to becoming the chief product officer and dusting off that old builder's toolbox. First, the project will benefit from your years of expertise. Your attention to the nitty-gritty details will set a fresh tone for the organization. Everyone needs to dive deep and understand the details from top to bottom. You can skip freely around the organization's hierarchy. Develop personal relationships and influence team members at all levels, some of whom you might not normally work with in an active manner.

For example, Musk reportedly spends half a day each week working directly in the studio with Tesla's design guru Franz von Holzhausen.[2] Musk remains up to his elbows in problem solving on product. He is part of the creative process. He is on a first-name basis with the team creating the products for whom he is the highly recognizable face. This is intentional.

As chief product officer, you too must lead by example. But it is not enough to offer expertise and maintain an acute eye for detail. You must also demonstrate accountability, primarily through a scorecard of metrics. There is nothing worse than a leader who grades himself or herself on a different scale than other members of the team. You are all in this together, and as chief product officer, it is up to you to prove it.

It's important that your team understand you are in the trenches with them when it comes to creating an excellent product. However, as we will discuss in the next chapter, if you are going to create game-changing innovation, you must be willing to be misunderstood by the critics.

QUESTIONS TO CONSIDER

1. Do leaders dive down into the details of the product and customer experience?

2. Do leaders understand good design and create an environment where design matters?

3. Is there enough attention to detail in product design to create an insanely good product?

ARE YOU WILLING TO BE MISUNDERSTOOD?

Lessons from Amazon's Biggest Innovations

And the haters gonna hate, hate, hate, hate, hate.
—Taylor Swift

What are Amazon's greatest innovations? Drones? Cloud computing? Echo and Alexa? These are impressive; some are even revolutionary. However, I believe Amazon's greatest innovations are the ones that have changed the basics of competing to the point where they now sound mundane.

My top list of greatest Amazon innovations includes Free Everyday Shipping, Prime Loyalty, and Item Authority. Deceptively simple, Item Authority signed up multiple sellers of the same item to increase item selection, availability, and price competition. It was the "killer feature" that led to Amazon overtaking eBay in the mid-2000s as the destination site for third-party sellers. Amazon received negative feedback from many constituencies, internal and external, as they were implementing.

What are the common traits each of these innovations share, other than that they come from Amazon? For one, they are all customer experience and

> **idea 11:** The most impactful and underappreciated aspect of innovation is challenging common and long-held assumptions about how things work. When you create an alternative to these assumptions, expect many doubters.

business model innovations. They are not really that technical. What they also have in common is the fact that incumbents and industry pundits woefully underestimated their impact on the industry and the bottom line. These innovations were implemented when Amazon was young, small, and neither respected nor feared by the industry the way it is now. Here are just a few examples:

- "Amazon is pulling everyone into the gutter to play that [free shipping] game." —Bob Schwartz, former president of Magento and founder of Nordstrom.com[1]

- "There's many moments where a voice assistant is really beneficial, but that doesn't mean you'd never want a screen. So the idea of [Amazon Echo] not having a screen, I don't think suits many situations." —Philip Schiller, senior vice president of worldwide marketing for Apple[2]

- "While recent stories and reports of a new entity competing with the three major carriers in the United States grab headlines, the reality is it would be a daunting task requiring tens of billions of dollars in capital and years to build sufficient scale and density to replicate existing networks like FedEx." —Mike Glenn, executive vice president of FedEx[3]

- "We do not believe our vendors selling product directly on Amazon is an imminent threat. There is no indication that any of our vendors intend to sell premium athletic product, $100-plus sneakers that we offer, directly via that sort of distribution channel." —Richard Johnson, CEO and chairman of Foot Locker[4]

- "When you think about the online versus the offline experience, we don't need AI in our stores. We have 'I.' We have living, breathing, 4,500 style advisors in our stores." —Marc Metrick, president of Saks Fifth Avenue[5]

- "What the hell is cloud computing? . . . I mean, it's really just complete gibberish." —Larry Ellison, executive chair and chief technology officer of Oracle[6]

- "I don't really worry so much about [AWS], to be very blunt with you. We need to worry about ourselves. We're in a great position." —Mark Hurd, CEO of Oracle[7]

All of these public statements from entrenched industry leaders remind me of the classic quote by Thomas Watson, chairman of IBM, who in 1943 said, "I think there is a world market for maybe five computers."

Over the years, as Amazon has upset the status quo and disrupted cozy business tradition after cozy business tradition with innovation, the establishment fought back with mockery and dismissals. In Bezos's mind, this is being "misunderstood." If you are going to innovate, you not only have to be willing to be misunderstood but you must also have a thick skin. To many of its competitors, Amazon makes no sense. "It's the most befuddling, illogically sprawling, and—to a growing sea of competitors—flat-out terrifying company in the world."[8] If you aren't upsetting someone, you likely are not disrupting much of anything:

> One thing that I learned within the first couple of years of starting a company is that inventing and pioneering involve a willingness to be misunderstood for long periods of time. One of the early examples of this is customer reviews. Someone wrote to me and said, "You don't understand your business. You make money when you sell things. Why do you allow these negative customer reviews?" And when I read that letter, I thought, we don't make money when we sell things. We make money when we help customers make purchase decisions.[9]

Consider the feature Look Inside the Book. In 2001, Amazon launched this program based on a simple concept—the idea of emulating the bookstore experience by allowing Amazon surfers to look at the pages inside of a book before buying.

Of course, this required Amazon to house book content in online form on the site, which raised some questions about whether this would expose book content to piracy. Publishers were worried and skeptical. The program would also be very costly. Each book would have to be scanned digitally and indexed, a huge logistical challenge.

Jeff gave the go-ahead for a large-scale launch, recognizing that this was the only way to see whether it would go over with Amazon's then 43 million active customer accounts.[10] The feature debuted with an astonishing 120,000-plus books. The database took up 20 terabytes, which was about 20 times larger than the biggest database that existed anywhere when Amazon was founded.

David Risher was Amazon's first vice president of product and store development, responsible for growing the company's revenue from $16 million to over $4 billion. He described the strategy behind the launch of Look Inside the Book this way: "If we had tried it in a tentative way on a small number of books, say 1,000 or 2,000, it wouldn't have gotten the PR and the customers' perception. There's an X factor: What will it look like in scale? It's a big investment, and a big opportunity cost. There's a leap of faith. Jeff is willing to take those gambles."[11] Ultimately, the publishers embraced the Look Inside the Book program as an asset to sales:

> Anytime you do something big, that's disruptive—Kindle, AWS— there will be critics. And there will be at least two kinds of critics. There will be well-meaning critics who genuinely misunderstand what you are doing or genuinely have a different opinion. And there will be the self-interested critics that have a vested interest in not liking what you are doing, and they will have reason to misunderstand. And you have to be willing to ignore both types of critics. You listen to them, because you want to see, always testing, is it possible they are right? But if you hold back and you say, "No, we believe in this vision," then you just stay heads down, stay focused, and you build out your vision.[12]

A current example of Amazon being willing to be "misunderstood" is its overall healthcare strategy. By partnering with Berkshire Hathaway and JP Morgan Chase to start the yet unnamed healthcare company headed by Atul Gawande, how will Amazon strive to change healthcare and insurance for their employees? Is their strategy to sell supplies to hospitals? Is it to integrate the PillPack acquisition into a Prime benefit and give customers cheaper prescription deliveries (along with a new book)? Or is it to transform the overall customer experience of healthcare and healthcare insurance and change the cost structure, which is a huge drain on both businesses and employees? Or is it something else? I doubt that Amazon will clarify this in the short-term, and I actually expect that they will add more healthcare investments to their portfolio.

There are two sides to "being misunderstood" to consider. The first is that if your goal is *big* innovation, in which the customer experience and business model are dramatically changed, then if established stakeholders are not being naysayers, you should be worried. The second side is in planning and preparing your stakeholders, such as investors and partners, for the negative reactions. Amazon, often through the annual shareholder letter, consistently reminds investors that Amazon will look for long-term business results, not sacrifice long-term value for short-term results, and it will be misunderstood, often. Are you willing to be misunderstood?

QUESTIONS TO CONSIDER

1. When was the last time you did something that benefited customers but upset the traditions of business?

2. What aspects of your customer experience would be different if you started over?

3. What business model innovations could be applied to your industry?

GET TO YES

Finance, Tax, Legal, and HR Teams That Matter

> *If I had an hour to solve a problem,*
> *I'd spend 55 minutes thinking about the problem*
> *and 5 minutes thinking about solutions.*
> —Albert Einstein

Within most traditional organizations, a topic or project or function is "owned" by a core business team. In this model, the core group receives support from functional teams such as finance, legal, and human resources.

Organizationally marginalized and narrowly defined, these support teams are often considered expert only in their specific discipline. Naturally, these functions come to see themselves the way they are seen, and they decline to contribute much beyond the constraints of their job description.

Often, these are the people who will give the core business team reasons a goal can't be reached, or they will give very specific requirements to achieve the goal. In other words, they tend to be gatekeepers and represent just another hurdle for your core business team.

How many times has negotiating within your own company felt like the most daunting part of a project? At prior firms, many of my colleagues referred to our legal team as the "deal avoidance team." While managing legal risk is part of the job, the safest course of action is no action. As a result, no becomes the legal team's default answer to any problem if the terms are not the preferred or default terms. Similarly, when faced with a challenge, I've also heard a lot of technology leaders or CIOs say, "It's the business's decision" as if the business were an entirely separate entity. "Guess what, Sparky?" I want to tell them. "*You* are the business as much anyone else."

> **idea 12:** It is everyone's job to figure out how to get to yes. Traditional support capabilities need to understand that they are in the business of helping their internal clients get to yes. Spend more time understanding the real objectives, and more options will become available.

THERE IS NO "NO"

When Kimberly Reuter joined Amazon, she was an expert in international logistics and compliance with more than 15 years of experience at leading freight forward companies. Because of this expertise, Amazon tapped Reuter to dramatically expand Amazon's cross-border business for customers and third-party sellers. At the time, Reuter saw customs and compliance as a transactional system of prescribed procedures and regulations. However, in her new role as Amazon's director of global supply chain and compliance, these processes and procedures were expected to scale. Radically. The model she brought with her to Amazon was suddenly far too slow and unwieldy.

"It was really disorienting. I spent the first few months saying, 'No, that's not possible' a lot. I was really frustrated when I first joined, and no one was listening to my decisions," said Reuter. "My mentor sat me down and informed me that there is no 'No' at Amazon. If I was going to be successful, I had to figure out solutions, no matter how complicated—and I needed to do it quickly."[1]

Her mentor told Reuter that if she was going to innovate, she had to be able to present options, choices, trade-offs, and opportunities. The bottom line is that, at Amazon, no one defers responsibility. Everyone works to get to yes. Amazon requires the mindset that "we" must get to yes. All of us. It's everyone's job to get to yes. It was Reuter's job just as it was the job of HR or legal or finance. Everyone has the same amount of ownership and accountability about getting to yes as the core business team.

REFRAME THE ISSUE

How do you get your team to yes? Finding solutions isn't always the obstacle. Frequently, it's truly understanding the situation, problem, or requirements. Is the issue, "Why did this fail?" or "How do we design something that allows that component to fail?" Is the right question, "How do we avoid this risk?" or "How do we accept and mitigate this risk?" These slight tweaks in the problem statement make all the difference in how you find solutions. What steps do you take to get to yes more effectively? Here are some suggestions:

1. Reframe the issue, and ask more questions about the situation and objectives.

2. Dive deep on the real root-cause factors versus symptoms. Ask the five whys (see Idea 5).

3. Outline and challenge your assumptions in a very deliberate way.

4. Articulate and quantify the real risks. Often the perceived risks can be mitigated, making the hurdle a minimal factor.

5. Bring in external, unbiased, cross-domain expertise to complement the expert mindset in the room.

6. Create a contest or hackathon for developing alternatives and solutions.

There are many obstacles to creating a yes culture. First and foremost, it requires direct and honest communication within an organization and viewing yourself as a co-owner of the business result. You have to get to yes. What is the mortal enemy of direct communication? Bureaucracy.

QUESTIONS TO CONSIDER

1. Are your support organizations like HR, legal, and finance true partners in the business?

2. Do support organizations participate throughout an initiative, or just at certain junctures?

3. Do you have problem-solving and brainstorming meetings where the mindset is, "There is no 'No'"?

BLOW UP THE ORG CHART

Don't Let Your Organizational Structure and Titles Get in the Way

The perfect bureaucrat everywhere is the man who manages to make no decisions and escape all responsibility.
—Brooks Atkinson

What is Amazon's senior leadership's biggest concern for their business? A competitor? Cybersecurity? Government regulation or interference? They certainly take all of these into account as they execute their seemingly unstoppable march to change every industry in the world. However, I believe the threat of creating a bureaucratic quagmire that bogs down the innovation machine driving Amazon is their greatest concern.

Bureaucracy is insidious. It can grow and flourish like a cancer. It can creep through your organizational chart with a grim determination until it has choked your company's efficiency and innovation.

> **idea 13:** Organizational charts, titles, and job descriptions serve important purposes. Use them to do the right thing. Don't let them get in the way of doing the right thing. Set up strategies to counterbalance organizational structures.

No matter how carefully you design the organizational chart, no matter how often you do a reorganization (hopefully not annually), and no matter how much job design expertise you bring to the table, you are—at best—organized for predictable situations and today's business. When things go sideways or when a change initiative is underway, you are at high risk of a cross-functional, bureaucratic chokehold.

In his 2016 letter to shareholders, Bezos warned that the quickest way to become a dreaded Day 2 company was to rely on process as proxy. Good process serves the business so the business can serve customers, Bezos said, but if you're not careful, the process will consume the outcome. "This can happen very easily in large organizations. The process becomes the proxy for the result you want. You stop looking at outcomes and just make sure you're doing the process right. Gulp. It's not that rare to hear a junior leader defend a bad outcome with something like, 'Well, we followed the process.' A more experienced leader will use it as an opportunity to investigate and improve the process. The process is not the thing. It's always worth asking, do we own the process, or does the process own us? In a Day 2 company, you might find it's the second,"[1] wrote Bezos.

CONWAY'S LAW AND THE CONSULTING ORGANIZATION

Conway's law states that "organizations which design systems . . . are constrained to produce designs that are copies of the communication structures of these organizations." Although it reads like a Zen koan, this 1967 computer programming adage has a useful corollary to business. In short, it states that multiple authors must communicate frequently with each other to ensure a software module's function. Because the design that occurs first is almost never the best possible, the prevailing system concept may need to change. Therefore, flexibility of organization is important to effective design.[2]

According to Nigel Bevan, a usability expert, Conway's law is evident in the design of many corporate websites. "Organizations often produce websites with a content and structure which mirrors the internal concerns of the organization rather than the needs of the users of the site," Bevan says.[3]

The way a consulting practice is organized and deployed offers helpful concepts here. A consulting practice is often aligned to one core axis such as geography or industry, and then a second axis such as solution. These long-lived organization alignments are used for talent management—hiring and training—and the development of intelletual property (IP). A consultant often is a assigned a performance manager as part this organization alignment. But the business of consulting is based on clients and projects or a mission. A project often requires people in a way that cuts across the primary organization structure. A project has a beginning and an end to it. And a project has one leader. So the formal organization chart helps to guide messaging to the market; it helps define and hire for the right industries and solutions; it cultivates expertise and communities around this expertise; and it helps people grow. But it's not the way real projects with clients get done. In the real world, the project team reports to the client engagement leader. When done correctly, everyone pitches in on all topics to achieve the right results for the client. Serving the client, getting the project mission done, is the primary orientation, not the organization charts within the business.

Nonconsulting organizations should borrow from this playbook. Maintain your normal organization model and reporting hierarchy. But when there is a project or a mission to accomplish or a problem to solve, report to the leader of the initiative. Project success is measured only by the success of the initiative, hopefully to the delight of customers. This "all hands on deck" approach is clean, clear, and simple. It cuts down countless hours of meetings and extraneous communication. It leverages the most experienced talent on your team. It promotes a culture of yes.

Even with Amazon's small-team organizational structure, the leaders sometimes find their organization chart and job descriptions not serving the immediate situation. When this happens, they will quickly form project teams pulled from across the organization. The second leadership principle, "Ownership," states that a leader never gets to say, "That's not my job." Customer obsession and metrics support the mindset of not letting job descriptions and the organizational chart get in the way of doing the right thing.

MAKE IT THE EXPECTATION

So how do you institute a culture of antibureaucracy? At Amazon, these cultural norms and expectations are not assumed or taken for granted. They are reinforced and passed on in a dynamically growing organization through communications, tribal lore, and leadership examples. Don't assume that communicating this idea once is going to get the job done. Repeat, repeat, repeat—just like brand messaging, you must always be on message.

I'm guessing you've heard the old saying, "It isn't work if you love it." Much of this book is about inspiring your team to love solving problems, to love turning a challenge around and around like a Rubik's Cube, examining every possible permutation until the perfect solution falls into place. This passion for problem solving focuses energy on the right types of results and collaboration, and it explodes the bureaucratic mindset that organizational charts and dynamics can create. This is how innovation happens. This is how yes happens. The stakes are high, but it's all still a game. Teach your people to love to play. They don't always have to win. They just have to win a lot. What games might help create innovation?

QUESTIONS TO CONSIDER

1. Do job descriptions and organizational charts at your company reduce the effectiveness of solving problems, driving operational excellence, or serving the customer?

2. What strategies to reduce organizational boundaries could you pursue to create faster results?

3. Does your organizational structure ever get in the way of innovation? If yes, how do you counterbalance this?

GAMES FOR INNOVATION

Spur Invention in Fun Ways

The present is theirs; the future,
for which I really worked, is mine.
—Nicola Tesla

One of the most valuable honors an Amazon employee can earn is a puzzle piece made of clear or blue acrylic resin. Outside Amazon, the thing is basically worthless. Inside Amazon, it is a medal of honor. These are called "patent awards." Amazon inventors receive a clear puzzle piece when one of their inventions is filed. If a patent ensues, they receive a blue puzzle piece with their name, the patent number, and the date of issuance.

Some of the most successful inventors at Amazon have large puzzles with dozens of pieces on their desks. But no one out-invents the big dog. Walk into Jeff's conference room, and you'll find the word "patent" in blue puzzle pieces framed by clear puzzle pieces.[1] Digital versions of these patent awards are also displayed on the company's intranet. They distinguish an employee's profile in much the same way experience points or collected items distinguish a gamer's video game profile. This is not by accident.

> **idea 14:** *Patent* is just a word for "a great idea that adds value." For most organizations and teams, pursuing patents is not core to strategy or realistic, but creating incentives for coming up with "great ideas that add value" is. Find fun but consistent ways to incent and recognize innovating.

Video game designers have long understood that if you build an interaction into your game, the player is going to interact with it. Anytime a game responds to its players, they are going to keep playing. Give them a door, and they will walk through it. Give them a weapon, and they will use it. Give them an incentive to invent, and they will invent. It's human nature. Simply put, that's how Amazon generates an absurdly large number of inventions and patents. They gamified the process (Figure 14.1).

Figure 14.1 Congratulations on Being an Amazon Inventor!
Source: Adapted from Todd Bishop, "Legal Puzzle: Amazon and Former Employee Set for Trial in Unusual Patent Dispute," *GeekWire*, July 8, 2013.

THE FUTURE GAME

In his 2013 letter to shareholders, Bezos described Amazon as a "large, inventive team" with "a patient, pioneering, customer-obsessed culture." He described great innovations, large and small, happening every day on behalf of customers at all levels throughout the company.[2] "This decentralized distribution of invention throughout the company—not limited to the company's senior leaders—is the only way to get robust, high-throughput innovation. What we're doing is challenging and fun—we get to work in the future," wrote Bezos.[3]

Of course, in every game there are winners and losers. This does not bother Bezos. In fact, he embraces the fact that failure is part of invention.

He understands that failure is not optional. "We understand that, and believe in failing early and iterating until we get it right. When this process works, it means our failures are relatively small in size (most experiments can start small), and when we hit on something that is really working for customers, we double-down on it with hopes to turn it into an even bigger success. However, it's not always as clean as that. Inventing is messy, and over time, it's certain that we'll fail at some big bets too."[4]

WHAT DO I WIN?

When you are an employee of a company, the intellectual property you develop is typically owned by the company. So what's in it for the employee? Sometimes recognition is enough, especially if your employee has bought into your culture and is playing for the future (and future stock options). But there is no end to the ways you can motivate employees and gamify innovation in your organization.

In addition to finding a way to recognize innovation—such as a chunk of acrylic resin—there are many approaches to inspiring people to collaborate and be excited about the process. Games and contests can be exciting because they allow for a different mindset and a break from the operational status quo.

A *hackathon*, in which you put "work" aside for two or three days to focus on a specific challenge, is one such approach. Frame the contest in a way that is suitable to your goals—a new business model, a way to improve a customer experience, or a way to eliminate an operational quality issue or risk. The constraints are that it must be done within a specific time frame. This gets people hacking, looking for shortcuts and new ideas.

Named for the Japanese term meaning "change for the better," Amazon's Kaizen program allows employees to join small teams to identify waste and streamline processes. In 2014, more than 2,300 associates participated in 725 kaizen activities, according to the Amazon website. "A team at Amazon's Las Vegas, Nevada, fulfillment center streamlined the customer returns process, improving productivity 34 percent, eliminating excess walking distance by 128,000 ft. per day, and reducing work in process by 46 percent."[5]

In a detailed survey and study of workers at an IBM research lab published by the *Journal of Socio-Economics*, behavioral economists Susanne Neckermann and Bruno Frey found that naming an award's recipients and holding a public ceremony had as much of an effect in motivating people as increasing the cash value of a reward from $0 to $1,000.[6]

Amazon hands out a wide variety of awards and recognitions. Many of these honors are presented at the quarterly all-hands meetings by Jeff Bezos or another senior leader. Each has its own subtext. For example, the Just Do It Award is given to an employee found demonstrating the leadership principle of ownership. The subtext of this prize is that it's never "not your job" to do the right thing. The Bar Raiser Award is bestowed upon those employees who can identify and hire talent guaranteed to markedly improve the company's collective IQ, capacity, and capability. The subtext of this award is that the engine driving Amazon is constant improvement. Jeff famously put the philosophy of the Bar Raiser Award this way: five years after an employee was hired, that employee should think, "I'm glad I got hired when I did because I wouldn't get hired now."[7]

It doesn't always need to be an award. Every holiday season as the logistics operations organization prepares for another peak of inventory and orders to manage, Jeff Wilke wears flannel shirts to recognize the hard work and sacrifices that the hundreds of thousands of people working in the Amazon fulfillment centers are doing and to send a safety-first message.

Then there's the "empty chair." Bezos is known to leave one seat open at a conference table to inform all attendees that they should consider that seat occupied by their customer, "the most important person in the room."[8]

Ultimately, these symbolic gestures are highly calculated and often repeated messages created to reinforce Amazon's leadership principles. It's a tactic Bezos has used since the beginning. He has proven time and again that if you give an employee—any employee—a door, he or she will walk through it. And in some cases, these incentives will have a considerable impact on your bottom line. Which brings us to the door desk.

QUESTIONS TO CONSIDER

1. Do you recognize teams and people who go beyond expectations?

2. Could a hackathon help spur ideas for innovation?

3. Could unstructured time dedicated to problem solving and innovation bring different results to your organization?

THE DOOR DESK

Forcing Innovation Through Frugality

Frugality includes all the other virtues.
—Cicero

Jeff Bezos has long believed that one of the great forcing functions for innovation is frugality. As he has put it, "One of the only ways to get out of a tight box is to invent your way out."[1] Every dollar saved is another opportunity to invest in the business. Eliminating cost structure from the business drives low prices, which drives the virtuous flywheel. He also believes that attention to frugality minimizes what he fears and loathes most: complacency.

Bezos is big on symbols. One of the iconic symbols associated with Amazon is the *door desk*. Early in the company's history, Bezos was adamant that the organization did not need offices with huge, elaborate desks. He figured that all anyone needed was a place to work, and that included senior leadership. Somewhere along the line, someone hammered legs onto spare doors to create desks. Eventually the door desk became Bezos's symbol for the low-cost, egalitarian culture he was trying to create. In fact, the company still hands out the Door Desk Award, an award given to select employees who have a "well-built idea" that creates significant savings for the company and enables lower prices for customers.[2]

While this concept has humble origins, the door desk is key to understanding how a company as complex and wide-ranging as Amazon has been able to scale to such absurd heights.

Bezos recognized that saving money is just a side benefit of frugality. The real value comes in the form of efficiency.

idea 15: Savings are more than a competitive matter. Frugal does not mean cheap. Embrace thrift to build a culture of efficiency and innovation. Designing to constraints, such as cost, helps to reframe the situation and drive innovation.

THE LONG VIEW

Because frugality is one of the core values of Amazon, it is also directly tied to the idea of the Day 1 company and the long view. In his 1997 letter to the shareholders, which he has appended to every letter to the shareholders since, Bezos explained that Amazon made decisions and weighed trade-offs differently than some companies. He then shared Amazon's fundamental management and decision-making approach with his shareholders.

The first on the list was this: "We will continue to focus relentlessly on our customers." The second? "We will continue to make investment decisions in light of long-term market leadership considerations rather than short-term profitability considerations or short-term Wall Street reactions." He continued, "We will work hard to spend wisely and maintain our lean culture. We understand the importance of continually reinforcing a cost-conscious culture, particularly in a business incurring net losses."[3]

Frugality informs an attitude of being lean, scrappy, humble, and innovative, creating a culture that pays attention to details and understands operational excellence. Frugality and customer experience are the magic ingredients to both innovation and scaling. To this day, Amazon's insistence on remaining frugal helps keep at the front of employees' minds that Amazon is purposefully a different company with a mission focused on customers and innovation.

THE DOOR DESK 69

QUESTIONS TO CONSIDER

1. Frugality is just one type of constraint. What constraints could you put in place to support operational excellence and innovation in your organization?

2. What symbols, like the Amazon door desk, could you use to support the constraints you want in the business?

3. Would an exercise like answering the question, "How could we cut costs by 50 percent and improve customer satisfaction and revenue?" result in potential innovation?

Part II
Strategy

INTRODUCTION TO MISSION IMPOSSIBLE

Being Digital

We are an impossibility in an impossible universe.
—Ray Bradbury

I could write an entire book examining the definition of *digital*. I could frame, define, argue, and create frameworks outlining the many aspects, variations, categories, and nomenclature. I don't see what I would be adding.

What most managers, leaders, and teams are struggling with is not what digital is, or knowing that their businesses need to evolve, but *how to do it*. What do you and your organization need to do differently? If these are your questions, then you are in the right place. And despite the title of this chapter, it's not "mission impossible." It can just seem that way.

> **Idea 16:** Being digital is about changing and improving not just the organization but also yourself. Being digital is about speed and agility, not just for your customer but in how you get work done and collaborate as an organization. To drive permanent and lasting change, be deliberate in the different habits your direct team starts to practice as part of this mission.

BE OPEN TO CHANGE

Secret 1. Compete Differently

It's said that the only people who like change are babies. But an appetite for change is what separates innovators from laggards, entrepreneurs from bureaucrats, and digital winners from digital losers. The professionals, teams, and companies who learn to love change, who are addicted to challenging *everything* about the status quo, are the digital winners. You must wring out the last drop of capability every single day until you and your organization are *great*. Then wash, rinse, and repeat.

Why? Because digital is neither the technology nor the social networks. Digital is competing differently by leveraging new customer experiences, lean business practices, and innovative business models, which are powered by the convergence of a wide range of technology and computer science capabilities such as cloud computing, social and mobile collaboration, and artificial intelligence and predictive analytics. Repeat. Digital is not the technology. It's about competing differently.

Secret 2. This Time, It's Personal

What people often don't understand is that digital transformation is not just about organizational change—it's also about *personal* change. You must be, as Gandhi said, the change you want to see in the world. The entire organization cannot be transformed if you fail to change your own personal habits.

Digital transformation is both the organizational change and personal change needed to thrive as a business or a professional in the digital era. Digital transformation is new beliefs, new management philosophies, and new techniques, at both the organizational and personal level. The personal changes typically needed are encapsulated in many of the ideas in this book— being a builder, writing narratives, designing metrics, seeking root causes, and innovating by solving a problem. And while you can't do it all by yourself, you need to be much more of an owner or direct contributor rather than always delegating.

Secret 3. Speed Matters

On paper, it's simple. Digital equals speed and agility. Speed is operational excellence. Agility is the ability to make change happen. To win in digital, make everything faster and more nimble.

This includes what you offer your customers and how you go about your work. Both inside and outside, you need to deliver and get things done with shorter time frames, and you need to be able to adapt, react more nimbly, shorten cycle times, and improve the data from the customer experience and your processes.

MAKE IT EASY

Being digital is about competing differently. How are innovative companies doing it? The overarching strategy that defines the digital era is making things *easy*. And by "easy," I mean easier by factors of 10 or 100. Perhaps the real value proposition of Amazon is giving back time to its customers. Customers save time by not going to the store. Merchants save time by not having to market or brand to get customer exposure. Logistics leaders save time by leveraging Amazon fulfillment to deliver orders. "Easy" also means giving your customer far more data, insight, and control vis-à-vis their interactions with your organization.

Take the cloud, a technology-disrupting traditional hardware and software industry. First, you pay only for what you use. Cloud computing changes the purchase from a fixed and capital expense to a variable and operating expense.

Second, cloud computing removes cycle time from procurement, setup, and installation, and it delivers immediate scaling. The elasticity to scale up and scale down easily allows organizations to save vast amounts of time, resources, and expense. Scale was once the great advantage of incumbents. No more. Platforms such as Amazon's Mechanical Turk or WeWork allow small teams to have an immediate and scalable workforce. When I ran two businesses at Amazon, the trait I admired most was that every function had a plan to improve and scale. Not all these plans were funded, but every leader had a plan and a chance to pitch that plan for funding and resources.

Finally, cloud computing abstracts complexity and makes infrastructure management exponentially more accessible than running your own. As I said, easy.

Digital competition is about convenience and choice for the customers, empowering them to choose how and when they want to do business with you. It's about erasing steps that do not add value, cut costs, improve quality, or save time. For example, "fast fashion" companies like H&M have cut lead time from idea to product to six weeks. It's also about providing transparency and access to your customers. Travelocity disrupted the world of travel agents and travel through one killer feature: making all options and prices available to the consumer.

"Technology today is creating totally new business models. Uber, the largest limo company, owns no vehicles. Facebook, the largest news company, develops no content. Alibaba, the largest retailer, doesn't have inventory. Airbnb, the largest hotelier, doesn't own hotels," says Terry Jones, founder of Travelocity and Kayak. "These companies are drop dead easy. There's a slogan in Silicon Valley: Step one, install software. There is no step two. That's it. That's how easy you have to be."[1]

FIND AND HIRE DIGITAL LEADERS

There's a common belief in sports that you can't coach speed; you were either born fast, or you weren't. Training and technique can develop, hone, and refine that speed, but nothing can make a slow athlete fast. Fortunately, that's not the case in business. Speed can be coached, but you need the right coaches.

Finding leaders with the critical eye and instincts necessary to innovate and execute digital transformation is tough—it's a magical skill set. Why? Mature organizations have solved their customers' problems and now measure success by profit, which means an increased focus on operational efficiency. As a result, innovation suffers.

"Such practices and policies ensure that executives can deliver meaningful earnings to the street and placate shareholders. But they also minimize the types and scale of innovation that can be pursued successfully within an organization," wrote innovation researcher Maxwell Wessel in the *Harvard Business Review*. "No company ever created a transformational growth product by asking: 'How can we do what we're already doing, a tiny bit better and a tiny bit cheaper?'"[2]

In other words, asking the same teams and people to be both operators and innovators will fail. The two things a company leader (be that a CEO or middle manager) is best positioned to do are to communicate vision and allocate resources. For enterprises to combine operational excellence and systematically create innovation, to help give permission to move quickly and "fail forward," leaders must create the environment to nurture tiny seeds.

"Both [Amazon Retail and AWS]," Bezos explained, "were planted as tiny seeds, and both have grown organically. . . . One is famous for brown boxes and the other for APIs. . . . Under the surface, the two are not so different. They share a distinctive organizational culture that cares deeply about and acts with conviction on a small number of principles." Those principles, as designed by company leadership, have created the scaffolding for a culture of forward failure that carries success across Amazon's many lines of business.

The key to innovation, within Amazon or your own company, is to imagine and build your own scaffolding of trial and error. According to Bezos, "You need to select people who tend to be dissatisfied by a lot of the current ways. As they go about their daily experiences, they notice that little things are broken in the world, and they want to fix them. Inventors have a divine discontent. . . . You want to embrace high-judgment failure—this was worth trying, it didn't work, so let's try something different. All of our most important successes at Amazon have been through that kind of failure: Fail, try again, and repeat that loop."[3]

At the risk of oversimplifying, if digital is best described as speed, then digital transformation is best described as making your organization and yourself fast.

QUESTIONS TO CONSIDER

1. How do you define *digital* in your organization?

2. Can you measure and track progress in becoming digital?

3. What is hard to do today that should become easy?

EXPERIMENT, FAIL, RINSE, REPEAT

Plan and Operate Your Experiments for Digital Success

*I have not failed. I've just found
10,000 ways that won't work.*
—Thomas Edison

I love the history of products that overreach with glorious names. Like an apartment complex named "The Lakes" situated on a barren section of land with one tepid, artificial pond. Products that aimed for the stars but imploded on the tarmac such as the Apple Newton, Google Glass, Microsoft Bob, New Coke, and the Amazon Fire Phone.

My current favorite buzzword is *agile methodology*: an approach for iterative incremental solution design and delivery. I've worked with and managed several technology programs using an agile methodology. Key participants in the initiatives apparently define *agile* as "the methodology of no accountability." Scope, time, cost? You can't hold us accountable because we are *agile* (wink, wink). They are wholly noncommittal when it comes to doing what they say they're going to do. Yet the greatest semantic travesty occurs when *agile* is used as an excuse for not getting *real* results—the kind that actually matter for customers and for the business.

"Move fast and break things." Facebook's internal mantra encourages quick action when it comes to new ideas. Overthinking such things can sacrifice competitive edge in an industry moving at light speed.

idea 17: Digital success depends on moving quickly and measuring the impact of changes through tests. It depends on identifying the right type of failure versus the wrong type of failure and carefully deciding how to define a test and evaluation. Senior leaders need to be personally involved in defining the test and reviewing results and implications.

THINKING BIG, NOT BETTING BIG

I led the launch of the third-party business at Amazon in 2002. This platform allowed retailers to sell their products through Amazon's website. Today it supports 3 million sellers, and it is responsible for 50 percent of all units shipped and sold at Amazon. Having and holding a big vision for creating an outstanding customer and seller experience was critical in laying the foundation for success.

As we built the third-party business, we focused on three core principles that would allow it to grow. First, the customers' experience with these third-party sellers needed to be indistinguishable from their experience buying directly from Amazon, the retailer. Second, the experience of selling on Amazon's third-party platform had to be intuitive and easy, even though the process was relatively complex. Third, we had to design the platform for and strategize around supporting hundreds of thousands—not tens or hundreds—of sellers. Managing your business at Amazon had to be self-service.

Because of our strategy, the data and transaction choreography between the sellers and Amazon had to be more complex. We built tools, examples, test environments, and lots of supports to make selling as intuitive and efficient for sellers as possible. We also had to think through topics of scale. Amazon had parity agreements in place with its third-party sellers, requiring them to list items on Amazon at the same price and availability as any other sales channels they might be using. How could we keep track of whether sellers were living up to this obligation?

The most obvious but least scalable and effective option would have been to rely on manual audits or reviews. That would have been an expensive process that only allowed us to review a subset of items. Instead, we built an automated system to verify that sellers were living up to their parity obligations. Using the item information sent to Amazon, we were able to crawl their website and any other sales channels to verify the consistency of their pricing and availability.

We were thinking big, really big. But we did not confuse "thinking big" with "betting big," and neither should you. While my summary of how we built Amazon's third-party business platform sounds like it was smooth sailing in the deceivingly concise paragraphs above, the fact of the matter is that the voyage was littered with failures. However, none of these sharp reefs succeeded in sinking the ship. The business and art of innovation lie in the many failures—the learning, adjusting, and moving ahead—that come along the way. The principle you'll find below the waterline is about how to scale failure.

STARTING SMALL

The better you become at creating ways to test repeatedly in small ways, the more likely you are to achieve big success. In other words, think big, but act small.

It took years before the third-party business became the force that it is today. Before I even joined the Marketplace team, Amazon had already tried—and failed—to build two other third-party seller platforms. Before Amazon Marketplace, there was Amazon Auctions and then the zSHOP. The first two were failures; the third is now a huge success.

And although Amazon certainly invested in the Marketplace business, it was not a high-risk investment. Instead, leadership invested in relatively small individual experiments that would improve Amazon's long-term understanding of the winning formula.

What do those smaller experiments look like? At Marketplace, we thought up front that customers would want to shop through seller-specific storefronts, so we built the infrastructure to enable sellers to create branded online storefronts. Once we actually launched storefronts, though, we found customers were actually more likely to shop by category across Amazon's entire site. As a result, we wound up deemphasizing merchant-specific storefronts and focusing instead on improving Amazon's core browsing and searching capabilities.

It wasn't until Marketplace eventually found the right long-term formula—through this and many other experiments—that the company shifted its focus to growth.

Successful innovators execute on lots of small experiments, and they have a patient, long-term approach to product and business success. It is rare, though not impossible, that innovation and short-term profits go together. Executed well, these kinds of small experiments help you understand your customers' needs and how your product might fit the market. Executed poorly, they can be worse than not experimenting at all.

TACTICS FOR ACTING SMALL

A failed experiment could just as easily be the result of bad execution as it could be a valid test of your hypothesis about a product. Luckily, Amazon and others have developed tactics for acting small and moving iteratively to help you avoid this trap.

Low-Fidelity Prototyping

If you've ever created something that only partially works just to test a few critical components, you've created a *low-fidelity prototype*. Google's Cardboard is an example of a low-fidelity virtual-reality (VR) prototype: sticking their phones inside a cardboard VR viewer, users can test and experiment with VR.

The first version of this was likely hacked together with a few off-the-shelf parts and a cardboard box. Today, Google is using Cardboard to build its developer community and to test the popularity of virtual reality without spending valuable time and money creating a more complex VR product. Consider ways you can test the effectiveness or viability of your experiment without actually producing it. Low-fidelity prototyping can be useful as a visual demonstration of how a product might work and as a way to get buy-in for a full prototype development.

Minimum Viable Product

The idea of a *minimum viable product* (MVP) was popularized by Eric Ries's 2011 book, *The Lean Startup*. In it, Ries encouraged business owners to identify and test the critical assumptions behind their businesses and solutions.

Inspired by the work of his mentor, Steve Blank, Ries popularized the idea of using a minimum viable version of your product to help you prove or disprove assumptions about your business and customers through carefully constructed trials.

The key for the MVP is articulating, as succinctly as possible, what part or feature of your bigger vision needs to be validated or tested first (or next) and making the scope as closely limited to that feature as possible. This is the process of defining and measuring to hypothesis and quickly getting customer or real-world feedback on that test, then proceeding in as incremental or agile a manner as possible to the next test.

At a conceptual level, this sounds easy to do. But in practice, there are many forces and realities that come into play and work against the small-as-possible MVP. Among these challenges are accurately understanding and defining what the correct hypotheses are and in what order they should be; finding ways to build just to the capabilities needed versus the many surrounding capabilities needed for a market-ready product; finding ways to let real customers use a minimal product without undercutting your brand; and finally, avoiding the likely impact to other enterprise applications and processes (including potentially avoiding the centralized information technology group) until the right time.

The key suggestion is avoiding committees and group decision-making as much as possible. Trusting one strong voice helps cut through the layers, shrink time to market, and minimize scope. But that one voice does need to be mostly right.

Fail Fast and Fail Forward

Build a team that can make the most of its failures—and that knows how to create new learning for itself. This comes down to one thing: encouraging smart, quick failure.

Your job is to make sure your team understands the difference between a failure that drives learning and a failure of execution. The first gives you valuable data. The second wastes your time.

THE FIRE PHONE AND THE ECHO

"One area where I think we are especially distinctive," Bezos wrote in Amazon's 2015 letter to shareholders, "is failure. I believe we are the best place in the world to fail (we have plenty of practice!), and failure and invention are inseparable twins. To invent you have to experiment, and if you know in advance that it's going to work, it's not an experiment. Most large organizations embrace the idea of invention but are not willing to suffer the string of failed experiments necessary to get there."[1]

Amazon's most prolific failure was the Fire Phone, launched in July 2014. It was a short-lived market miss that resulted in a $170 million inventory write-off.

"What the hell happened with the Fire Phone?" asked stock analyst Henry Blodget in a *Business Insider* discussion with Bezos.[2]

The Fire Phone, like all of Amazon's projects, was an experiment, Bezos coolly replied. In his mind, its failure was a learning experience—another chance to iterate or pivot. The phone, Bezos explained, was just one more entry in Amazon's "device portfolio." The operative word in that phrase was "portfolio."

"It's early," he told Blodget. "And we've had a lot of things we've had to iterate on at Amazon. One of my jobs as the leader at Amazon is to encourage people to be bold, . . . to create a shield around the teams innovating so they can focus on the hard things they are accomplishing and minimize the noise and concerns of detractors within the company."[3]

Amazon launched its next round of smart devices according to the standard playbook: launch a product or service quickly, don't make too big a deal of it, and spend almost nothing on marketing. Instead, get customer feedback and make adjustments or cut quickly. Launch more experiments. After all, Bezos views every project as an investment in Amazon's portfolio.

The Amazon Echo was an invitation-only product for Amazon Prime customers. It was advertised as a beta product, and it was available in limited quantities. This kept expectations low and company learning high. Amazon followed the same playbook for the Dash Button. Only when feedback and reviews of the Echo and Dash Button were fantastic did Amazon make them available to everyone. It's the same strategy that theater producers use. Tour the production around the country in select markets as a workshop production. If the reviews are good enough, open on Broadway. If the audiences hate it, pretend it never happened and move on to the next project.

YOU STILL HAVE TO BE RIGHT, A LOT

Amazon's Leadership Principle 4 is "Leaders Are Right, a Lot." It reads, "Leaders are right a lot. They have strong judgment and good instincts. They seek diverse perspectives and work to disconfirm their beliefs."

Creating and adopting a test-measure-adjust mentality is not without risk. Using it as a crutch for either bad judgment or poor execution can spell the death of your enterprise. Just as "agile" has been allowed to become the development methodology of no accountability, "fail fast" can become the excuse for more failing than needed. Just because many opportunities to become digital exist in the business, that doesn't mean you can afford repeated attempts at something that you should get right the first time. "Failure" has become an excuse and almost an expectation; this is the risk of the current innovation models.

The difference between a *test failure* in which you learn and an *execution failure* is sometimes obvious, sometimes really subtle. The more involvement you have, the better your odds of knowing which one it is. Marc Andreessen noted, "We are biased toward people who never give up. That's something you can't find on a résumé. We look for courage, and we look for genius. There's all this talk about how important failure is, which I call the failure fetish. 'Failure is wonderful. It teaches you so much. It is great to fail a lot,' people say. But we think failure sucks. Success is wonderful."[4]

To win in digital, you have to have a strong product or business vision and the ability to listen to others, but you must also take command, and clearly and simply articulate what is needed. This creates the "think big but bet small" strategy to drive innovation.

QUESTIONS TO CONSIDER

1. Do you understand how to define and test the critical hypothesis in your innovation initiatives?

2. Does your organization understand the difference between testing failure versus execution failure?

3. Do you have a one-speed project approach? Or do you adapt your project approach based on the situation?

idea
18

SO YOU WANT TO BE
A PLATFORM?

Platform Strategy for
the Rest of Us

> *I think that not only do saints make poor role models,*
> *they are incapable in one sense of identifying radically*
> *with those of us who are mere mortals.*
> —Martin Luther King Jr.

A *platform* is a business model and capability that can be accessed and customized by external users. Often, these external users leverage this platform in ways you could never imagine, let alone sustain and serve. Amazon consists of more than a dozen thriving platform businesses, including AWS, Fulfillment, Payments, CreateSpace, Direct Publishing, Audible, Advertising, Flex, Instant Video, Kindle, and Mechanical Turk, to name a few.

Outside of Amazon, who are the dominant digital platform companies? In addition to Amazon, Facebook, Apple, and Google are typically considered those with a lock on the foreseeable future. Scott Galloway refers to them as the "Four Horsemen."[1] Each offers core capabilities and access to customers with a strong network effect. With each additional participant, the network grows stronger and smarter. It's hard to understand how anyone would compete with them on broad platform capabilities.

idea 18: Thinking about how your core capabilities could be offered as a platform might help you identify a future business strategy. It's not for everyone. Regardless, deeply understanding what it would take will give you great ideas for improvement and innovation.

What are some attributes of a platform business model? It abstracts complexity. It democratizes access and use. It has high fixed costs. It has low (zero) marginal costs. Its inventory is owned by others. It's on demand. It features by-the-sip pricing. It has a network effect. It owns the means of connection. It is not the means of production. It features user-generated content and *other people's work* (OPW) (see Idea 23). It is marketplace enabled. It has level and clear rules. It is programmable.

Amazon stresses one more attribute, perhaps the "killer feature" that adds value to users and to Amazon. That attribute is self-service. Using a company's platform (or service) should not require you to talk to someone in that company. In fact, successful platform businesses innovate through contact avoidance. You should be able to discover, implement, and consume without an "engagement." It should be zero provisioned. Much like aspiring to perfection in your customer experiences or operations, zero provisioning is an aspirational goal. Some capabilities can truly be self-service. For others, it simply is not feasible. "When a platform is self-service, even improbable ideas get tried, because there's no expert gatekeeper ready to say, 'That will never work!' Guess what? Many of those improbable ideas do work," wrote Bezos in his 2011 letter to shareholders.[2]

SHOULD YOU DEVELOP A PLATFORM?

Maybe. Maybe not. What you absolutely must do is carefully evaluate if you should take a core capability, or set of capabilities, and invest and transition to be a platform business:

1. **Identify your core capabilities as a business.** Can you define precisely what gives your company competitive advantage? How easily can it be imitated? How do you deliver value to your customers?

Evaluate your business as a set of processes and capabilities. Be clear on the definition, and break down big processes into smaller functions and services.

2. **Identify the services.** Think through what the service, and the API for the service, might be. How do you make it a "black box"? In other words, how will you protect it from replication and theft?

3. **Where's your advantage?** How would you offer best-in-class commercial terms? Commercial terms include cost, speed, availability, quality, flexibility, and features.

4. **Can it be profitable?** Would these commercial terms and capabilities be viable in the market? Would it be a viable profitable business for you?

5. **Test and evaluate.** You have a critical and fact-based understanding of your core capabilities, their gaps, and the potential benefit (or lack thereof) of a platform. Build your agile approach to testing, learning, and building value as you go.

Developing a platform service takes effort and careful inspection. Whether you decide to proceed with a platform strategy or not, doing this exercise will give you honest and current insights into how to improve and innovate your capabilities.

QUESTIONS TO CONSIDER

1. What are the true core capabilities and processes in your organization?

2. Could you make them into self-service platform capabilities serving internal and external customers?

3. Could you make these capabilities highly available, zero provisioned, and competitive in the market?

idea

19

YES, YOU ARE A TECHNOLOGY COMPANY

Decentralize Your Way to Digital Greatness

*The only way to control chaos and complexity
is to give up some of that control.*
—Gyan Nagpal

In his 1979 letter to shareholders, Warren Buffett explained that Berkshire's financial decisions are acutely centralized at the very top of the organization. Operating authority, he continued, is widely delegated to key managers at the individual company or business unit level. "We could just field a basketball team with our corporate headquarters group," explained Buffett. The Oracle of Omaha admits that this approach occasionally produces a major mistake that might have been eliminated or minimized through closer operating controls, but it produces wide-ranging benefits.

"It also eliminates large layers of costs and dramatically speeds decision-making," said Buffett." Because everyone has a great deal to do, a very great deal gets done. Most important of all, it enables us to attract and retain some extraordinarily talented individuals—people who simply can't be hired in the normal course of events—who find working for Berkshire to be almost identical to running their own show."[1]

idea 19: Centralized IT serves one set of purposes for an enterprise. As more connected experiences are integrated into your products and services and more technology-enabled innovation is needed throughout, put technology resources closer to customers, and embed these into the business, where they are part of the team and product.

The command-and-control mindset, which includes the common belief that "my CIO is going to manage my technology operations *and* deliver digital transformation" is yesterday's management model and mindset. As your products and services become more digital, you need to develop a balanced understanding of what functions and decisions should be owned by the CIO (aka centralized IT) and what should be built at the edges of the business with technology capabilities built and operated.

WHAT REMAINS CENTRAL

Before we shotgun the IT department to the furthest reaches of your organization, let's touch on aspects of IT that likely should remain centralized: systems, standards, and operations.

First, certain systems and technology teams—especially those with high legal and investor obligations, operating infrastructure for all technology teams, and "order-to-cash" systems—should remain centralized. One could argue that these systems should be decentralized to the finance and controllership organization, but they are best left in central IT.

Typical applications and capabilities to consider centralizing in your IT organization include financial systems; systems owned by key support organizations such as finance, HR, and legal; systems with highly sensitive customer data (personally identifiable information, or PII); key infrastructure such as the data center, cloud, database, and messaging systems; employee and vendor enablement; integrated deployment environments; office productivity applications and desktop and/or device support; and perimeter and cyber threat detection technology. The operations central IT might continue to provide include operations to all the systems above, a program management office for large programs, and key vendor management operations.

Second, it's important to point out that the shift to decentralized technology capability does not mean that everybody does things in different ways. In fact, *standards become even more important, perhaps vital, in a decentralized model*. If we can create standards and principles under which every team deploys and operates, this will greatly enhance the speed, interoperability, and quality our teams will produce. As a result, the shift to decentralized IT will mean that the mission of central IT will grow in its ability to lead by influence through standards.

What types of standards are needed? Standards for system design; metrics and SLAs, APIs, and interoperability; technical documentation; tool and programming language; security (see Idea 36); program management including risk and program governance; quality, testing and release management; and support and operations, availability, performance, and graceful failure.

Finally, not only does central IT need to define these standards, they also need to evangelize these standards to their customers (the other technology teams); review and sign off on both designs and implementations using these standards (they are an enforcement organization); and keep a scorecard of adoption (what's in compliance and what is not in compliance). Holding others accountable through a "trust but verify" approach is vital. All functions and leaders need to invite IT to partner and drive these standards.

TO THE EDGE

I often hear people say, "Amazon's information technology team must be huge." On the contrary, Amazon's centralized IT team is actually quite small, but the technology capability is pervasive, huge, and with scarce skill sets where more is always needed.[2] So if the technology skills are not in a centralized IT team, what should be decentralized?

First, technology that is part of products or core services can be distributed to these teams. Second, marketing, sales, and supply chain systems are great candidates to be integrated into their respective business organizations. These organizations need to have greater ownership over integrating technology and data into their processes and capabilities.

Even if technology teams and systems still report into a centralized IT organization, many of the same outcomes can be achieved if these teams operate as if they are part of the functional teams by colocating them with the business and breaking down physical and communication barriers. Every function needs to become better at incorporating technology to serve customers better, to enable new business capabilities, and to adjust to the market and your vision. Find ways to break down the barriers between the business owners and the technology skills those business owners need to serve customers, grow their business, and innovate faster.

QUESTIONS TO CONSIDER

1. Is your IT organization a world-class partner to the business it supports?

2. Is there opportunity to decentralize technology capability to create speed and agility?

3. Do business owners have enough control of technology delivery to meet their needs?

PIZZA FOR ALL!

The Magic of Small Autonomous Teams

> *You better cut the pizza in four pieces*
> *because I'm not hungry enough to eat six.*
> —Yogi Berra

When it comes to Amazon's famous Two-Pizza Teams, most people miss the point. It's not about the team's size. It's about the team's autonomy, accountability, and entrepreneurial mindset. The Two-Pizza Team is about equipping a small team within an organization to operate independently and with agility.

At Amazon, Two-Pizza Teams work like semi-independent entrepreneurial hothouses. Insulated from the greater organization's bureaucracy, the Two-Pizza Teams encourage ambitious leaders, provide opportunity, and instill a sense of ownership.

As established in Idea 13, bureaucracy is a killer to innovation. What's more, high-performing employees are not attracted to companies or divisions in which they cannot make a difference. Small teams truly own something—a product or feature, a service like the checkout cart, or a process like the warehouse receive process. Each team defines its business plan, metrics, and product road map. This drives motivation and continuous improvement while providing transparency and accountability for future investment and results. Each team has a keen sense of customers, even if they are internal customers, and the most important orientation is to gain adoption and provide value to these customers.

idea 20: Organize the digitization of core capabilities and services to be owned by small teams. This team will engineer, build, and operate a capability valued by both internal and external customers. Creating small teams results in more innovation, higher-quality work, and a stronger culture.

Two-Pizza Teams are organized around capabilities and services as opposed to projects. Work is expected to continue for more than two years at a minimum, and it is improved through iteration. There are hundreds of Two-Pizza Teams at Amazon today. Many are very technical in nature, owning underlying technology services powering the business. Some are more functional, bringing together and integrating other technical services to fulfill a business objective. An example of this type of team might be the promotions team or the image team. These teams build a world-class and configurable capability that business units can use in their business. Amazon does not create all teams as Two-Pizza Teams, but it does strive to break up organizations into well-defined, mission-oriented teams. Be fixed on the vision and flexible on model to serve your needs.

BUILDING A PIZZA

Of course, for any team to operate, it needs the right personnel. This is especially true for a small band of operational ninjas like a Two-Pizza Team, which should be no larger than 10 people. The optimal size, incidentally, is one person operating independently.

First, the business owner is the leader of the team. For a technology pizza team, the programmers become the customers and the implementers; they are both writing the spec and implementing it. The team is composed only of A+ people. At Amazon, this is enforced indirectly through the Bar Raisers Award (see Idea 43).

The Two-Pizza Team is autonomous. Interaction with other teams is limited, and when it does occur, it is well documented, and interfaces are clearly defined. It owns and is responsible for every aspect of its systems. One of the primary goals is to lower the communications overhead in organizations,

NEVER SAY NEVER

Don't Let Past Positions
Create a Trap

When the facts change, I change my mind.
—John Maynard Keynes

I used to tell people I wasn't a California guy. I lived in the Northwest, and like most Americans, I enjoyed mocking Californians. "I'll never live in California," I'd tell anyone who would listen. "I love visiting, but I could never live there." Then in 2016, we moved from the Seattle area to Southern California for both professional and family reasons, and now I can't imagine *not* living there. Of course, several of my friends remind me of my hypocrisy every chance they get. And there's not a whole lot I can do but shrug and admit I changed my mind. I may change it yet again!

Of course, this is not a particularly uncommon situation. How many times have you not only said something but completely believed it, only to regret it later? It happens all the time, yet changing our minds is ingrained as a flaw or a weakness in our culture. Not at Amazon.

> **idea 21:** For most companies and teams, "becoming digital" requires change at all levels: strategy, business models, teams, partners, and others. Do not let your past positions be a limiting factor in what the right strategy is going forward. Things change.

Amazon and Jeff Bezos have flip-flopped on many long-held positions and strategies without batting an eyelash. "Advertising is the price you pay for a mediocre product," Bezos said at the 2009 shareholders meeting.[1] For the first couple of decades of its existence, Amazon spent essentially nothing on TV or print advertising, and the marketing budget went to fund free shipping. Today? You can't watch an NFL or MLB game or walk through an airport without seeing an Amazon Prime or AWS commercial.

When *Fortune* Executive Editor Adam Lashinsky asked Bezos if the company was becoming less frugal in 2016, Bezos replied, "Some things are so hard to measure that you have to just take them as articles of faith." As Lashinsky pointed out, this response would undoubtedly be read as flip-flopping or rationalizing from a politician. From Bezos, it's called "evolution."[2]

When I was at Amazon, we believed not having physical retail stores was a natural advantage to our business model. During those years, a store footprint seemed as unnecessary as, I don't know, an in-house film studio making Oscar-nominated feature films and TV shows. Today, Amazon has not one but *several types* of retail stores: Amazon Lockers, Amazon Bookstores, Amazon Go convenience stores, and, of course, 480 Whole Foods Markets across the United States. Oh, yeah, Amazon also has an in-house film studio making Oscar-nominated feature films and TV shows.

Many great companies have landed in the gutter by guzzling their own dogmatic Kool-Aid. It's easy to mistake strategy with core competence. Times change and situations change, so strategies need to change, and management better be willing to change along as well. Be very careful that your options are not limited by the commitments you make because the ability to change can mean the difference between survival or extinction for your organization.

I can list many brands on Amazon that at one time claimed they would never sell on Amazon. Most were forced either to reconsider or to lose control of the channel. Think you'll never go direct to customers? I promise you that continuing to go solely through distributors may be a tough one to remain committed to in the years ahead.

YOUR ECHO CHAMBER

Have you ever heard of "confirmation bias"? Confirmation bias is the natural human tendency to find the data, stories, and people who validate how you see the world and what you believe to be true and credible. To an innovator, this is a dangerous and limiting set of inputs and approach to processing them. You won't hear what your real risks and weaknesses are. These are your blind spots.

Amazon Leadership Principle 4 states, "Leaders are right, a lot. They have strong judgment and good instincts. They seek diverse perspectives and work to disconfirm their beliefs."[3] Being aware of confirmation bias and that leaders need to actively seek out diverse opinions and data in order to override this human tendency to confirm what they already believe is perhaps the most unnatural requirement asked of leaders at Amazon. But this is how you identify risk and see through your bias.

Because of Amazon's employee size—over 500,000—they are a target of publicity on employee topics. In 2018, criticism of hourly employee pay led by Senator Bernie Sanders was being levied at Amazon. Amazon was defensive about the benefits, wages, and working conditions at first. But behind the scenes, Amazon heard the message, and change was quickly afoot:

> In September 2018, Amazon announced a $15 per hour minimum wage, more than double the required amount, and made it effective worldwide starting November 1. "We listened to our critics, thought hard about what we wanted to do, and decided we want to lead," said Jeff Bezos, as the company announced the new pay scale. "We're excited about this change and encourage our competitors and other large employers to join us."[4]

What's your echo chamber? Ask yourself, "What are the assumptions, strategies, beliefs, or values that might have been the right perspectives for yesterday's business but could limit us going forward?" Try to view your business model objectively. Hire people who will continue to ask *why*. The days of doing things one way because they've always been done that way have gone the way of Kodak, the poster child for squandering digital opportunity.

Kodak never capitalized on the digital camera tech it helped create. Kodak also profoundly blew it when it came to accommodating consumers who wanted to interact with their photos. They whiffed on the accompanying technologies, and the surrounding market forces.[5] I'm willing to bet Kodak wishes it could rewind the last 20 years and admit it was wrong a little sooner than it did.

Think it can't happen to you?

QUESTIONS TO CONSIDER

1. Do your senior leaders work to actively disconfirm their beliefs?

2. Are there core assumptions limiting how you define your business?

3. What blind spots might you have in your strategy?

RELENTLESS.COM

Next-Generation Operational Excellence

We are what we repeatedly do. Excellence, then,
is not an act, but a habit.
—Aristotle

The media often use the phrase "the Amazon effect" to describe how Amazon has affected an industry, typically retail, or to talk about how customer expectations have been significantly changed by Amazon.

While Amazon's endless trail of disruption is always good clickbait, the Amazon effect is really just operational excellence. Sure, Amazon profoundly affects industries, but the true force behind its success is its incredible selection, great pricing, fast delivery, trustworthiness, no-hassle return, and warranty. How does Amazon deliver those intangibles every day, to 99.9 percent of customers, at an incredible scale of categories and geography? It's relentless.

At Amazon, everything—every process, every customer experience, and every function—has an improvement plan and road map. The majority do not get funded, but they all have a plan. Compare that with the typical company

> **idea 22:** Customer expectations are rising across all sectors and experiences. Delivering to those expectations and competing in the digital era are enabled by operational excellence. Digital experiences and the *Internet of Things* (IoT) offer opportunities to enhance your operational excellence programs.

where, other than the occasional reorganization, processes that aren't broken stay largely the same from year to year. Improvements are often driven by the enterprise-resource-planning (ERP) system-upgrade cycle.

You can find nods to this focus on continuous improvement throughout Amazon's leadership principles and history. Bezos originally named his company Relentless.com. In fact, type www.relentless.com into a browser and it will still take you to Amazon.com. While he ultimately decided against such a literal moniker for his company, "relentless" still perfectly encompasses Amazon's nature. The company is dead set on constantly exploring and reinventing itself through key leadership principles and an undying belief in the power of technology. Amazon's dedication to continuous improvement is a key part of company culture.

David Wood, a good friend of mine, is the founder of Eventene, a company that sells an application that assists the coordination of complex events. He and I were discussing what "being digital" meant. David said he believes that being digital is largely the "relentless pursuit of reducing inefficiencies." *Inefficiencies* is not a euphemism for cost-cutting and layoffs. It can refer to quality issues, cycle times, and customer contacts and problems, among others. These are opportunities to innovate by using data to solve problems that affect customers, worker safety, competitiveness, and profitability. That's a great summation of Amazon's eternal pursuit.

This companywide expectation is reinforced by Amazon's evaluation process, which assesses employees for traits such as their commitment to continuous improvement: "Always looks for ways to make Amazon better. Makes decisions for long-term success. Investigates and takes action to meet customers' current and future needs. Not afraid to suggest bold ideas and goals. Demonstrates boldness and courage to try new approaches."

Of course, Amazon is just one of many companies that have found value through a focus on continuous improvement. It's likely you're at least familiar with one or more of the following business methodologies "continuous improvement" has inspired:

- **Lean:** The philosophy of creating more customer value with fewer resources.

- **Toyota Production System (TPS):** A management approach intent on eliminating all waste. TPS includes key strategies such as just-in-time (JIT) inventory demand and management signals.

- **Statistical process control (SPC):** A system of attaining and maintaining quality through statistical tools. SPC emphasizes root-cause elimination of variation.

- **ISO 9000 quality management systems:** A set of quality certification standards based on eight management principles, including continuous improvement and fact-based decision-making.

- **Six Sigma:** A data-driven methodology for eliminating defects, lowering costs, and reducing waste.

These strategies empower employees to gather data and to act on the insights that data provides. The employees are encouraged to drive change and improvement from within. The introduction of ubiquitous connected devices has changed the rules of the data game, creating the possibility for real-time feedback loops that power continuous improvement programs. This technology injects the search for operational excellence with rocket fuel. Instead of living in a world of manual data collection, which creates limited, slow, and stale data sets, organizations can harness an exponential stream of affordable real-time data. That flood of data empowers companies to focus on making continuous improvements to their internal systems, saving them time and money while increasing productivity and consistency.

HOW AMAZON TOOK OPERATIONS
FROM GOOD TO GREAT

Today Amazon's operations—the way they fulfill, ship, track, and deliver your orders—are world class. But they didn't start out that way. Amazon measured, refined, and executed its way to greatness. It embraced continuous improvement as a way of life.

By building that dedication into its company culture and creating an operational improvement heritage, Amazon has been able to build consistently high-quality, low-cost facilities all around the world. They now boast 300 fulfillment centers across 14 countries.[1]

That kind of consistency gives Amazon the confidence and competence to guarantee incredible service: Amazon Fresh, Amazon's home grocery delivery service, lets customers schedule delivery within a 15-minute window. That kind of customer service takes incredible forecasting and execution capability—ability built on the back of Amazon's world-class supply chain heritage.

That level of precision wouldn't be possible if Amazon hadn't made a concerted effort to take advantage of connected devices and the data they provide.

In the early 2000s, the leaders of Amazon's fulfillment and operations capabilities decided to implement Six Sigma, a data-driven, five-step approach for eliminating defects in a process. Define, measure, analyze, implement, and control—or as it is referred to in Six Sigma, DMAIC. This is the root improvement cycle, and it sets up the methodical, measured steps and mindset to squeeze out defects, costs, and cycle times.

Six Sigma was introduced by Bill Smith, an engineer at Motorola, in 1986. In 1995, Jack Welch used it at General Electric to much success. The term itself is used to describe a manufacturing process that is defect free to six standard deviations. In other words, the process is 99.9996 percent accurate.

One of the challenges of completing a Six Sigma initiative is that so much of the effort—generally up to 25 percent—lies in collecting data. Depending on the project, manual data collection can be not only difficult but inaccurate. The data itself is often of questionable quality, skewed by bias or cut short due to time and effort. Because of these challenges, Six Sigma certifies professionals in a set of empirical and statistical quality management methods to help them execute on the process successfully. These professionals are installed in an organization during a Six Sigma process to make sure everything is completed successfully.

There are several levels of Six Sigma certification, but the most involved is called a Black Belt. Black Belt practitioners have received significant training and are deeply vested in applying Six Sigma. Black Belts are generally nimble problem solvers, good project managers, and facilitators. They are crafty at collecting data, and they have a strong background in statistics and math.

As you can imagine, people who have these skills are also highly sought after and well compensated. Creating a team of Black Belts within your organization is one of the biggest cost drivers of Six Sigma initiatives.

That's where digital comes in.

Using connected devices to collect data frees up the Black Belts in an organization to tackle more projects. It also leads to faster Six Sigma initiatives and a much richer, more reliable data set.

Connected devices can bring visibility to your company's operating conditions, giving you real-time insights into the flow, status, and state of key items in your process. Not only does this enhance your understanding of needed improvements, but it builds a way to scale operations with active quality and measure built into the process.

At the time Amazon integrated Six Sigma into its operations, the company was experiencing a disconnect in a process it calls SLAM. SLAM stands for the ship, label, and manifest process. Every time something, say, a printer, is ordered on Amazon, that printer is placed in a box in an Amazon fulfillment facility, labeled, sorted, and shunted through the fulfillment center, until eventually it's placed in an outbound truck. That's the SLAM process. At peak, Amazon ships over 1 million packages a day.

When Six Sigma was introduced, packages were labeled and moved down conveyor belts before being manually sorted and delivered to the correct docking station. This worked well most of the time, but there was no final confirmation that the package had actually made it onto the right truck, and there was no visibility—for the company or the customer—about where exactly a package was in the outbound process. As a result, packages were occasionally missorted.

An occasional missort doesn't sound like a big deal, but over the course of a year, missorts can cost a company like Amazon millions of dollars. More important, even one missort breaks Amazon's underlying promise to its customers: that all of their orders will arrive in their hands on time.

For Amazon, the solution was to create a *positive automated confirmation*, or "visibility," that a package had moved correctly through all logistics checkpoints after its shipping label had been applied. The change was simple in concept but incredibly complicated in implementation.

To execute, Amazon installed sensors and readers across its conveyor system. The sensors would automatically scan a package's bar code as it moved through the SLAM process. Since packages were scanned to destination-specific staging areas, the sensors allowed Amazon to track the whereabouts of specific packages at any given time in the SLAM process. Furthermore, as Amazon employees loaded those packages into the outbound trucks, scanners on the bay doors would alert them if a package was about to be loaded into the wrong truck.

By creating a positive-confirmation system for its packages, Amazon lowered its missorts to within Six Sigma's 0.0004 percent accuracy range. That's fewer than four packages missorted in every million.

Perfection is the goal, but it is never attained. It's exhausting and humbling. What's the trick to keep going? You must be relentless . . . and leverage *other people's work* (OPW).

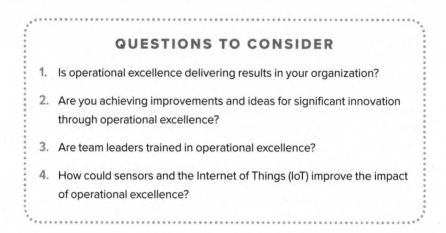

QUESTIONS TO CONSIDER

1. Is operational excellence delivering results in your organization?

2. Are you achieving improvements and ideas for significant innovation through operational excellence?

3. Are team leaders trained in operational excellence?

4. How could sensors and the Internet of Things (IoT) improve the impact of operational excellence?

OPW

The Strategy of Other People's Work

*I choose a lazy person to do a hard job. Because
a lazy person will find an easy way to do it.*
—Bill Gates

Original ideas are in short supply. However, anyone can fill a toolbox with existing great ideas and learn how to apply the right ones at the right moments. When I was a consulting partner at Arthur Andersen, I knew someone else had created a methodology, tool, proposal, or analysis that could get me going. I just needed to know how to find it.

As Jim Collins has pointed out, best beats first. "The pattern of the second (or third or fourth) market entrant's prevailing over the early trailblazers shows up throughout the entire history of technological and economic change," Collins wrote in 2000, listing IBM, Boeing, American Express, and Disneyland as proof for his theory.[1]

Why? Because the first to market doesn't always get it right. The products that follow directly behind tend to get everything the pioneer did, without the expensive mistakes. If you've ever climbed up a hill through deep snow, you know it's a lot easier to be number 2 than to be the guy post-holing up the slope.

While Collins's theory operates on a macro-organizational scale, it also applies in many ways to granular operations within an organization. Even Amazon can't automate a majority of business activity. One of my favorite strategies for dealing with this fact is the utilization of *other people's work* (OPW). In many cases, the best way to scale an unavoidable residue of manual labor is to enable and motivate other people to do it.

> **idea 23:** For work that is repeatable and poised to grow significantly or experience dramatic spikes, find ways to get other people to do it for you. By finding ways to get others to be key contributors in a core capability while protecting your brand and the customer experience, you will transform the underlying technology and operating philosophy.

OTHER PEOPLE'S WORK AND THE MECHANICAL TURK

Consider just two of the many tasks that must be done when building an e-commerce website with a virtually infinite array of products: (1) evaluating the quality of product images and (2) writing clear and accurate product descriptions. Neither can be handled effectively by a computer. Instead of hiring a vast army of people to perform these small but essential and practically endless tasks, Amazon handed that task over to its customers and partners. It created a product image management tool that collected customer feedback, allowed customers to compare images, and enabled them to report offensive or irrelevant content. It worked extremely well.

Before long, Amazon was using OPW to manage other processes that couldn't be automated. Customer reviews, which were controversial when Amazon first introduced them, are probably the best-known example of OPW. It allows thousands of Amazon customers to handle the task of describing, rating, and categorizing products for the benefit of millions of other users.

With the right approach, almost every company can find opportunities for OPW. Many of my current clients are finding that letting vendors, customers, or business partners carry out activities for which they have greater motivation and better expertise can be a powerful step toward transforming their businesses while dramatically cutting costs.

Eventually, Amazon's basic OPW concept was retooled into a platform for others to use named Amazon Mechanical Turk. It's an online marketplace that provides businesses access to an on-demand, scalable, flexible army of freelancers they can hire to tackle small, manual tasks. Countless companies use this platform daily to leverage a worldwide employment base, and of course, Amazon makes money every time they do.

Today, companies like Uber and Airbnb have taken the concept of OPW a step further. In addition to using other people's work, they also use these people's assets—namely, their cars and their homes.

OPW AND THE THIRD-PARTY
SELLING PLATFORM

When I joined Amazon with a mandate to create its third-party selling platform, the dominant third-party selling marketplace was eBay. eBay's mentality was very laissez-faire; they simply connected buyers with sellers, taking little accountability for customer experience or trust between merchants and shoppers. If you searched for a specific model of camera, you might get pages and pages of individual listings that offered no help in understanding how the items or the offers to sell compared. (Incidentally, eBay has since significantly changed and improved in many of these areas, primarily due to the pressure from the success of Amazon Marketplace.)

By contrast, we defined three main design principles that were important to us in building our third-party marketplace business:

1. Present the customer with a single item accompanied by an easy-to-compare list of offers to sell that item. We called this design principle "item authority." Create a single definition of the item, which would allow multiple sellers, including Amazon, to make offers to sell the item. We wanted to create a marketplace where sellers would be competing for the order in a way that worked to the customer's benefit.

2. Make it possible for customers to trust our third-party sellers as much as they trusted Amazon itself. We operationalized the concept of "seller trust" in several ways.

3. Provide great seller tools, including multiple selling methods and rich data to help merchants operate their businesses at Amazon. For small sellers, simple tools were needed. For more sophisticated high-volume sellers, different types of integrated capabilities should be provided. Documentation, operational metrics, testing environments, and professional service partners should be developed to help sellers be successful while keeping the Amazon team small.

Obviously, this was an ambitious program that required a highly complex integration between sellers and Amazon. It was clear to me that Amazon simply didn't have the human resources to manually govern a platform like this at scale. We had to make the third-party marketplace self-service. We had to provide simple-to-use, highly intuitive tools for sellers, as well as a system that would somehow cull subpar sellers from the marketplace in order to keep customer trust high.

We quickly realized that the only way to accomplish all this was by taking a page from the OPW book. Fortunately, Jeff Bezos smiles upon projects designed to scale a business on a self-service platform.

Amazon continues to use OPW as a "first principle" or fundamental concept in building strategy. For example, Amazon Flex, which has independent drivers picking up packages for delivery at Amazon fulfillment centers, is OPW at its core. Amazon Flex is akin to Uber for package delivery. An independent person with a car signs up to deliver for Amazon. This driver arrives at an Amazon fulfillment center, gets assigned orders to deliver, and puts the boxes in his or her car. Drivers use the Flex application to navigate and confirm delivery of the packages to customers' doorsteps. This independent agent model allows Amazon to have yet another last-mile-delivery option for their retail business.

What are your capabilities that need an OPW strategy? Simply hiring contractors is one way, but it typically does not provide the leverage, economic advantage, or scalability that technology does to equip a flexible workforce that has the right incentives to do the work. Don't forget that you are still responsible for quality and results, and part of what your technology needs to do is build great metrics and tracking to ensure quality.

One of Bezos's favorite techniques to accomplish this is the *forcing function*—a set of guidelines, restrictions, or commitments that force a desirable outcome without having to manage all the details of making it happen.

QUESTIONS TO CONSIDER

1. What manual activities in your business could benefit from an OPW strategy?

2. Could you build the right tools to create and manage small pieces of well-defined work? Would this provide improvements even if the work were done externally?

3. How do you create flexibility for the spikes in your business? What digital strategy could help?

THE MAGIC OF FORCING FUNCTIONS

Get These Right, and Your Teams Will Take Off

If you want a thing done well, do it yourself.
—Napoléon Bonaparte

How does a leader get the right results without micromanaging? How does a business develop agility while maintaining high standards for success? How do you empower the team while minimizing risk? Put too much governance on these teams, and you slow them down and stunt their growth as leaders. Pay too little attention and oversight, and you might be held accountable for poor outcomes. One of Amazon's secrets? *Forcing functions.*

A forcing function is a set of guidelines, restrictions, requirements, or commitments that "force," or direct, a desirable outcome without having to manage all the details of making it happen. Forcing functions are a powerful technique used at Amazon to enforce a strategy or change or to get a difficult project launched.

Many of the ideas outlined in this book are forcing functions. For example, having deep conversations on metrics with a team up front allows a leader to pay a little less attention to the team because she or he knows the team is measuring for the right results. Forcing functions must be done early and designed strategically, and accompanied by open and consistent communication. Let the team know "this is a forcing function."

Simply put, the forcing function is a behavior-shaping constraint not much different than the barrier separating lanes on a freeway. It exists to keep your project or objective from swerving into oncoming traffic.

> **idea 24:** To balance getting the right results and avoiding bureaucracy and centralized management, leaders should develop approaches that assist in getting the right results, while not having to pay as close attention to the team or function. These approaches are called *forcing functions*. Designing these strategies early in a program or strategy aligns expectations and empowers the leaders of the program to operate with clear authority and expectations.

THIRD-PARTY SELLERS: INVENTING A PLATFORM AND MAKING IT SIMPLE

One of the best examples of the principle of invent and simplify is the business that brought me to Amazon in the first place, the development of the third-party seller platform.

In late 2001, I was working at a technology startup in Seattle and actively looking for the next big thing—both in my own career and in the world of business in general. Jason Child, a colleague of mine from my Arthur Andersen days, introduced me to Jason Kilar (who later became the founder and CEO of Hulu). They invited me to interview at Amazon. The successful candidate, I was told, would lead a business responsible for designing and operating a capability that would allow third parties to sell at Amazon.

Over the next two months, I had 23 interviews at Amazon. It was, without a doubt, the most exhaustive, intense hiring process I have ever experienced. What we were really doing in these interviews was refining strategy and brainstorming the requirements of a third-party selling business. A precursor already existed. Unfortunately, zSHOP was largely defined by its horrible customer experience and shoddy inventory. I remember thinking, "Well, the idea is there, but I'm hearing some fairly vague plans and expectations."

Eventually, I was hired to lead the launch of the third-party business as Amazon's first director of merchant integration. I had direct accountability managing all the merchants (aka sellers) we were going to bring on board for the opening of the apparel category in late 2002, including brands like Nordstrom, Gap, Eddie Bauer, and Macy's. But I was also responsible for making the Amazon third-party seller experience just as effective and frictionless as the customer experience. We realized that, without a seller experience culture, the new business would not succeed, and we adopted "seller success" as our mission.

We put a forcing function in place using a *future press release* (Idea 45). The future press release stated that "a third-party seller, in the middle of the night without talking to anyone, would be able to register, list an item, fulfill an order, and delight a customer as though Amazon the retailer had received the order." This simple sentence imposed a tremendous amount of integration and operations coordination between Amazon Marketplace and our sellers. And we needed to scale this to tens of thousands of sellers without adding that many employees at Amazon. It had to be done in a self-service manner. This forcing function did its intended job. We devised tools, processes, metrics, and monitoring to enable sellers to launch and operate their business at Amazon with surprisingly little support from Amazon. Yet we knew and the seller knew whether they were serving customers in the quality manner Amazon demanded.

Another example of a forcing function was the concept of direct versus indirect headcount. The *direct headcount* for a project would typically include system development engineers (SDEs), technical program managers, and people who negotiated contracts, such as vendor managers. In Bezos's mind, these were the essential skills to build a scalable company. All other headcount—all the people who don't directly create a better customer experience—was considered indirect. The forcing function was that acquiring direct headcount was relatively easy to get approved. However, indirect headcount was constrained and had to be justified by demonstrating that it would decrease with scale in the business.

In building the third-party business, my indirect headcount consisted of the account managers I hired to help assist merchants complete their integration into Amazon. These account managers initially launched 15 to 20 merchants at a time, but before long they were launching 50 to 100 merchants. Eventually the number became astronomical. This was enabled by a number of strategies, including building a variety of ways for sellers to integrate into Amazon, creating great documentation and examples, providing a test environment and certification process to enable the seller to evaluate when they were ready to launch, and building an ecosystem of partners who could help sellers who needed consultation. The forcing function did exactly what it was intended to do—it enabled us to build capabilities and processes that scaled well and became more efficient over time.

Our merchant integration team built tools, metrics, dashboards, alarms, and other capabilities to help the sellers meet all of their contractual commitments to us and live up to our marketplace's high standards and ultimately, the expectations of their customers. We also built various technological and operational tools for monitoring their performance. For example, we policed the price and availability of an item on the seller's own website to ensure that it was not less expensive or easier to purchase on that website than it was at the Amazon Marketplace, and we flagged sellers who made unreasonable commitments or failed to keep their promises.

Eventually we built a seller's trust index based on all the touch points between the merchant and customer, as well as all the promises a merchant made. Every seller could track the answers to questions like these: "Is my content good?" "Am I fulfilling orders on time?" "Am I managing returns correctly?" "Is my customer feedback good?" All of this was then rolled into an aggregated index yielding a score for each seller. We used many functions and algorithms to reward high-performing sellers—for example, by having them vault to the top of search results. In this way, the third-party marketplace evolved into a highly efficient, largely self-governing meritocracy. If a seller's score was really low, our management team would have various discussions with them before eventually removing them from the platform.

Equally important was Item Authority. Deceptively simple at first blush, Item Authority was perhaps the merchant program's quintessential invent-and-simplify innovation and a major reason for our success. In order to increase item selection, availability, and price competition, we signed up multiple sellers of the same items. Item Authority reconciled onto one page all of the various content from sellers selling the same item. This forced sellers to compete on price, selection, and convenience while markedly improving the customer experience. Instead of having to look through pages and pages for the best deal on a single item—which is essentially how eBay worked at the time—customers were presented with the most competitive offers all in one place.

Taken together, all these innovations worked remarkably well. Today, there are over 2 million third-party sellers on Amazon Marketplace, accounting for approximately 50 percent of all Amazon units shipped and sold.

YOUR FORCING FUNCTION IDEAS

What are the types of forcing functions that can be put into place early in a strategy or program that will empower the leadership of the initiative to drive with more autonomy and empowerment?

A quick outline includes narratives (Idea 44) and future press releases (Idea 45) dictating clear requirements or a desired state. Describe the requirement or outcome, not how it is accomplished. Key performance targets and metrics can be great forcing functions, but you need to be smart. Focus on input metrics—metrics more within the control of the team, than output metrics, like revenue. So a goal like "decrease quality errors by 90 percent" or "maximum system latency of 0.5 seconds" might be appropriate, but "drive revenue to $2 million in Q1" might not be a good forcing function. It might be a great goal, but it does not constrain or dictate how this happens—it does not force the result.

How will you know if your forcing functions are working? They will begin to accelerate your innovation, you will execute and attain hard results better, and suddenly the business flywheels will begin turning faster. So what's a flywheel?

QUESTIONS TO CONSIDER

1. Are you using forcing functions in your organization? Are they doing their job?

2. Where could forcing functions help deliver a better result?

3. Do you keep track of the commitments made and feature these in reviews?

WHAT'S YOUR FLYWHEEL?

Systems Thinking in Strategy Development

The consumer is the most important point on the production line.
—W. Edwards Deming

Amazon's retail flywheel is famous. Yet what is it exactly? Simply put, it's a self-reinforcing loop or systems diagram driven by key objectives or initiatives. The flywheel metaphor refers to a huge, heavy mechanical device that slowly rotates, gathers momentum—building and storing energy—before achieving a semblance of self-perpetuation. In a factory, this looks like kinetic efficiency. In business, it looks like ever-increasing growth or adoption. It is a virtuous cycle.

At Amazon, leaders work to reinforce the flywheel by investing to make it spin faster, and they keep developing it. Teams at Amazon today still explain how their proposals or ideas reinforce or are tied to the flywheel. To paraphrase Jim Collins, some efforts may have been bigger than others, but any single heave—no matter how large—reflects a small fraction of the entire cumulative effect upon the flywheel.[1]

Thinking about your business as a flywheel—determining what factors will generate and sustain the most momentum in creating growth—will help you identify its most important levers.

idea 25: Study and analyze either your industry or the situation you are trying to improve using systems thinking. Once you have an idea or hypothesis on how to achieve your goal, create a simple version of your system, often called a "flywheel," to assist in testing your strategy and then in communicating your logic and plan to others.

SYNERGIES OF THE FLYWHEEL

The volume and variety of Amazon's retail business may be the stuff of legend, but the Amazon retail business is centered on the concept of the flywheel, which Jeff Bezos may have borrowed from strategy guru Jim Collins, author of *Good to Great*. In addition to a powerful business strategy, the flywheel idea is a useful tool for communicating the company's decisions that are sometimes puzzling to employees and outsiders.

In early 2002, the momentum of the Amazon flywheel was limited. I was tasked with dramatically affecting a major part of that flywheel—adding thousands of sellers, who would add millions of items to Amazon's selection. At the time, essentially all selections (stock keeping units, or SKUs) were in one of three categories—books, music, and video—and almost all of those products were being purchased and resold by Amazon, with limited third-party sellers participating.

Amazon had already tried to launch a third-party seller program twice. Both attempts failed. Bezos has described it this way: "Marketplace's early days were not easy. First, we launched Amazon Auctions. I think seven people came, if you count my parents and siblings. Auctions transformed into zShops, which was basically a fixed price version of Auctions. Again, no customers."[2]

The main reason these early versions failed was because Amazon hadn't made things easy or simple enough for either set of customers they were trying to attract. Tools for the seller (customer 1) were limiting and hard to use, as were the discovery and shopping tools for the consumer (customer 2) who was forced to check out and pay separately for third-party products.

A big part of my new job as director of merchant integration was to bring "seller obsession" to the business, a new twist on Amazon's fundamental "customer obsession" principle. We knew that we had to make great tools and a great business for sellers if we wanted to create the virtuous cycle we had pictured.

To achieve this, we did something pretty radical for the time. We took our most valuable retail real estate—our product detail pages—and let third-party sellers compete against our own retail category managers.

"It was more convenient for customers, and within a year, it accounted for 5 percent of units," explained Bezos. "Today, more than 40 percent of our units are sold by more than 2 million third-party sellers worldwide. Customers ordered more than two billion units from sellers in 2014."[3]

The success of this hybrid model accelerated the Amazon flywheel. Customers were initially drawn by our fast-growing selection of Amazon-sold products at great prices with a great customer experience. By allowing third parties to offer products side-by-side, we became more attractive to customers, which drew even more sellers. This also added to our economies of scale, which we passed along by lowering prices and eliminating shipping fees for qualifying orders.

Having introduced these programs in the United States, we rolled them out as quickly as we could to our other geographies. The result was a Marketplace that became seamlessly integrated with all of our global websites.[4] Now, let's revisit how Amazon thinks about and uses the flywheel.

THE MECHANICS OF THE FLYWHEEL

The original flywheel looks simple, but in reality it's quite nuanced (Figure 25.1). Lower prices and a great customer experience will bring customers in, Bezos reasoned. High traffic will lead to higher sales numbers, which will draw in more third-party, commission-paying sellers. Each additional seller will allow Amazon to get more out of fixed costs like fulfillment centers and the servers needed to run the website. This greater efficiency will then enable it to lower prices further. More sellers will also lead to better selection. All of these effects will come full circle back to a better customer experience.

Figure 25.1 Amazon's Original Flywheel
Source: Amazon.

While I was at Amazon, we used the flywheel to develop, rationalize, and coordinate important investments and understand how other companies, which on one hand might be viewed as competitors, could actually be leveraged as important partners to accomplish long-term goals. A flywheel can help you see unobvious opportunities and help you prioritize partners and clients. Bezos has often said, "We are willing to be misunderstood for long periods of time."[5] These areas of being "misunderstood" are often key leverage points in Amazon's systems dynamics–based strategy.

DESIGNING YOUR OWN FLYWHEEL

The value of creating your own flywheel is threefold: Gain a deeper and broader understanding of your industry that includes opportunities, risks, and dead zones. Define your strategy, and prioritize specific actions. Create a model that will help you communicate this strategy to others.

> ## Six Steps to Designing Your Own Flywheel
>
> 1. Create a preliminary definition and scope statement.
> 2. Outline the key nouns and variables.
> 3. Rationalize and group the nouns and variables.
> 4. Build a causal relationship diagram.
> 5. Keep working the model and simplify it over time.
> 6. Identify the implications of the model.

How long will building your flywheel take? Longer than you might think. It does not tend to be an afternoon exercise. Jerry Seinfeld, in his documentary *Comedian*, talks about "going to the sweaty gym" to refine your craft. These types of models and strategies have to be pressure tested and worked at— you have to go to the sweaty gym and grind away time and again to define, improve, and derive value from your flywheel. If you haven't had a few aha moments, then you're likely not digging deeply enough. When in doubt, look for ways to *reduce friction* to make your flywheel accelerate.

QUESTIONS TO CONSIDER

1. Do you have a systems model of your industry or business?

2. Does the systems model help define or communicate strategy?

3. Does the systems model uncover opportunities to create a virtuous business cycle?

4. Are you able to easily and consistently communicate the essence and mechanics of your strategy?

WHY IS THIS SO HARD?

Innovate by Reducing Friction

Is there anybody in there?
Just nod if you can hear me
Is there anyone at home?
—"Comfortably Numb" by
David John Gilmour and Roger Waters

Terry Jones, founder of Travelocity, once told me the most innovative thing Amazon has ever done is sell used items right next to new items on the same web page. That's not some huge transformative technology. That's a nontechnical capability.

Surprisingly, a great many of Amazon's game-changing innovations are not technical in nature. Many happened relatively early in Amazon's business. Many, like the listing of old items beside new ones, just don't feel like innovations anymore because everyone has copied them, and they are now standard operating procedure for digital retail.

What else do these innovations have in common? They reduce friction by allowing customers to do business the way they want to do it. Revolutionary, right? Give them what they want. Jeff Bezos will tell you, customers are going to do these things anyway, so why not grease the skids? It may feel unnatural at first, but when you start with the customer, when you reduce a source of friction and you create a fresh perspective, groundbreaking innovation is possible.

idea 26: When most of us hear "innovate," we think of a technology innovation. Many of Amazon's most impactful innovations have leveraged technology, but the real innovation has been its success in reducing customer friction.

If you want to be innovative, pay attention to the friction of your product or service. What's harder than it should be? Look for the root cause of customer frustrations and the irritating aspects of your service or product to which we have become "comfortably numb." Improve the customer experience, and typically you will improve your operations and support costs at the same time.

AMAZON'S WAR ON FRICTION

No company has every attacked friction with the gusto and resolve of Bezos and Amazon. In addition to selling used items next to new items, my favorite examples include Free Everyday Shipping, authentic customer reviews, multiple selling offers against the same item, and Where's My Stuff.

It's hard to imagine, but before the growth of e-commerce, ordering from a print catalog was the alternative customers had to going into a retail store. When ordering from a catalog, shipping times were long, often 10 to 14 days, and it was difficult for customers to know where their order was. This point of customer friction was the inspiration for the brilliantly named Where's My Stuff capability at Amazon. "Has my order been shipped? Has my order arrived? How do I deal with a missing or damaged item?" These are all the friction points customers can easily resolve for themselves in the Where's My Stuff area of Amazon's website.

To develop your own strategy to reduce friction, you must become a new customer with a neophyte's mindset. This will allow you to ask, "Why is it this way?" and truly question everything about the experience and any assumptions or bias shaping your insights. Dive deep into your customer's experience, with the neophyte's mindset, and you'll find points of friction to eliminate. Take, for instance, the customer experience at a pharmacy.

PLEASE, AMAZON,
OPEN A PHARMACY. PLEASE!

It's a sunny Saturday morning in Southern California. I stop at my local pharmacy, a large national chain, to pick up a prescription following a doctor's appointment. The store is quiet. A lone customer speaks to the clerk at the pharmacy pickup window. Another customer, an elderly lady in a jogging suit, stands in front of me, waiting to be served. In addition to the clerk serving the customer, two pharmacists work in the rear. A fourth employee peruses the 10-foot-high aisles behind the pharmacist's counter. This should be quick, I think. The employees outnumber the customers.

The clerk calls out "I'll be right with you" to us as a fourth customer joins the queue behind me. Despite being a respectful 10 feet behind the customer at the counter, we can't help but overhear the conversation he is having with the clerk. It's slightly embarrassing for everyone. I look at my shoes. The clerk calls the pharmacist over for a new prescription consultation.

Five minutes pass before the customer at the counter receives the correct ointments and pills. He leaves, and the elderly lady in the jogging suit approaches the counter expectantly, stating her name. Nodding, the clerk rifles through the alphabetically ordered plastic bags hanging in the pharmacy for her prescription order. No dice. The lady states her name again, and the clerk rescans all the bags. Sometimes orders are hung in the wrong place, the clerk tells her. The elderly lady says she received a text an hour ago saying her order was ready. The clerk grabs a big red basket containing filled prescription orders that have not yet been placed on the hangers. The clerk checks the entire basket one by one.

"Found it!" she says triumphantly, lifting the lady's prescription into the air like a winning lottery ticket.

Now it's time to pay. The clerk asks the customer if she has the rewards program card. The lady shakes her head. She doesn't want or need the hassle. She just wants to leave with her prescription. Who can blame her? She pays for the order without connecting the transaction to her history or loyalty number.

Now it's my turn.

"Name?" the clerk asks.

"John Rossman."

"Grossman?"

"No, Rossman. R, O, S, S, M, A, N."

The clerk finds the order and brings it over. She asks for my insurance card. When I hand it to her, she sees I have new coverage. She instructs me to take a seat over to the side.

"Why?"

The clerk doesn't answer, so I obediently sit. And wait. As I wait, I notice the aisles of retail items at the large pharmacy store contain everything from mouthwash and hair care products to books and coolers. It seems like every other item has both a normal price and a handwritten "price reduced" tag taped to the shelf. In addition to the employees in the pharmacy, the store has six checkout counters and three or four store clerks. In total, there are seven customers in the store, five of whom are here in the pharmacy.

"I'll be right with you," says the clerk again to the ever-growing pharmacy customer line. The clerk is apparently the only pharmacy employee allowed to directly serve customers. The two pharmacists are filling prescriptions, and the other clerk is placing them in the red basket.

After waiting another five minutes, I stand up and approach the counter. The pharmacist had forgotten to come over. I complete the transaction, and I'm on my way. I still don't understand why I had to sit.

After Amazon announced the acquisition of Whole Foods in the fall of 2017 and Bezos made it clear he was going to improve the customer experience and perfect a creative and seamless "omnichannel" execution, my experience at the pharmacy immediately came to mind. The pharmacy industry was a sitting duck for Amazon. How might Amazon improve the customer experience and business operations of the traditional retail pharmacy?

Automate the prescription filling and inventory management system. Between its Kiva robot and sortation expertise, Amazon would dramatically improve the speed, accuracy, labor efficiency, and costs of this activity—and likely improve the pharmacists' job satisfaction as they would be able to spend their time on helping customers and other impactful activities.

Deliver prescriptions to the home, likely within an hour of ordering. I should never be forced to go to a pharmacy for a prescription again, unless of course I want to.

But what if I need to talk to a pharmacist when having my prescription delivered to my house? Two ideas come to mind. First is to use the Echo to leverage voice-to-pharmacist. The second is to use the Echo Show device. This is an Echo but with a screen and video capability. With this, Amazon could enable face-to-face video with a pharmacist.

Need to reorder your prescription? How about either a reminder for reorder from Amazon, or using a custom Amazon dash button?

And price? Come on, this is Amazon's bread and butter. Amazon would dramatically lower the price charged to consumers for prescriptions because their business model is used to lower margins and Amazon would create a more efficient and lower cost structure. A typical pharmacy generates most of its revenue and margin from prescriptions. Typical prescription drugs offer a high margin, and Amazon would use that margin either to lower prices on the drugs or to drive prices even lower on ancillary items.

Amazon might disrupt the pharmaceutical industry if it ever decides to create private label drugs and products. After all, Amazon owns private label products in most every retail category, from the Amazon Basics brand for electronic accessories, to Pike Street bath and home products and Strathwood outdoor furniture. Over time, Amazon would surely find opportunities in private label generic drugs.

With the acquisition of PillPack, Amazon now has the ability to fulfill and deliver prescriptions. PillPack presorts prescriptions into daily doses for customers, so instead of customers needing to open and correctly dose for each medication, their medications come in individual packages presorted to make life a little bit easier. Customers could choose to have the order delivered either to their home or to a Whole Foods store. Imagine ordering groceries online and stopping by to pick up the combined grocery and pharmacy order, or having them delivered to your house within two hours. Think I'll add a book to my order too!

Finally, consider how Amazon's data and information prowess could improve the customer experience with insurance coverage transparency, providing information on what is covered and options for generics. The best that happens today is the pharmacist *might* recommend a generic or equivalent to a customer, but typically this happens only for new prescriptions, and the customer is dependent on the pharmacist to share that information.

On the heels of Amazon's acquisition of Whole Foods and more than 400 Whole Foods stores, and the aforementioned PillPack acquisition, Amazon now has the footprint to add a pharmacies counter. And why not? No existing retail pharmacy enterprise will reinvent and disrupt itself. "Retail-first" organizations can't win over a "technology-first" enterprise. Companies are not truly capable of disrupting their own business, and even if they were, they lack the ability or will to manage through the process. And they don't have the supply chain or automation expertise to fulfill this vision. Amazon had 76 supply chain patents last year alone. No wonder I'm begging Amazon to get into the pharmacy business!

AMAZON GO

Of course, a discussion of Amazon's quest for the frictionless customer experience would be seriously remiss if I did not mention Amazon Go. Amazon Go is the revolutionary brick-and-mortar store with Just Walk Out Technology that uses sensors, fusion vision, and artificial intelligence to allow customers to walk in with their smartphone, choose items off the shelves, put some back if they choose, and just walk out. Your account at Amazon is automatically charged. The only thing easier than Amazon Go is opening your own refrigerator. Amazon has plans to open 3,000 of these stores by 2021.[1] Now that's what I call reducing friction.

Reduce friction in your business and give the customers what they want. Check. What's after that? Think about your favorite superheros and their superpowers.

QUESTIONS TO CONSIDER

1. Are you resetting the industry standard for customer experience?

2. What are the points of friction in your services or products that your customers, your ex-customers, or the customers who don't choose you would prefer not to deal with?

3. Where are there small points of friction in the customer's use of your product or service? Are you paying attention to these?

GRANTING CUSTOMERS SUPERPOWERS

Dreamy Businesses and Durable Needs

He who knows others is wise;
he who knows himself is enlightened.
—Lao Tzu

One way to tell the story of my life is to chronicle the TV series of an era. There tends to be one that stands out every few years, and my simple mind uses that TV series as the marker for that period in my life. Pathetic, I agree. Right now, it would likely be the HBO series *Silicon Valley*. The 1990s were marked by the sitcom *Seinfeld*. One of the great recurring themes was Jerry's obsession with Superman. As George said, "His whole life revolves around Superman and cereal."[1] Innovation can be inspired by the same super-hero fascination.

How? Well, to differentiate yourself from the competition, you must grant your customers a superpower that is completely unique from what other companies give them. You may have parity or offer most of the same features as your competition. To win, there needs to be a superpower. The power of flight, x-ray vision, time travel . . . you must pick a couple of capabilities, features, or processes at which you are *super*.

idea 27: Challenge yourself with the questions, "Who are my customers, and what superpowers will we grant them?" These need to be a few differentiated core competencies that power your strategy. Invest to make and keep these "best in class" and ahead of the market.

I once heard Jeff Bezos tell a large retailer client that he couldn't imagine a world where a customer wanted a higher price, a slower delivery, or a smaller selection. Throughout Amazon's existence, much of its strategy has been driven by providing superpowers to its customers. Lightning speed! The ability to shrink (prices)! The power to make anything appear! What's more, these superpowers delivered on durable customer needs.

Take logistics and delivery. Amazon is relentless in building multiple approaches to equip their supply chain, give customers choices, flexibility, and transparency, and remove friction so that delivery is fast and reliable. For example, in 2014 Amazon partnered with the U.S. Postal Service (USPS) to offer Sunday delivery to select cities. Sunday delivery by USPS? Now that's a superpower. Even Superman has to respect that.

When commercial carriers couldn't support Amazon's peak volumes, Bezos created his own fast, last-mile-delivery capabilities, including the Amazon Delivery Service Partner program announced in June 2018. This program empowers entrepreneurs to start a delivery business dedicated to delivering Amazon packages, and it includes offers for "technology and operational support to individuals with little to no logistics experience the opportunity to run their own delivery business. To help keep startup costs as low as $10,000, entrepreneurs will also have access to a variety of exclusively negotiated discounts on important resources they'll need to operate a delivery business. The deals are available on Amazon-branded vehicles customized for delivery, branded uniforms, fuel, comprehensive insurance coverage, and more."[2]

When delivery infrastructure wasn't yet mature in India and China, Amazon called upon an army of bike couriers to deliver packages throughout major cities. And when UPS and FedEx couldn't keep up with holiday peak deliveries, Bezos amped up his spending to build more fulfillment centers, Amazon-dedicated delivery capabilities, drones, and blimps. He is willing to try *anything* to satisfy the durable customer need of faster delivery.

DREAMY BUSINESSES

If Superman is the ultimate superhero, what is the Superman of business models? In his 2014 letter to shareholders, Bezos described this paragon as the "dreamy business":

> A dreamy business offering has at least four characteristics. Customers love it, it can grow to very large size, it has strong returns on capital, and it's durable in time—with the potential to endure for decades. When you find one of these, don't just swipe right, get married. . . .
>
> We'll approach the job with our usual tools: customer obsession rather than competitor focus, heartfelt passion for invention, commitment to operational excellence, and a willingness to think long term. With good execution and a bit of continuing good luck, Marketplace, Prime, and AWS can be serving customers and earning financial returns for many years to come.[3]

YOUR CUSTOMERS' DURABLE NEEDS

Focusing on specific and durable customer needs is similar to the core competencies process outlined in C.K. Prahalad and Gary Hamel's *Harvard Business Review* article "The Core Competence of the Corporation." A core competency exhibits at least three characteristics. It (a) provides potential access to a wide variety of markets; (b) should make a significant contribution to the perceived customer benefits of the end product; and (c) should be difficult for competitors to imitate."[4]

So what are your customers' true durable needs? And what is your promise in meeting those needs? This is truly what your brand strategy needs to define. If you design and manufacture surf apparel, maybe the durable need is "fashionable attire that withstands saltwater."

You can see from Amazon's success that having more selection, having a platform that allows for sellers (including Amazon Retail) to compete on price, and building increasingly speedy delivery have been the components of a consistently high-achieving brand and investment strategy for over 20 years. Yet I could argue that no customer need for Amazon has been bigger than trust.

Don't ever stop trying to discover your customers' durable needs and how to meet and exceed their expectations by granting them superpowers. Marginal improvement won't do it! It can take a while, and it can be a grind, but if you can figure it out, you might be able to turn these into a dreamy business.

QUESTIONS TO CONSIDER

1. What is the superpower your customers would most appreciate?

2. Is there an example of a killer feature in your industry? What can you learn from that?

3. What are your customers' durable needs? Can these help organize your innovation efforts?

THINK DIFFERENTLY

Improve Your Questions
for Disruption

*[The Hitchhiker's Guide to the Galaxy] taught me that
the tough thing is figuring out what questions to ask,
but that once you do that, the rest is really easy.*
—Elon Musk

Yes, Napoléon died by poison while in exile on Elba, but I can guarantee you he knew precisely why. Perhaps he wished he had asked a few more questions before invading Russia in the summer of 1812. Yes, Napoléon's downfall was caused by arrogance. After so much innovation and success on the battlefield, he did not think he could lose.

Similarly, business leaders tend to think their industry and business experience will give them the insights for innovation. While important, the skill of developing breakthrough ideas is in asking different and better questions. Amazon Leadership Principle 5 is "Learn and Be Curious." This principle encourages leaders to actively disconfirm their assumptions, to avoid an expert mindset that is not open to new perspectives, and to stay humble. This is not an accident. It is a habit, and it is a skill.

> **idea 28:** Asking different questions will result in seeing the customer and the opportunity with a fresh lens and different constraints. You must be thoughtful and purposeful in how you ask and ponder these questions. This is a skill that takes practice.

IDENTIFYING OPPORTUNITIES
ACROSS THE VALUE CHAIN

How can you follow Amazon's lead in building a conglomerate set of businesses and capabilities utilizing a value chain mentality? What can you learn from Amazon's strategy or planning to continue a growth rate that, at Amazon's size, is incredibly hard? How does Amazon plan to become not just the biggest retailer but perhaps the biggest company on earth?

There are no simple answers, of course, but you can set yourself on the right course by adopting a belief held by Bezos: "Your margin is my opportunity."[1] If you can create a better, lower-cost, more flexible self-service way to do what another company is doing, that space is a good one to enter as a competitor.

If you carefully consider each of these questions, with a bias toward challenging the status quo and starting with the customer, you'll be well on your way to identifying some of the top opportunities in your industry for moving up and down your value chain.[2]

To create a business culture modeled after Amazon's dogged pursuit of innovation, I suggest doing as Amazon does—entering an industry at one point in the value chain, looking upstream, looking downstream, and then asking five fundamental questions:

- First, where is there a broken customer experience? Lack of integration, lack of price and availability transparency, and arcane business practices are signs of a broken customer experience.

- Second, what service or technology is your company paying for today that you could build and operate yourself to make your business more profitable?

- Third, how do you build those services and products well enough that other outside parties can also use them?

- Fourth, where do these conditions exist where there are attractive margins?

- And finally, how could sensors and the Internet of Things either fix a broken customer experience, help you deliver services or technologies at a lower cost to yourself and others, or allow you to create a different value proposition for your target customer?

QUESTIONS FOR INNOVATION

Einstein had a famous way of building and explaining difficult and impossible-to-test concepts through a technique of "thought experiments." These scenarios would help to demonstrate a point or hypothesis by imposing constraints. When formulating the questions to help you innovate, one technique is first to outline the thought experiment using a set of constraints. For example, "What would have to be true to reduce cycle time by 90 percent?" or "For setup and implementation to be 98 percent self-service, what would need to happen?" Imposing these constraints dramatically challenges the status quo, gives a small allowance for not being "100 percent" automated, and frees the conversation so that you can pursue new approaches and paradigms.

Many of the chapters in this book help ask different questions, in particular, Idea 15, "The Door Desk," Idea 18, "So You Want to Be a Platform?" and Idea 24, "The Magic of Forcing Functions." Each of these chapters defines scenarios or constraints that compel us to ask different questions and remove the limitations binding us to the present during brainstorming moments. In my experience, starting with a radical idea like, "How could I reduce customer contacts by 90 percent?" and then walking backward to something more attainable *always* produces more ideas than asking the question, "How could I reduce customer contacts by 10 percent?" Incremental questions produce incremental results.

Take, for example, Elon Musk's Boring Company, which hopes to improve the urban gridlock crisis by building tunnels. The starting challenge with tunnels is that they cost in the neighborhood of $1 billion per mile or more. Boring Company states, "Tunnels are really expensive to dig, with some projects costing as much as $1 billion per mile. In order to make a tunnel network feasible, tunneling costs must be reduced by a factor of more than 10."[3] This mindset has allowed them to rethink everything about how tunnels are designed, built, and operated.

Carefully crafting the scenarios, questions, and constraints will help you see the opportunities early and lead the disruption.

QUESTIONS TO CONSIDER

1. Is your leadership team asking the right strategic questions?

2. Would a retreat with significant time spent outlining and prioritizing questions you should be asking create different perspectives on risk and opportunities?

3. What constraints can you use to ask different questions that challenge business as usual (for example, "Reduce the cycle time from two days to 10 minutes").

LAUNCH AND LEARN

Business Expansion the Amazon Way

Show me a good loser, and I'll show you a loser.
—Vince Lombardi

In March 2018, Amazon announced it would be venturing into the retail banking business by offering consumer checking accounts. Stop me if you've heard this one before. That's right, Amazon is launching consumer banking services such as checking accounts through a partner model. It does not envision becoming a bank *today*. Classic. It's interesting to note, however, that the *Wall Street Journal* described Amazon's foray into the consumer checking account business as that of a partner, rather than a disrupter.[1]

Bezos isn't tied to the notion that Amazon must be *l'enfant terrible* with every new business move. Sometimes immediate disruption isn't necessary. It's far more important that Amazon's innovation and growth come from constant exploration and strategic bets in new products and services. The Amazon way to identify those products and services is typically to start with an existing product and/or service and move up and down the value chain.

You may partner to start, but use those partnerships to learn the business, reach customers, and build brand. As you begin to understand the entire business ecosystem, look for opportunities to innovate and serve customers in ways beyond the original partnerships. In other words, "launch and learn." The key, of course, is learning to evaluate if and when it makes sense to expand and build beyond the partnership.

idea 29: "Launch and learn" new industries and adjacencies to your existing businesses. Find a way to get started in new businesses, and from there, find ways to expand not just the size of the business but the ways you participate in the value chain of the industry.

THE VALUE CHAIN

A *value chain* is the end-to-end set of processes and activities for an industry. When Amazon first started, it was focused on being a first-generation e-commerce retailer. The company initially allowed others to sell used items, books, and compact discs on the same item page as new inventory. Then it moved to allowing third-party sellers to create new items to sell at Amazon and multiple sellers of the same item through the Marketplace platform. From there, Amazon expanded rapidly into new retail categories including apparel, sporting goods, and even musical instruments. Amazon then began creating proprietary brands of products. Amazon enables third-party sellers to effectively outsource logistics and delivery capabilities to Amazon. The list goes on and on.

The most recent iteration of Amazon's value chain expansion is into the transportation industry. The company has begun leasing its own jets to transport its retail inventory more cost effectively and with greater control. Analysts have estimated that this will save the company upward of $400 million a year.[2]

When it comes to healthcare, Amazon will have a multipronged strategy that follows a pattern of making thrusts into different aspects of the industry value chain. At some point, a large integrated capability will be created, like a jigsaw puzzle coming together. At first, it's unclear how the pieces create a picture. With progress, the picture becomes clear, and placing the next piece becomes easier.

There are formal ways of understanding an industry in this manner. *Harvard Business Review*'s classic "How to Map Your Industry's Profit Pool"[3] outlines the process of mapping your industry's value chain, including revenue and margin percentage at each step of the way. The summary is as follows:

1. Define the industry and value chain. Create boundaries for the industry you are evaluating.

2. Define the size of the revenue and profit pool. For each major step in the value chain, estimate the size of revenue, profits, or margin percentages.

3. Create a visualization. This is typically accomplished by lining up the industry value chain from left to right and creating a bar graph for each step of the industry or process. Assume the Y axis is "margin percentage" and the X axis is "revenue size."

Voilà! The launch-and-learn strategy. You're entering an industry from one business point and learning the industry to identify new opportunities. Sitting down and walking through this value chain analysis will enable you to understand and evaluate your business options.

STUDENT BODY LEFT

In college football, "student body left" is a classic basic end-sweep play in which the quarterback pitches the ball to the tailback and everybody blocks as he runs to the left. Defenses usually know it's coming—but when each player does his job and the play is executed with a running back with speed and power, it is not just successful. It also demoralizes the defense if it is run multiple times with success. In business, "student body left" means getting everyone on the same page relative to an important change or project and everyone executing his or her job.

When I worked at Amazon from early 2002 through late 2005, it was a relatively simple company. There were roughly 3,000 employees at corporate headquarters (not including customer service and fulfillment associates). Almost all our annual revenue, which at the time clocked in at just below $4 billion, came from retail sales in three categories—books, music, and video retail (primarily DVDs). There were just five Amazon fulfillment centers in North America. As Amazon looked to expand beyond books, music, and videos (BMVs) in the early 2000s, my team ran a series of launch-and-learn strategies that were very much "student body left" plays. Some not only shaped the business but, in many ways, also shaped the retail industry.

In the toy category, Amazon started a partnership with Toys R Us in 2000. Although Toys R Us eventually declared bankruptcy in 2017, in 2000, the toy company was still a Goliath. Believe it or not, the original partnership terms dictated that the "Toysrus.com" website address would lead directly to an Amazon toys website where customers would use or create an Amazon account and purchase toys from Amazon. Some toys were delivered by Amazon; some items were delivered by Toys R Us. "Under the terms of that deal, Toys R Us agreed to stock a wide variety of its most popular toys on Amazon in exchange for being Amazon's exclusive seller of toys and baby products. The companies also agreed that Toys R Us would give up its online autonomy, with ToysRUs .com redirecting to Amazon. Toys R Us paid Amazon $50 million a year plus a percentage of its sales through the Amazon site."[4] Yes, they basically gave the future of the business away to Amazon right then and there.

The next important launch and learn was in the apparel business. In fall of 2002, we launched the first category using the new Marketplace platform. We had about 30 partners at the launch, and we implied to them that "Amazon would not plan on being an apparel retailer." It was not too many years later that Amazon not only became a retailer in the apparel category but also launched private label products in apparel. It is estimated that Amazon sells roughly five times as much apparel and footwear as the next largest online seller, Walmart, and it is on track to being the largest retailer combined.[5]

The formation of AWS, the market leader in cloud technology, started out as a simple move to improve technical efficiency. When I was at Amazon, each team owned, engineered, and operated its own computing infrastructure. What became apparent was that we were not taking advantage of economies of scale: custom configurations and nonstandardized hardware led to more expensive servers; infrastructure sat idle a large portion of the time (with no load sharing, infrastructure had to be designed for peak use); and each team developed its own operating and support approach.

Eventually, we decided to separate out computing infrastructure into a central function. This was an important start, but the separation itself wasn't going to make our technology infrastructure world class.

Always the rationalist, Bezos would say something like, "You know, this split may be a good idea, but it's only by having external customers that we'll have the feedback and expectations to turn this into something world class. So what we're going to do is to turn this around and expose it to external developers because that's what's going to make the infrastructure good enough for our internal teams."

It didn't take long for Amazon to see that external developers loved this service and that it could be a great business. AWS was born, and the rest is history.

Through this kind of search for operational efficiencies, Amazon has expanded into a wide range of conglomerate businesses, building new tools and services that both its internal teams and outside customers can use. At Amazon, the breadth of these conglomerate businesses includes the following:

- **Acquisitions:** Amazon has acquired over 64 businesses, including Kiva Systems, a warehouse robotics company; Zappos, an online footwear company; and Annapurna Labs, a system-on-a-chip microelectronics company selling to hardware original equipment manufacturers (OEMs).

- **Private label brands:** Amazon designs, markets, and manufactures or contracts for manufacture many consumer brands currently for sale at Amazon, including apparel brands such as Lark & Ro and North Eleven, outdoor-furniture brand Strathwood, electronics brand AmazonBasics, and Prime Pantry, a consumables brand.

- **Website brands:** Amazon also owns and operates many other websites, including IMDB.com, Woot.com, Zappos.com, Diapers.com, Fabric.com, Twitch.tv, dbreview.com, and Endless.com.

- **Products and services:** Beyond retail services, Amazon sells all of the following as independent capabilities:

  - **Order fulfillment services:** Fulfillment by Amazon (FBA) allows sellers to warehouse and fulfill orders from Amazon fulfillment centers.

  - **Payments processing:** Retailers use Payments by Amazon as a trusted payment gateway.

  - **AWS S3 (Simple Storage Service) and EC2 (Elastic Compute Cloud):** These are two of the many AWS cloud computing products.

- ○ **Amazon Fire Stick:** This is a proprietary device used by customers on their TVs to access Amazon and many other content providers, like ESPN.

- ○ **System on a Chip Design:** Annapurna Labs is a company that designs and sells specially designed computer chips used in networking devices.

- ○ **Amazon Publishing:** This full-service book publishing arm of Amazon cultivates authors and books.

- ○ **Amazon Advertising:** This service allows sellers to bid for product-placement ads at Amazon.

- ○ **Twitch:** This live video service and social platform enables customers to watch events, primarily eSport events, centered on popular online games like *Call of Duty* and *Counter-Strike*.

There are also several major internal capabilities Amazon has today that it could one day decide to offer to other companies:

- **Electronic device (phone or tablet) design:** Could Amazon figure out a way to democratize device design and manufacturing by removing obstacles and gatekeepers, perhaps similar to the way CreateSpace has opened up book publishing and distribution?

- **Content production, including TV shows and games:** This area has a strong potential for creating a platform business by removing the barriers and complexities of original-content production and distribution. This could be a huge win for both Amazon and people who want to tell stories via video or game production.

- **Robots used in warehouses:** Kiva was an acquisition, and it had external customers. For competitive reasons, Amazon has made this a proprietary and internal capability only. Will they reopen it to others at some point?

- **Retail store solutions:** Based on the Amazon Go store concepts, it's easy to see AWS taking aspects of the sensors, vision systems, and Just Walk Out Technology and offering these managed services to other retail store operators.

- **Photography studios and image services:** Driven in particular by the apparel category, Amazon has developed scalable processes for creating and managing images. This would be a valuable "as-a-service" capability for other brands to leverage.

Major new businesses and capabilities are being hatched right now. Amazon's proprietary air logistics capability, Prime Air, will deliver Amazon cost savings and control for parcel logistics. Amazon shipping is focused on international product-sourcing logistics, like oceangoing freight. Amazon Business Supplies is selling business products and supplies, and Amazon's machine learning makes it easy, in relative terms, for any developer to include machine-learning capabilities in their products through such on-demand cloud services like Sage Maker and AWS Rekognition.

These are the big bets that might become Amazon's next "dreamy businesses."

QUESTIONS TO CONSIDER

1. Are you trapped in one primary business?

2. Are there opportunities to expand into new industries or new ways to serve existing clients?

3. How could a launch-and-learn strategy be used in your business?

DON'T GIVE AWAY THE OPERATING SYSTEM

Partners, Vendors, and Strategy

Gary went flying.
—Bill Gates

On July 8, 1994, Gary Kildall—the American computer scientist and microcomputer entrepreneur who created the CP/M operating system and founded Digital Research, Inc.—suffered traumatic injuries when he fell or was beaten at a biker bar in Monterey, California. He died in a hospital three days later. An autopsy indicated Kildall suffered symptoms associated with chronic alcoholism.[1] An ignominious end to the man many believe is the "real" Bill Gates.

What's that? Never heard of Gary Kildall? Unfortunately, he's perhaps best known for an apocryphal tale at the birth of the personal computer revolution. Kildall was the genius behind CP/M, the original and dominant operating system at the time. In 1980, IBM approached Kildall with an offer to license CP/M for their stealth PC business. According to lore, Kildall was not present when the IBM representatives showed up unannounced. Kildall was a pilot, and he was out flying, but to another business appointment. That's not really what happened, of course. At the time, Kildall's wife handled negotiations, and based on the advice of their lawyer, she allegedly balked at signing a nondisclosure agreement. Ultimately, the delay in negotiations gave the Bill Gates we know today enough time to propose an alternative operating system, 86-DOS, which borrowed heavily from CP/M. Later in life, Kildall would call idea 30: Don't outsource strategic or critical decision-making. Create processes, data flows, decision trees and algorithms, and systems seeking to optimize critical functions across the enterprise. Use partners and vendors for tactical execution, and build the rules and optimization engine as your intellectual property. Integrate real-time data to feed into this decision-making.

DOS "plain and simple theft," and he would point out that its first 26 system calls worked the same as CP/M's.[2]

But don't feel too sorry for Kildall. He sold his company for $125 million and lived a lavish lifestyle with a Lear jet and mansions in Pebble Beach and Austin, Texas, before his premature death in Monterey. But think about what he gave away. The story of Digital Research remains a cautionary tale. Don't give away your operating system.

AMAZON'S OPERATING SYSTEMS

What does an operating system do? At a conceptual level, two things. First, it runs, allocates, and optimizes system resources to all the users. Second, it abstracts complexity and takes care of common basics like error management for any service that wants to use system resources. An operating system is the strategic "smarts" of any computer system. It's an interesting parallel to make between how you leverage others, primarily partners and vendors, to help scale your business.

Is Amazon an operating system company? I'd never considered it until recently. In May 2018, I was preparing for the Institute of Supply Management (ISM) annual conference keynote address, and I was thinking about how a quiet, under-the-radar Amazon program could radically alter the supply chain by becoming an operating system. Drones, blimps, and fleets of Amazon vans get all the press and attention, but I look at the potential for Amazon Seller Flex, and it is different. It could become an operating system for supply chain management.

Amazon Seller Flex (not to be confused with Amazon Flex, which is Amazon's Uber-like on-demand delivery service allowing independent drivers to deliver packages for Amazon) is a program that invites either vendors or third-party sellers to manage transportation by using Amazon's logistics management capabilities, technologies, and negotiated contracts in their warehouses.

Here's how it works: To ensure the two-day-or-less Prime delivery expectation, the Amazon Prime–eligible selection needs to be in Amazon's fulfillment centers. Third-party sellers are able to make their selection Prime eligible by sending inventory to Amazon fulfillment centers and letting Amazon manage the order delivery, typically using FedEx, UPS, and USPS. The Amazon Seller Flex program now extends the Amazon fulfillment management scope into the third-party seller's fulfillment center by offering software to the third-party seller, who is often a brand company and/or a retailer too.

By using Amazon Seller Flex software, the user can have Amazon orders allocated directly to them for shipping, leveraging Amazon's negotiated rates for transportation. This has benefits for every party involved as it avoids having to send and receive inventory into the Amazon warehouses. The seller can also use the capability for non-Amazon orders. Amazon gets more shipping volume running through their transportation contracts, giving them even more power in the relationship. The seller gets not just Amazon transportation capability but all the "smarts" behind it, including optimization for how best to ship the order to meet the customer expectation. By embedding software within the seller and giving this software a core operating capability, Amazon is spidering even deeper into the commerce ecosystem. Don't be surprised if in 10 years Amazon Seller Flex will have become another big business for Amazon and that it will have created an "Internet of Supply Chain and Logistics," like the Internet of Things, driving much of our commerce, whether we are buying products directly from Amazon or not.

Companies adopting Seller Flex leverage Amazon's market-leading negotiated rates and options to transportation providers. Amazon gains more consolidated volume through its control of the transportation providers, plus likely some fees.

But here's the killer strategy for Amazon. First, they will control more spending to the transportation providers, providing Amazon even more leverage in these relationships. Second, Amazon will get even more data about products, volume, and customers. Seller Flex is the equivalent of an operating platform. It optimizes and allocates resources, and it abstracts complexity to the participants. Over time, Seller Flex has the potential to be a transportation operating system controlling a significant amount of the package delivery volume. Is it another of Bezos's "magical" businesses? Maybe.

Another Amazon "operating system" in early development is called Green-grass. A product of the AWS division, AWS Greengrass is software (Amazon is careful to not call it an operating system) that runs on "smart products." It allows local computing, messaging, data caching, syncing, and machine-learning (ML) inference capabilities for connected devices. It also allows users to run IoT applications across the AWS cloud and local devices using AWS Lambda and AWS IoT Core.[3] All of the AWS and the general cloud architecture have been about centralized capability. Greengrass is the first product that allows for the capabilities of AWS to be utilized in a decentralized manner. Wow! Play that thought forward. Greengrass is the operating system that allows for the device usage of AWS capabilities that would compete with the likes of Android, Microsoft, and other device operating systems. A huge strategy advancement from a pure cloud approach.

AND THE POINT IS . . .

Did you know that Yahoo! had the opportunity to acquire Google? Actually, twice: once in 1998 for $1 million and again in 2002 for $5 billion.[4] Instead, Yahoo! licensed Google to be Yahoo!'s search engine. Oops. They essentially "outsourced the operating system" of a core piece of their business to Google. Despite several attempts to correct this decision, Yahoo! has never recovered.

Whether allocating orders to warehouses, interpreting demand signals for deciding what products to design and manufacture, or engaging in customer personalization and market segmentation, it's smart and necessary to leverage other partners and vendors to provide services and lend their expertise in support of your goals. But here's the flip side: don't outsource or give away the smart decision-making key to your business. This key is the "operating system" of your management. You need to build, codify, support with algorithms, and scale these essential leverage points of resource allocation within your management structures.

Don't let your legacy be overshadowed by what you didn't do. Don't repeat history with your own "Gary went flying" story just to become a footnote.

QUESTIONS TO CONSIDER

1. Are there strategic capabilities or decision-making processes that you've outsourced to others?

2. What would an operating system in your industry look like?

3. What history lessons could help identify the digital strategy options in your business?

Part III
Business and Technology

LIES, DAMN LIES, AND METRICS

Use Metrics to Build a Culture of Accountability and Customer Obsession

> *Gentlemen, we are going to relentlessly chase perfection, knowing full well we will not catch it, because nothing is perfect. But we are going to relentlessly chase it because in the process we will catch excellence. I am not remotely interested in just being good.*
> —Vince Lombardi

I deliver scores of keynotes and presentations in meetings with business executive teams. These meetings cover broad territory and topics, but I always try to emphasize a few key points: the importance of patience, and that transformation is as much about your personal habits and beliefs as it is about changing your organization. I stress that Amazon's playbook is a system based off principles. It is not based on a set of steps or a single linear approach.

Inevitably, someone will raise his or her hand and ask me to pick the most important play in Amazon's playbook. I understand the need to give a starting point. So while explaining that "it's a system," there is an answer to the question "What's the one thing to get me started?" The critical fundamental, the "championship habit" above all else is this: metrics.

idea 31: Use metrics to relentlessly pursue root-cause understanding and correction. Measure the customer experience aspect of your business as well as the operational and financial aspects. Design processes and systems to collect granular and real-time data that will feed into your metrics. Create a drumbeat of meetings centered on metrics to drive accountability and action. Designing your metrics is a skill and takes constant effort. The design of metrics is never done.

IN GOD WE TRUST.
ALL OTHERS MUST BRING DATA

In 2004, I attended a senior executive team meeting at Amazon that just so happened to coincide with the Salesforce initial public offering (IPO). During the meeting, one of the other executive team members casually commented that Salesforce was the world's largest customer relationship management (CRM) technology company.

Big mistake.

"We are the world's largest CRM company!" a senior Amazon leader (guess who) yelled in response.

Like a CRM company, Amazon is obsessed with managing and analyzing the data on customer interactions to improve its relationships with them. And it is doing it on a much bigger scale than Salesforce. The digital nature of Amazon's business and its focus on collecting obscene amounts of data make it significantly different than the average e-commerce company. Metrics is seamlessly woven into the culture of Amazon.

W. Edwards Deming's famous quote is a mantra: "In God we trust. All others must bring data." Teams spend as much or more time defining and agreeing on how to measure a new feature, service, or product as they do designing the feature itself. Weeks are built into project management schedules for the consideration of an operation's inputs and outputs; to identify what data might be needed to run that operation; and to understand its complex internal workings. Metrics are the answer. Metrics are the question. Metrics are the vehicle to relentlessly pursue root cause.

"DID MY CUSTOMERS HAVE
A GOOD DAY TODAY?"

At Amazon, having a balanced, well-engineered scorecard of metrics that is consistently reviewed day over day, week over week, provides deep insights into what works and what doesn't. It also places sole responsibility for success and failure on you as a leader.

Repeatable, consistent performance reflected in metrics is the gold standard for success. Without access to a consistent set of metrics, an Amazon leader would be flying blind, and such risky behavior is not acceptable at the company. Real-time metrics are the lifeblood flowing through the veins of Amazon. Real data and real insights from the customer experience are used continually to answer the question, "Did my customers have a good day today?" If your metrics are in place, if they are in real time, and your team members and processes use them, this question yields a simple yes or no answer.

It takes foresight to lead by the numbers correctly. You must embed real-time metrics from the very start of a program because they are nearly impossible to retrofit. The Amazon experience shows us that the single biggest opportunity for companies operating today is to completely rethink their concept of metrics. Most companies use what's called "batch architecture" to record large sets of transactions or other quantitative updates and to process them periodically (daily or weekly is typical). Batch architecture is very last century. Today, you need real-time data, real-time monitoring, and real-time alarms when trouble is brewing—not lag-time metrics that hide the real issues for 24 hours or longer. Your business should operate like a nuclear reactor. If a problem arises, you need to be aware of it immediately.

SPEND MORE TIME DESIGNING
YOUR METRICS

Think about where time is allocated at a company at the executive and management levels—lots of time spent on budgeting, financial reviews, HR, and compliance, and so on. These are important. But do they really help serve customers, drive operational excellence, or spark ideas for innovation? Here are three quick steps for designing your metrics:

1. Spend time talking about what your metrics should be.

2. Have meetings that use those metrics to constantly review your business. Always look for root causes. Turn metrics to action.

3. Get as granular and real-time data as possible.

METRICS IS A VERB

Having great metrics is ammunition, but the wars are fought in the daily combat of using metrics to drive to perfection. The theater for these battles is meetings we called "metrics meetings." The entire operational rhythm of life at Amazon is a set of weekly metrics meetings. Typically starting with the lowest-level services and capabilities and building up to the worldwide senior meetings at the end of the week, an operational leader at Amazon attends a series of metrics meetings over the course of a week. Every week.

Although they are called "metrics meetings," they are really meetings of shared accountability where the "owners" of related metrics discuss the most recent trends and issues in their metrics. Leaders are expected to know the details of their business, to be vocally self-critical, and to discuss plans or progress for improvement. Although successes might be recognized, the general modus operandi is to "celebrate for a nanosecond" and then focus on the issues and errors in the business. Even when things are generally good, they're never perfect.

Meetings are organized around key services, processes, and groups of capabilities. For example, I ran the Marketplace metrics meetings, even though from an organizational standpoint, only a subset was part of my organization. I would include leaders from key capabilities affecting the Marketplace business, such as the catalog team, order pipeline team, and payment and fraud team.

The finance partners at Amazon play a key role in making sure all metrics, not just financial metrics, have been prepared, and they partner with the functional leader to take notes, assign responsibilities, and drive results and improvements to be delivered. The finance partners are critical in keeping the meetings "honest" and ensuring that people deliver results. I think of them as the independent accountability officers ensuring that the metrics meetings are doing their job of defining and reporting on progress to improve our performance.

INSTRUMENTATION:
REAL-TIME, FINE-GRAINED DATA

Once a team's metrics and SLAs are in place, the focus turns to data collection that will inform those metrics and SLAs. At Amazon, there are very specific standards for the quality and type of data a team should collect. Amazon's executive team refers to those standards as "instrumentation."

Expectations on data collection—or instrumentation—at Amazon are twofold: First, data should be fine-grained in nature. You can always summarize and aggregate data, but you can't go back and derive more detail from a data set. Second, that data should be available in real time. You can always batch data or slow it down, but you can't speed it up. Design for no time lags and no batch systems.

There are many reasons this is important. Let's say a grocery company uses a refrigerated storage bin to keep its fruits and vegetables fresh. Suddenly, over the course of a day, all the lettuce goes bad. If the company has been collecting fine-grained data—for example, any changes in temperature or pressure and their time stamps—that grocery company might actually be able to figure out what it was that caused the lettuce to go bad. Otherwise, they're stuck wondering about the possible variables and causes in that situation.

Of course, it's not possible to collect fine-grained real-time data in every situation. There are limitations to the nature of the data that you're able to collect in a specific situation, but at Amazon it's expected that you will work vigorously to achieve instrumentation.

Finally, never stop reevaluating and building metrics. Frequently check to make sure that your metrics are still explicitly linked to goals, and don't hesitate to change metrics when they stop driving change in your organization.

Why?

Because good metrics create good processes that minimize bureaucracy.

Designing Metrics and Metrics Meetings—
the Amazon Way

Figures 31.1 and 31.2 contain the key points on metrics definition and design and how to use metrics in the business.

Your metrics are never done.

- Spend more time debating and defining your metrics.

- Build metrics from the customer experience.

- You should be able to answer the question "Did my customers have a good day today?" with metrics.

- Metrics are designed to go "up and to the right."

- Make it easy to read "at a glance" to know the trend and which metrics need discussion and investigation.

- Metrics always have a comparison prior period, trends, and SLAs.

- Have a balanced scorecard of metrics.

- Have a clear, common definition of each metric.

- Avoid manual metric preparation. Metric decks should be "one click" and automatically generated.

- A metric is owned by one person in the organization.

- SLAs are typically increased each year. Performance needs to improve!

- There are different types of metrics for different purposes and types of conversations:

  - Metrics for operational and customer experience
  - Metrics for financial results and targets
  - Long-term adoption and customer delight metrics

Figure 31.1 Metrics: The Rhythm of the Business

Guidelines for Metrics Meetings

- Metrics meetings involve a consistent set of people to discuss a line of business, a technology service, or a program.

- Meet on a consistent basis—typically weekly.

- People attend and pay attention. They should put away phones and computers.

- Come prepared, knowing the key issues with answers and explanations.

- Good leaders have an "open kimono" and are vocally self-critical (Amazon Leadership Principal 11, Earn Trust).

- Metrics meetings are really meetings of root-cause discovery and holding each other accountable.

- The finance team does not run the meeting, but typically they keep everyone honest.

- Action items are published after each meeting.

- Try to avoid escalating or asking for permission to "do the right thing."

- It's everyone's job to lead with and understand the customer's impact and perspective.

- Deep review and discussion on a consistent set of metrics over time yield operational excellence and ideas for innovation.

- Just like your metrics, metrics meetings are thoughtfully designed and are not static. Evolve your metrics meetings as needed to keep creating value.

Figure 31.2 *Metrics* Is a Verb

QUESTIONS TO CONSIDER

1. Can your core teams answer the question "Did my customers have a good day today?" with metrics and monitoring?

2. Do you have robust customer experience metrics to complement your operational and financial metrics?

3. Could you use metrics to drive better accountability and quality?

PROCESS VERSUS BUREAUCRACY

Creating Processes That Scale

*Scaling up is every entrepreneur's dream—
and nightmare. Hypergrowth is terrifying, and it's
most often success that kills great companies.*
—Verne Harnish

What's your pet peeve? I have several, but the one I'm thinking about is that I quickly get frustrated when something doesn't make sense, we all recognize that it doesn't make sense, yet no one is empowered to make a change or the right decision. It's like dealing with customer service when all they can say is "I'm sorry this is affecting you, but our policy states that . . . " You know what that is? Bureaucracy with rigid rules that are typically outdated, and with no empowerment to change.

The third leadership principle of Amazon is "Invent and Simplify." Most find it curious that "simplify" shares the top billing with "invent" and is not buried somewhere in the description of the leadership principle. Operational leaders at Amazon think about how to scale core capabilities, knowing that keeping processes simple is the key to being able to scale them. I cannot overstate the importance of keeping it simple.

At its most basic, the ability to scale results in the production of more "units" through your process, on a declining cost per unit. Whether your unit is an order, a customer, or a byte, being able to "do more on a declining unit cost" helps you figure out how to scale the process without always just adding

> idea 32: Well-defined processes help prevent bureaucracy or expose it if it exists. Build your core processes in a deliberate way as a key enabler of scale. Part of designing your processes is identifying the key services that are used in multiple ways across the enterprise. Force simplicity to triumph over complexity. Have high standards for building and operating key processes to prevent bureaucracy.

more people to it. These types of core processes could be services that help drive the online customer experience, such as the payments service or the image service, or they could be key back office capabilities like the inventory forecasting process or the server procurement process. These are essential capabilities that need to be world-class for the business and customer experience to excel. Not everything in the business needs to be as wired or world-class, just the essential processes differentiating your business.

There are certainly processes at Amazon that are too manual and too messy and that could be improved and automated. But creating world-class processes takes critical talent, and that talent might be better directed toward other more strategic work, so you allow noncore processes to suffer less innovation and automation. These are important trade-off decisions. An example of processes at Amazon that are important but not core are capabilities like site merchandising or adding new features to the Prime program. While these need to be done right, the amount of work does not increase with the increase in business, and thus these processes can be stabilized at an acceptable level of manual, suboptimal effort. The engineering talent that it would take to better automate these processes is deemed better utilized on programs that do need to scale, such as increasing automation in Amazon fulfillment centers.

WHAT IS BUREAUCRACY?

One of the great observations I heard from Jeff Bezos came during one of our all-hands meetings, held at a local movie theater. Bezos took a question from an employee about avoiding bureaucracy while still ensuring that certain rules were in place. Bezos responded, "Good process is absolutely essential. Without defined processes, you can't scale, you can't put metrics and instrumentation in place, you can't manage. But avoiding bureaucracy is essential. Bureaucracy is process run amok."

Bezos understood that A-level performers hate bureaucracy and will leave organizations where it encroaches upon them. By contrast, C- and D-level performers, many of whom typically reside in middle management in any given organization, love bureaucracy because they can hide behind it, acting as gatekeepers and frequently creating the kind of friction that can bog down an entire company. Strong processes with measurable outcomes eliminate bureaucracy and expose underperformers.

So how do you recognize bureaucracy and distinguish it from well-defined process? When the rules can't be explained; when they don't favor the customer; when you can't get redress from a higher authority; when you can't get an answer to a reasonable question; when there is no service-level agreement or guaranteed response time built into the process; or when the rules simply don't make sense—when any of these circumstances occur, the chances are good that bureaucracy is beginning to spread.

Having high standards and paying attention to detail to avoid these symptoms and driving accountability and world-class capability may sound unreasonable—and it is. This is the type of unreasonable expectation that Amazon has for its leaders. It is also one of the reasons Amazon is not a great place to work for many people because they will be exposed if they don't live up to the high standards. Bureaucracy lets underperformers hide, and that's why they like it. In his 2017 letter to shareholders, Bezos explained the benefits of high standards:

> Building a culture of high standards is well worth the effort, and there are many benefits. Naturally and most obviously, you're going to build better products and services for customers—this would be reason enough! Perhaps a little less obvious: people are drawn to high standards—they help with recruiting and retention. More subtle: a culture of high standards is protective of all the "invisible" but crucial work that goes on in every company. I'm talking about the work that no one sees. The work that gets done when no one is watching. In a high-standards culture, doing that work well is its own reward—it's part of what it means to be a professional. And finally, high standards are fun! Once you've tasted high standards, there's no going back.[1]

As you work to invent and perfect processes, always remember that simplicity is an essential bulwark against the creeping onslaught of bureaucracy.

THE RECIPE FOR A PROCESS THAT SCALES

Here's the checklist for great processes that scale:

1. **The process CEO:** A process has a leader—call the person a "process CEO." This person is responsible for building a world-class capability. This does not mean that this person runs the process in all locations. For example, the "inventory receive process" is a critical fulfillment center process. The "process CEO" does not run the inventory receive process in the hundreds of Amazon fulfillment centers, but he or she delivers a world-class capability that is used by every fulfillment center.

2. **The Two-Pizza Team:** A dedicated and small team, the Two-Pizza Team is typically a cross-functional team of no more than 10 people. We explored this in greater depth in Idea 20.

3. **Customers:** Customers are both internal and, as Amazon's platform strategy shows, external. Your company must have deep understanding of your customers and their plans, road maps, and needs. Build personas for these customers, and deliver to them a compelling capability.

4. **Self-service:** A process should be self-service. Someone using or wanting to use your process should be able to discover, contract, implement, manage, and optimize utilizing your service without talking to you. This is a forcing function to force teams to define and explain their process. For more about forcing functions, see Idea 24.

5. **Definition:** Create a deep, written definition of your process, with emphasis on the connections and interfaces. Think of the process as a black box. While not understanding the details of what goes on in the black box, define exactly what the inputs to the box are, the outputs the box delivers, and then the metrics.

6. **Metrics:** This includes daily and operational metrics, as well as longer-term metrics. Long-term metrics were sometimes referred to collectively as a "fitness function" at Amazon. A fitness function, which is a set of metrics, showed how a process or capability was delivered over a long time period. Metrics on adoption, scaling, cost, and quality were the key topics carefully debated and approved before a fitness function could be approved.

7. **Application programming interfaces (APIs):** Part of making your capability self-service, APIs are the programming interfaces that allow other systems to integrate into your capability. APIs interface with the upstream and downstream business partners and systems, and they define the choreography and business rules between processes and capabilities. Designing these interfaces is a key part of the process engineering that a team does, and as such it is a core business concern.

8. **Road map of possibilities:** A process has a road map of potential innovations and improvements for the capability. This road map is always updated and added to as part of an ongoing conversation with the team and partners on potential new ideas and features. This is not the approved or funded road map but, rather, a list of cataloged ideas to keep the team thinking about the future and getting them to write down these ideas. Making it a habit to critically ask questions about how to scale key capabilities, how to improve your operating metrics, and how to increase quality and writing these ideas down will enable you to develop better ideas over time. When a detailed and committed plan is needed, you will be ready with the best ideas because you have already been putting in the hard work, which cannot be rushed.

Think about your core processes. Is there an opportunity to raise the bar on what your processes deliver and how they affect the business? Start with careful consideration and debate on which of your core processes need to scale, review the ingredient list, and begin engineering your processes.

Of course, any process you put in place is useless if you don't first do the math.

KEY QUESTIONS TO CONSIDER

1. Where could you start the concept of a small team owning a critical service in your business?

2. Where is scaling important in your business? Could these functions be improved with this "recipe for a process"?

3. What resistance can you predict? How might you get ahead of the change challenges?

DO THE MATH

The Path to Automation and AI Starts with Formulas

*Mathematics is not about numbers, equations,
computations, or algorithms: it is about understanding.*
—William Paul Thurston

Do you know the formula for your business process? Do you know what the input variables are versus the output variables? Working with my clients, I do a significant amount of process reengineering and process improvement work. An early discussion (and test) I give them includes the following three questions:

1. Do you have a sufficiently deep and accurate written definition of the process?

2. Can you walk me through a balanced (cost, quality, throughput) set of metrics for the process (and show me today's metrics in addition to last month's metrics)?

3. Can you show me a written formula for the process?

The answers tend to range quite a bit. Many clients have a definition of their process, but it's neither deep nor accurate enough to explain how their business really works. Most have some metrics, but they're generally single sided or unbalanced, and they typically have significant latency. As for that third question, I usually get curious looks. "What on earth is he getting at?" Most often, I work with clients who have no idea what a formula for their business might look like. What would it look like to really understand these things about your business?

> **idea 33:** In your journey of process improvement and automation, build the best mathematical equations you can for the process and subprocesses. These will help you understand and define the process, how to measure, and put you on the path to automation and artificial intelligence (AI).

HOW TO GET STARTED IN YOUR BUSINESS? DO THE MATH

Let's take a deeper look at the case of Clifford Cancelosi, an ex-Amazon leader and former colleague of mine. Until recently, Clifford was a leader at a national home service appliance installation and repair business. When Clifford started in the home repair business, customers were consistently waiting 7 to 10 days for a scheduled appointment with a technician. This made it hard to create a business road map or even to prioritize the urgency of specific customers.

Luckily, based on his Amazon experience, Clifford knew what to do. He calls it "Do the math." He set to work creating a set of equations to determine his daily effective repair capacity. After some thought, he realized that at a high level, the company's effective daily repair capacity for each technician was a function of three variables:

- The mean time it takes a technician to complete a job
- The mean time it takes a technician to move from job to job
- The percentage of times a repair job was completed in one visit

The formula for the effective capacity of a technician is then this:

(8 hours × percentage first-time completes) / (mean time to complete job + mean routing time between jobs) = effective daily capacity

If the mean time to complete the job is 2 hours, the mean time to move between job locations is 0.5 hours, and the percentage of first-time completes is 75 percent, the effective capacity becomes this:

$$(8 \times 0.75) / (2 + 0.5) = 2.4$$

That's 2.4 effective jobs per eight-hour day.

Once Clifford had this equation, he could turn each variable into a metric: first-time completes, mean routing times, and so forth. He tracked each to keep tabs on that specific part of the business's operations.

From there, he analyzed the possible errors that might affect each metric. In the case of first-time completes, these included the following:

- Technician efficacy

- Wrong part on truck

- No part on truck

- Scheduling inaccuracy

The more the company grew to understand the subequations within the formula and what drove variations in each metric, the better it could improve business performance. That deep understanding allowed the company to build formulas to augment its manual decision-making.

Today, that home appliance repair business has significantly elevated its effective capacity formula. It has strengthened its first-time complete metric by creating a hierarchy of metrics that measures the critical customer experience and the root causes to improve each metric, reduce variability, and reduce costs.

If you're struggling to understand how to measure and improve your business processes, this is a great way to start:

1. Pick a key process or customer experience. (In the preceding example, the process was the number of jobs a technician could complete in a day.)

2. Define the hierarchy of metrics. (What are the factors that affect that process?)

3. Build a formula from the variables.

Once you have your basic formulas, it becomes much easier to understand which parts of the processes could benefit from more data collection by connected devices.

In Clifford's appliance repair business, for example, sensors were used to capture the following:

- **The actual routes of company delivery trucks and the actual time between stops:** Once the company had access to actual route and wait-time data via the tablets the company provided the delivery trucks, the company leaders overlaid it with a driver's planned route and expected routing time to identify factors that might improve the efficiency of drivers—for example, eliminating unscheduled stops, increasing productivity on each job, and creating more efficient routes for drivers.

- **The movement of key inventory using radio frequency identification (RFID) sensors:** RFID sensors allowed company leaders to see when key inventory was loaded on a truck and when it was removed. This not only helped eliminate shrinkage but also allowed the company to prepare for inventory needs.

The next step for the appliance repair business would be to work with appliance manufacturers to include connected sensors in the appliances themselves. That would allow the company to understand the problem with the appliance—and any needed parts—before the technician arrived, leading to better "first-time fix" metrics and, eventually, the ability to detect, model, and predict appliance failures.

CREATE EQUATIONS FOR KEY TOPICS AND PROCESSES

The hardest part of "doing the math" is getting started. It is a process that requires a deep understanding of your company's operating environment, a talent for math, and a willingness to be transparent—all of which the average person inherently finds reasons to avoid.

It's far easier to spend hours debating subjective reasons for the variances in your operating environment than it is to double down and perfect your equations.

One of the most important things to remember when getting started with the math is not to let the perfect be the enemy of the good. Don't let yourself get hung up on fully optimizing your processes right away. The concept of a fully optimized business process is intimidating for most people. Rather than setting yourself up to give up before you even begin, focus on "doing the math" to drive continuous improvement.

Keeping your eyes on the prize—a key business objective that can improve the customer experience, increase the efficiency of business operations, and scale these impacts financially—is critical to "doing the math."

QUESTIONS TO CONSIDER

1. Are there deep and accurate written definitions of your core processes and capabilities?

2. Do you have a balanced (cost, quality, throughput) set of metrics for the processes (and do they show today's metrics in addition to last month's metrics)?

3. Can you write a formula for the process?

CUSTOMER EXPERIENCE MATTERS

Design and Measure the Customer Experience to Win

If you don't appreciate your customers, someone else will.
—Jason Langella

I travel for both business and personal purposes, averaging a trip a week. When traveling, I really appreciate "ease." Priority boarding, ticketless travel, room service. Small delights that leave an impression and put a smile on my face.

Unfortunately, this is twice as true for the opposite of "ease"—operational "dis-ease," if you will. For example, I fly American Airlines, which is a partner of my preferred airline, Alaska Airlines. When I book the ticket at American, it allows me to select "Alaska" so I can use my partner airlines number. However, when I enter my Alaska number, I receive an error message. So every time I go to the airport to check in for my American Airlines flight, I need to remember to switch the flight to my Alaska airlines MVP number. This is obviously not a mission-critical matter, but it's something that I have to compensate for, and it makes me grimace when I think about it.

Yes, this may be just one small step in a long sequence of steps required to travel around the United States or the globe, but it grates on me. Every time. If I let it, this simple hiccup in the process might define my entire customer experience with American Airlines.

idea 34: The customer experience is not the website or mobile app. The customer experience is the entire life cycle of your customer in key scenarios involving your product or service, but it is not limited to your product or service. Build metrics specifically designed to measure the customer experience. Dive deep and understand the details of how your customers feel and react to the entire experience. You will gain ideas for improvement, and what's more, you will gain ideas for innovation and expansion.

A large healthcare provider that asked me to give a keynote for them recently wanted 1,500 signed copies of my previous book. I ordered the books from CreateSpace (easy!), signed them (hard on my hand!), and then had 15 boxes shipped to the event from my house. I was using one of the major carriers, and I soon figured out that I could not schedule from their website a home pickup for this many boxes. I called them, sat on the line for 10 minutes, and then discovered I would need to be home for a pickup "anytime between 8 a.m. and 5 p.m." Are you kidding me? Who runs their life like that? Even if I were at home for an entire day, I would never be ready at any moment to serve their pickup driver. I ended up making three trips to the carrier's local office to drop off the books. Yet another case of operational dis-ease.

THE EASY BUTTON

At the end of the day, what most of us want is an "easy" button. What does it do? For me, the easy button allows for business on my terms, through the channel of my choice. It is connected across all channels, with flexibility, proactive updates, and demonstrated respect for my most precious asset, time. The easy button could also mean guarantees, "outcomes," and ironclad service-level agreements, as opposed to my buying a product and just hoping it delivers the intended result.

Many organizations do an excellent job at this. Netflix seamlessly streams content you want with a single push of a button. Dropbox and WeTransfer make sending huge files a snap. Facebook makes connecting with friends and family quick and easy. Yet for companies like these, the challenge is continuing to enable new customer experiences and shooting for perfection in their operations affecting customer experience.

I recently dealt with a leading financial services organization that made me print, sign, and fax in a document instead of enabling an electronic signature. I didn't even know fax machines still existed.

Ordering an item online, having it delivered to your house, and not being able to return it to their store. Being told by the airline ticket counter, "The system seems to always be this slow on Fridays." All examples of companies without integration and without the easy button.

As Jello Biafra, a punk rock artist, once said, "Give me convenience or give me death." Yes, that was originally said ironically, but now it's true whether you like it or not. The modern customer is not going to put up with operational dis-ease. In this frictionless world, it will feel like death by a thousand cuts. We've all experienced too many great customer experiences to be satisfied with old-school and mediocre experiences. We sometimes settle for them because we have to, but we aren't delighted by the experience. I don't want to sound like a broken record, but this is worth listening to again and again because it's important: many organizations need to rethink, retool, and significantly upgrade the customer experience.

THE iPHONE RUINED US ALL

In my estimation, nothing has so dramatically changed customer expectations as much as the iPhone. I've heard it referred to as "life's remote control." We want an app for everything, with the unstated promise that the app is going to be modern, intuitive (no user manual), fast, easily procured through iTunes, secure, and trustworthy. We want these attributes now for everything in life, including experiences in business. While many do not hit this bar, that doesn't change the fact that our expectations are calibrated to a great mobile experience. And what is the direct result of unrealized expectations? Resentments.

Obviously, the website and mobile experience need to feature great attributes, but this is just the start, the baseline of customer experience. Customer experience also includes the discovery and shopping experience, the pricing and negotiation experience, the delivery process, the training, the use, the maintenance, the loyalty, the returns, the customer service, the billing and invoicing, the operating experience and quality, the integration to other capabilities, the upgrade, and the end-of-life experience. In other words, the whole life cycle. As a result, it should be no surprise that customer experience can also affect the business model.

DESIGN METRICS FOR
THE CUSTOMER EXPERIENCE

Review the customer experience metrics in your business. In my experience, most metrics we have are focused on the financial, operations, and process metrics aligned with the organizational structure. And, boy, do we work to optimize them. A leader at Alvarez and Marsal liked to say, "Show me your P&L and I'll show you your organization's dysfunction."

His point was that the need for financial and operational reporting, coupled with most executive compensation structures and the natural competitive streak in most of us, leads us to focus on and optimize along the P&L, which is typically our organizational structure. Do your customers care about your organizational structure? No! But all too often we make them aware of it and make them deal with it.

Complementing your typical metrics with customer experience metrics will improve customer obsession, help everyone break down organizational boundaries, and drive for operational excellence—in other words, perfection. What's an example of metrics designed for the customer experience?

PERFECT ORDER PERCENTAGE:
THE POP METRIC AT AMAZON

As we have firmly established, customer satisfaction lies at the core of Amazon's business model. To determine how well its sellers are doing, Amazon uses certain performance measures, including the *perfect order percentage* (POP) *metric*. In short, it tracks the number of perfectly accepted, processed, and fulfilled orders.

In Amazon's eyes, the perfect order is entirely devoid of operational disease. There are no A-to-Z claims (Amazon's satisfaction guaranty), negative feedback instances, charge-backs, cancellations, late shipments, refunds, or buyer-initiated messages.

Amazon "recommends" that a retailer's POP metric be above 95 percent. By "recommend," Amazon means they will bring down the hurt if a seller allows the following metrics to fall above these stated goals: order defect rate greater than 1 percent, prefulfillment cancellation rate greater than 2.5 percent, and late dispatch rate greater than 4 percent.

To remain in the 95th percentile or above, sellers need optimized listings as well as the best fulfillment options and customer services offerings. It means identifying the products with the poorest performance and eliminating them (Figure 34.1).

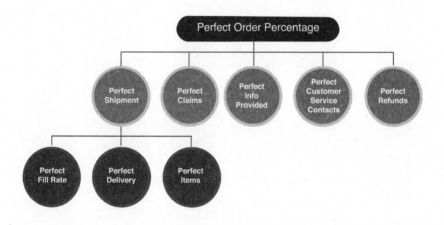

Figure 34.1 The Perfect Order Percentage (POP):
Percentage of Orders That Are Perfectly Accepted,
Processed, and Fulfilled

The POP metric system generally eliminates inaccurate listings, late shipments, missing tracking information, and canceled orders in the Amazon ecosystem. It's remarkable.

Focus on ways to set and measure the customer experience. Take the time to figure out how to measure the real interactions, and you will reap all types of benefits from these efforts. Figure out what "easy" and "perfect" mean for your customers.

QUESTIONS TO CONSIDER

1. How do you measure the customer experience in your business?

2. Do you have real measures, or are they proxies like surveys?

3. Are there standards set for what the customer experience needs to be?

4. How would you define and measure the perfect customer experience in your business?

WHAT'S YOUR JUST WALK OUT TECHNOLOGY?

Use the Internet of Things to Reinvent Customer Experiences

*Any sufficiently advanced technology is
indistinguishable from magic.*
—Arthur C. Clarke

Ever hear of the Amazon Dash Wand? Probably not. Launched in 2014, the Dash Wand was not a hit when it was first released. Designed for use in a customer's kitchen and pantry, the wand allows a customer to scan a universal product code (UPC), take a photo of an item, or speak to the wand to get product information or reorder an item. The Dash Wand was never widely available.

After a limited release, it quickly morphed into the Amazon Dash Buttons, small consumer electronic devices placed around the house and programmed to order consumer goods. It also begat the Amazon Dash Replenishment Service, which allows manufacturers to add a physical button or auto-detection capability to their devices to enable customers to reorder supplies from Amazon when necessary. In 2018, a revised Alexa-enabled version of the Dash Wand became a freebie for Prime members after Amazon acquired Whole Foods.

> idea 35: Using sensors and the Internet of Things, you can greatly improve your ability to understand the customer experience, to test new ideas and run trials, and to get your innovation engine running.

Of the many lessons to be gleaned from the humble Amazon Dash Wand, the first is that what might be deemed a failure at some companies is just a step in the innovation journey to other ideas at Amazon. Second, sometimes you just need to be patient. Some concepts require a generation or two to succeed. Sometimes the product needs to advance, sometimes the market needs to mature, or a combination needs to happen. The big lesson, however, is that the Internet of Things provides a new paradigm for improving your customer experience and for your business to innovate and grow.

AMAZON GO

"No lines, no checkouts, no registers. . . . Welcome to Amazon Go." Such is the promise and slogan of Amazon's new revolutionary stores, which literally make shopping easier than shoplifting. Check in with a quick scan of your Amazon Go app and begin shopping. Anything you pick up is automatically added to your virtual cart. Place it back on the shelf and it is removed.

How does it work? The short promotional video will tell you it's a combination of computer vision, deep learning algorithms, and sensor fusion, "much like you'd find in self-driving cars."[1] For obvious reasons, Amazon refuses to go into any more detail regarding the tech. However, they have branded this potent IoT cocktail Just Walk Out Technology. As the name suggests, when you're done shopping, you simply leave. Voilà! As I said, easier than shoplifting. In fact, shoplifting is really difficult with Amazon Go.

The first 1,800-square-foot Amazon Go opened in Seattle in January 2018. The *New York Times* described it as a convenience store that also carries some of the food usually found at Whole Foods.[2] It's been described as a seamless experience. The only signs of the Just Walk Out Technology are the arrays of small cameras positioned above the shelves and the subwaylike sensory turnstiles at the door.

As the *New York Times* piece aptly points out, the real question is what Jeff Bezos plans to do with this technology now that it exists. While more stores are being built and more than 2,000 Amazon Go stores are now reportedly planned, some suspect the Just Walk Out Technology may soon appear at Whole Foods. Perhaps Amazon's AWS division will package the capabilities to sell the system to other retailers and companies, "much as it sells its cloud computing services to other companies."[3] The point is that Amazon Go is just one stop on a potentially enormous road map leading far into the future of retail.

CUSTOMER OBSESSION

The Internet of Things won't get you anywhere unless you're obsessing over your customers and their experiences and how connected devices can solve their problems. As you may have already experienced in your own life, when the Internet of Things is done wrong, it can be really creepy. Remember that German, Internet-connected doll, "My Friend Cayla"? Made by Genesis toys, Cayla contained an internal microphone that hackers could use to listen in on children—and even speak through. That's the stuff of nightmares.[4]

So how does Amazon make a revolutionary and hugely ambitious project like Amazon Go work? By starting with lots of little Amazon Dash Wands. Obsessing over the customer means trying new things, many of which don't work out. It means sticking with things that do work or that might work instead of getting distracted by the lure of a shinier, more profitable short-term opportunity. Ignore the long-held traditions and assumptions of how retail works, start with the customer, and work backward.

Customer Reviews, Free Everyday Shipping, 1-Click Ordering, Look Inside the Book, Prime, AutoRip—each of these innovations was controversial or negatively perceived by industry traditionalists when launched. Naysayers didn't understand Amazon's long-term strategy: obsess over a better customer experience to build long-term trust. Because of that strategy, many of these innovations are now the standard by which customers measure all online shopping experiences.

PUTTING IOT TO WORK FOR YOUR CUSTOMERS

"This all sounds nice," you might be thinking, "but I'm not Jeff Bezos. My customers need very different things, and we have to generate a profit along the way."

In some ways, you'd be right—nailing the next Kindle or Dash Button for your industry won't be easy. But that's exactly why IoT has become a game changer for those willing to obsess over their customers. The technology and solution components are accessible to every team, the cost basis is much improved and continuing to drop, and you can try small experiments without betting the farm. The key technologies of most IoT solutions include sensors, connectivity, cloud storage and processing, analytics, and machine learning.

Finding even one big success will require lots of experimentation. Many of those experiments will likely fail—just look at Amazon's Fire Phone or its investment in Pets.com, one of the biggest jokes of the dot-com era. There are nearly unlimited opportunities to improve the customer experience by leveraging connected devices. What's the path?

Start with the Customer

Walk yourself through an entire day in the life of your customer. Not just with your product or service, but broadly and deeply. How might connected devices change the way that your product or service fits into that day?

Deep customer obsession is rooted in a company's culture. A way to start building that is through a voice of the customer program. Keep in mind that successful customer feedback loops aren't limited to any one product or channel. They span the enterprise and include a deliberate, ongoing mechanism for taking in data from and about your customers. (One survey is not enough.) The good news is that, in a world of connected devices, this is getting easier all the time.

The toughest—and most important—part of the program will be empowering it to create change across the organization. This will require buy-in and collaboration across departments.

Remove Friction

Your next move is to identify and remove points of friction. What problems do your customers face? Why do customers contact you? What parts of your product or customer service apparatus get in the way of solving those problems? And how could a connected device remove those pain points? Is there data you could be collecting that would give you or your customer new insight?

Sometimes the best way to create a great customer experience is to start by imagining a terrible customer experience. Imagine your grandmother trying to use a cell phone for the first time. No matter how intuitive the process, chances are good that something will go wrong. When it does, she'll spend 45 minutes on the phone with the nice customer service agent explaining that "the angry blinkie thingies keep looking at me." If that fails, she'll be forced to drive all the way to her service provider's physical location, or more likely, she'll put the phone away in a drawer until her teenage grandchildren come to visit.

How could you reinvent this experience for her?

Unsurprisingly, Amazon has already tried its hand at this—the Kindle Fire's Mayday feature lets customer service agents take over a user's screen remotely, with their permission, to see and fix problems for them.

As you think about how to reduce friction in your industry, start by recreating a terrible customer experience, and then think about how the Internet of Things or connected devices could improve that experience.

Think Broadly

The next most innovative move in your industry may not directly involve your current product—just think about Amazon's drones. Amazon is an e-commerce company, but it turned out that the design of online shopping sites and the products it offers are no longer the biggest pain points for customers. The speed and efficiency of their delivery is a vital part of the customer experience, and Amazon realized early on that it needed to control and innovate even when it heavily relied on partners for execution.

Think about the power of the Internet of Things to provide a new interface with your customers. Connected devices empower you to learn more about your customers and use these deeper insights to build better products and services for the environments in which they are used.

What data would help you understand your customers and their experience better? How can you collect that data? And, most important, how can you use that data, once collected, to create value and improve your customer experience?

Integrating this kind of thinking into your current customer planning is the key to transitioning from being customer focused to customer obsessed.

DON'T COMMIT TO SCALING

One of the biggest mistakes companies can make is to commit to scaling a new feature or capability before it has been thoroughly tested and perfected. Keep new approaches in a beta state and for a limited number of customers. Set their expectations to be realistic, telling them that this is new and a trial. Too often executives are pressured or too optimistic, and they commit to scaling, to revenue, and to a plan that have not been proven. Then they have to roll out a new product or service that is not fantastic, customers react negatively, projections are not hit, the initiative does not reach its vision or potential, and the enterprise becomes more timid about trying new things.

Companies like Amazon run trials for new features and products, sometimes for years, before scaling. They might have a plan for scaling, but they have certain goals to be reached, milestones and issues that have to be figured out, before the plan is started, budgeted, and announced. For example, Amazon Echo was in limited release for months before Amazon decided to scale it.

That's all well and good, but if you're still thinking about that creepy German doll Cayla, let me explain to you why information security must die.

QUESTIONS TO CONSIDER

1. How are you working to innovate the customer experience today?

2. Do you have a list of ideas on how IoT or other technologies could affect your customer experience?

3. How was the last failure in innovating the customer experience treated?

4. Do promising ideas and programs get committed to scaling or delivering revenue before they are proven? Has this affected the ultimate success of the idea?

INFORMATION
SECURITY MUST DIE

Making Security
Everyone's Job

Cybersecurity is much more than a matter of IT.
—Stéphane Nappo

Everyone likes easy answers. Everyone likes easy answers that assign responsibility to one person or team and that provide a clear scapegoat when things go wrong.

Everyone likes easy answers that promise this technology product will provide this outcome for us. And company leaders and boards especially like easy answers when it comes to cybersecurity. Why? Because they don't understand the risks and are scared. They desperately want to believe them. If I just described you or your leadership, sorry. You won't like the answer I'm about to give you.

> **idea 36:** Security is not a role. Security is not the elimination of risks. Security is an integrated development of requirements, people, process, and risk acceptance that must be woven into every team.

* This idea was cowritten with Larry Hughes.

Larry Hughes built Amazon's very first firewalls. He was Amazon's second security engineer and second worldwide head of web and enterprise security. He has since been a leader and consultant to many organizations on the broad topics of enterprise risk and cybersecurity.

Larry and I first worked together in 2002 when I was leading the launch of Marketplace at Amazon. Payments was our big risk area in that business, incidentally. When discussing the lessons Larry learned working on Amazon's cybersecurity, he notes that Leadership Principle 2, "Ownership," is never truer than on the topic of security. As a business leader, you don't get to pass the hot potato to someone else. You own it.

Here are some of the lessons and ideas Larry learned at Amazon, which still influence his work today:

1.   **Business-justified information security budget:** Business teams and internal service providers need to make the decisions and investments for security-related needs, just as they would for any other business-related expense. For example, the team that provides the enterprise its productivity tools like e-mail might say, "We need a spam tool," and the decisions and budget come from their team. Why? Because spam has an adverse operational effect on the single most common form of business communication. Why should we expect security to forecast or improve the operations of another team? This type of thinking breeds "learned helplessness," which remains one of the biggest enterprise security problems today.

2.   **Distributed ownership:** Just as the budget for cybersecurity should be allocated to the business teams, ownership for security lies with the leader and teams responsible for the service. They pull on the expertise and standards provided by the security team, but teams should own every aspect of their business.

3.   **Chief information security officer (CISO) role and team:** Just like tax, finance, and legal, the CISO organization is a service provider to business teams, and their job is to get to yes (see Idea 12). Larry's team motto was "We never say 'No!'" Sometimes you must provide a better route and restate the requirements or approaches to solutions.

4. **Integration:** The CISO team needs to invest significant time in engaging and knowing every stakeholder, particularly their pain points. They need to be integrated and involved early, providing guidance and expertise. This eliminates any semblance of "ivory tower" security decisions. Done right, integrating security into what other teams do should make their lives easier, not harder.

5. **Being secure by design:** Being secure is not a checklist or a step in a process. Security is just like any other set of requirements or capabilities. Throughout the design and management of a capability, the security requirements, scenarios, and risks need to be considered and articulated.

6. **Risk:** The CISO assists business teams in risk modeling and risk measuring. Security is about knowing your risks, and it's about quantifying the likelihood of risk occurrence with the value of the data or asset. Cybersecurity risk is just like any other type of business risk managed in the organization.

7. **Knowing your assets:** You must painstakingly categorize your enterprise data and assets. No one likes doing this, but it is necessary. If you don't know what your assets are, or if you do not have a notion of the value of the data, how can you make a proper business decision?

8. **Defending the data:** Unequivocal stewardship for all business-critical data needs to be established. Stewards should bear fully accountability for all aspects of the data under their purview, including its security.

9. **Security assessment and implementation process and framework:** The CISO provides the process and framework for security discussion and evaluation. Organizations like the Commerce Department's National Institute of Standards and Technology (NIST) are developing the frameworks, templates, and standard processes that the CISO can use to drive adoption within the enterprise.

10. **Just another defect:** The crowning touch is to think about a security problem as just another defect. Nobody sets out to design a system with bad security. When security problems rise to the surface, they should be rooted out with the same rigor that other defects are.

SECURE BY DESIGN

The approach of secure (or security) by design (SbD) is the mindset and approach that "means that the software (or system) has been designed from the ground up to be secure. Malicious practices are taken for granted, and care is taken to minimize impact when a security vulnerability is discovered or on invalid user input."[1] This approach of assuming the worst and having security at the heart of requirements and development, versus an audit and inspection, is critical. Having a strong security team participating, defining standards, and contributing expertise, but having the business and technical teams own security for their business and systems supports the decentralized and proactive nature of SbD.

One of the most famous cybersecurity incidents took place in December 2013 when Target was hacked and almost 110 million customers' personal and financial information was stolen. An in-depth analysis was conducted, and it's fascinating reading.[2] One expert summarized the *Target Kill Chain Report* as follows:

1. Attacks, defenses, and missed opportunities are described in plain English, with minimal technical details to disrupt the presentation.

2. As the story unfolds, it becomes clear that IT security can't be achieved and checked off. It's an ongoing, continuous effort that requires CEO and board-level leadership to move from mere compliance to true risk management.

3. The authors place appropriate emphasis on the importance of defense-in-depth, a key component of modern cyber defense. Start with a firewall to keep most threats out, but also use dynamic monitoring programs, internal barriers between systems, and other controls to detect and defeat malware that makes it through the first line of defense.[3]

Security, understanding and quantifying risk, and participating in the discussion and trade-offs are the job of the board and C suites. While framing the discussion and partnering, your CIO or CISO cannot own even a majority of the scope. So while "information security must die," security and risk management, embedded in all of your designs, processes, training, and thinking, must come to life. Security must become a habit.

QUESTIONS TO CONSIDER

1. Do you have a prioritized list of your data assets and the cybersecurity risks that pertain to them?

2. Is cybersecurity integrated throughout the design and management process, or is it a checklist item?

3. Does accountability for cybersecurity-related risk rest with the business leadership?

OP1

The Painstaking Process of Planning

Festina lente. (Make haste, slowly.)
—Emperor Augustus

Where do all of Amazon's ideas for scaling processes, innovating new services, improving customer experience, and rationalizing where to put headcount and resources come from? When do they say yes or no to all the great ideas they have to scale or innovate in their business? How does all of that happen? I often get asked variations of this question, and there is no single answer. There is, however, a specific time and place in the Amazon universe where these elements are evaluated and decided upon: the annual planning process generally known as Operating Plan 1 (OP1).

But let me stop you there. This is not a simple, clean, efficient process, nor does it immediately accelerate the organization. OP1 is messy, frustrating, painstaking, and imperfect. It's a classic example of the "go slow to go fast" approach to business. While knuckle-bitingly frustrating at times, the OP1 process helps the company collect, explain, and rationalize the best ideas, helps the executive team make the best decisions about what to go forward with and what not to fund, and helps the organization gain clarity and focus once decisions are made.

* This idea was cowritten with Clifford Cancelosi.

idea 37: Define a planning process that asks the questions "How did we perform?" "What is next year's plan?" "Which of our ideas will improve the business?" and "Which innovation ideas should we pursue?" and connects the answers to the headcount and other necessary expenses. In your discussion, include the business case and key operational and customer experience metrics and goals. Spend as much time as it takes to hash out these documents in development and to read, debate, and decide at the executive level. Be clear and announce to the organization which ideas and initiatives are being approved (a yes decision) or not approved or funded (a no or not now).

OPERATING PLAN 1 (OP1)

Summertime in Seattle is precious. Having borne the brunt of eight cold, wet months, each loaded with a mindless succession of short gray days, summer suddenly appears around July 4, and the Pacific Northwest becomes the most beautiful place on the planet. Alas, if you work at Amazon, you pretty much miss it. For in the months of July, August, and September, while also doing all the preholiday work before the retail peak season hits, you are spending your time meeting, debating, writing, and reviewing your next year's operating plans and ideas for scaling and innovating. That's right, summer and early fall is OP1 season.

While there are multiple opportunities to analyze and discuss ideas, plans, resource allocation, and critiques of the business throughout the year, OP1 is the tent under which all of Amazon's disciplines and strategies gather on an annual basis. Although structured, OP1 is messy. The time and effort required are hard to predict. OP1 is simply done when it's done. Genius requires truckloads of scribbles, crumpled up paper, and "wasted" time. And every year, this process not only brews ideas for inventions, but cements clear decisions and commitments:

The Basic Structure of OP1

1. Teams start reviewing their business results. They identify the goals for following years and the budgets and dependencies needed to meet those goals.

2. In addition, the executive team hands down detailed strategic business goals that all teams and businesses must be prepared to say how they will support. The objectives are detailed enough to allow teams to understand the specifics of how their business or service will need to respond (for example, retail will grow at 35 percent gross, resulting in $7.8 million incremental orders shipped).

3. Many of these goals are cross-functional, requiring teams across the company to work together to meet them.

4. Ideas for either incremental or new capabilities are captured.

5. The process encourages thorough and deep thinking.

6. Plans are written (see Ideas 44, 45, 46, and 47) in a variety of manners.

7. Oftentimes, meetings start with silence, allowing the participants to read and "grok" the plans.

8. The process creates alignment early on across the business regarding priorities, delivery timing, dependencies, and so on.

9. The process is designed to ensure that people and projects are tied to the overall strategy.

10. It encourages ownership by enforcing articulation of detailed and objective measurements of progress that can be tracked and reported on.

11. It allows executives to better understand what their peers are working on to avoid redundancy and to enable planning.

As I said, it's a messy structure, but the OP1 process enables a holistic review of the value of each team's business or service and its overall fit within the company's strategy. It also forces every team to think through and outline the road map necessary to support the overall growth objectives of the company.

The approach is bottom up. Every team in the company prepares its own documents. The SVPs subsequently roll up the most critical aspects of these plans and the full fiscal impact of all asks, growth, and so on into a summary OP1 for the entire operating area under their individual purview.

These plans are combined for a comprehensive, detailed, week-long review by the SVPs. The VPs and SVPs from other operating areas are invited to review and participate in these sessions to provide insights and critiques as well as to ensure buy-in and approval from dependent teams. In some cases, the leaders of these dependent teams cannot commit to the work, creating an opportunity to assess the importance of the ask and consider escalating for broader review.

The review meeting is typically four hours in length. Everyone spends the first hour of the meeting reading the document thoroughly. This is immediately followed by three hours of interrogation. Reviewers are expected to provide hard, but constructive feedback. Reviewers do their own math on financial assumptions, metrics, and so on. Mistakes are attacked vigorously. The process ensures that the thinking around the plan is as complete as possible.

The clarity of the commitments is equally important to the clarity of the thinking. Goals are agreed to, deliverables are estimated and committed to, and budgets can be reconciled and rolled up. Of course, there are always more ideas that can be pursued than can be funded. Clearly saying yes to approved initiatives means saying no or "later" to most ideas. It is better to commit and execute on a few key ideas than dilute your efforts across all the ideas.

A former Amazon product manager gave his thoughts on Amazon's annual planning process:

> Every year at Amazon, teams are forced to create and review a document with the executive team which outlines in excruciating detail their performance in the previous year and their plans for the upcoming year including resource asks. Operating Plan 1 (OP1) is typically a six-page narrative (with mountains of appendixes) looking at every angle of your business and can be the difference between your team getting a bunch of new resources or getting cut into oblivion (Bezos and crew aren't shy about killing teams that aren't performing well). While I used to gripe about the amount of our time this process would suck up, the reality is that this kind

of rigorous evaluation is probably one of the reasons why Amazon is able to be so focused in their investments and grow in businesses with relatively thin margins.[1]

YOUR VERSION NEEDED

It's no secret that competition is increasing in every industry, and the pace of change grows faster and faster. Have you realigned or defined how you will respond *every year* to this reality? It's not a one-time activity. Every year brings an entirely new set of circumstances. This is only one of the reasons why Amazon sacrifices its summer and early fall every year for OP1.

No process is perfect, but giving senior management the opportunity to impose constraints and objectives on the business from the top, getting ideas and involvement across the organization leveraging the best of everyone's thinking, and then putting it all together results in clarity and good decisions. This should be the goal of any planning process. You better get yours going!

QUESTIONS TO CONSIDER

1. What is your process for building and reviewing all the potential projects and investments you could make?

2. Are good and clear decisions made in your planning process?

3. Is appropriate time spent on planning the innovation initiatives in your business?

4. Can ideas come from anywhere in the organization? How are these collected and vetted?

STRATEGIC HEADCOUNT PLANNING

Scaling and Innovating Through People Allocation

Opportunity is missed by most people because it is dressed in overalls and looks like work.
—Thomas Edison

At Amazon, we used to joke that Jeff Bezos was like the Wizard of Oz, pulling levers behind the big curtain to operate his empire. And like the Great Oz, if Bezos could have his way, he would remain alone behind that curtain, free to manipulate the whole mechanism without interference or disruption. Alas, companies the size of Amazon don't work that way. As one of the largest employers in the United States, the dream of a fully automated company is no different than Dorothy's adventure—just a dream. What is real, however, is the pressure to scale, automate, and innovate at Amazon.

Scaling and innovating are not simple tasks. Yet most leaders overlook a critical tool at their disposal: headcount planning and allocation.

> **idea 38:** Define and account for the skills and headcount that "run the business" versus the skills and headcount that help "scale and innovate" the business, typically through technology and partners. As part of your planning process and decision-making, be deliberate in how you allocate and move the "scale and innovate" headcount and expense to accomplish that in the business.

DIRECT VERSUS INDIRECT
HEADCOUNT AT AMAZON

At Amazon, corporate employees are basically categorized as one of two types of headcount: direct or indirect. *Direct headcount employees* are skills and people who help scale a business or build new capabilities. This includes technical and software development skills, process architecture skills, and corporate development skills, as well as product managers and people who negotiate contracts. *Indirect headcount employees* are everything else: management, operations, customer services—basically everything else that hasn't been automated, perfected, or outsourced to others.

Ideas on how to scale processes or innovate are outlined during the Operating Plan 1 (Idea 37) process. The best ideas are allocated to direct headcount such as engineers, architects, and product managers for development. The indirect headcount is subsequently improved or eliminated to justify the allocation and to exhibit commitment to the project.

So what happens when strategic decisions are made annually to reallocate skills in ways that can build processes and technology to scale the business? Over time, the business becomes more and more defined, digital, and able to scale.

FULFILLMENT ROBOTS

As the *New York Times* pointed out in 2017, no company embodies the anxieties and hopes around automation better than Amazon.[1] As the company grows by leaps and bounds, it hires thousands more Americans every month. Yet Jeff Bezos realized long ago that Amazon's nearly 700 fulfillment centers across the globe represent a potentially disastrous hurdle to scaling.

In 2012, Amazon bought Kiva Systems for $775 million and rechristened it Amazon Robotics. Two year later, robots developed by Kiva entered the Amazon workforce at its warehouses. By 2017, Amazon had more than 100,000 robots in action around the world and has not stopped deploying them.[2]

In addition to delivering on a radically ambitious promise of Two-Day Shipping, the robots also alleviate monotony for the human workers by doing the most boring work and leaving the mentally engaging tasks to their flesh-and-blood counterparts. Have the Kiva robots displaced workers? Not according to Amazon, which told the *New York Times* that it had added 80,000 warehouse employees in the United States since adding the Kiva robots, for a total of more than 125,000 warehouse employees.[3] Go to the Amazon Robotics website and you will be greeted by the slogan, "We Reimagine Now," followed by invitations to train in the robotics field and to join a contest to encourage more innovation in the robotics category.

THE SHARK

Many competitors have likened Amazon to a shark over the years. It's an apt metaphor in the sense that sharks never stop moving. In Amazon's unprecedented journey to scale, Bezos and his people see the bottlenecks coming years in advance. There is never time to rest on one's laurels and smell the roses. When every day is Day 1, there is no end in sight.

As for your organization, carefully pick the processes you invest in. Make sure they are the true bottleneck or critical factor. Hopefully there will be many ideas, but you can only afford a few. After all, you never want to set out to build a single-bedroom home and end up with the Winchester Mystery House.

QUESTIONS TO CONSIDER

1. How is scaling managed in your organization?

2. Is headcount planning used as a tool to help digitize and innovate?

3. Can headcount be allocated and moved to fit business priorities?

ARCHITECTURE IS THE BUSINESS STRATEGY

Win Through Technology and Architecture

*Architecture is not an inspirational business,
it's a rational procedure to do sensible and
hopefully beautiful things; that's all.*
—Harry Seidler

The Winchester Mystery House, located in San Jose, was built by the widow of firearm company founder William Winchester. Although it had approximately 160 rooms, it was missing something critical: a plan. The house was built without an architect; the widow Winchester just kept adding on to the building in a haphazard fashion. As a result, the home contains numerous oddities such as doors and stairs that go nowhere, windows overlooking other rooms, and stairs with odd-sized risers.[1] Does this sound like your technology and data architecture?

I have worked with many companies on the intersection of business strategy and technology capabilities. The underlying challenge and frustration of most CEOs is that "it takes too long and costs too much" to make small changes that deliver business value. Most of the IT budget is devoted to keeping the current systems running, not to building new capabilities. I would often refer to their IT architecture as the "Winchester Mystery House"—lots of applications, lots of interfaces, but no master plan or architecture. When you want to quickly make changes, add features, or scale, you realize how rigid and ugly it is.

> **idea 39:** How your business designs, builds, and operates your data and technology architecture matters, and it will affect the value of your business. Architecture defines how nimble you can be and what types of risks you have. These are business considerations, and you need to make sure you are deeply involved. Don't underinvest the time, talent, or budget.

How is a solution or design typically approached? First, understand the user the solution is designed to serve and the problem the solution is designed to solve. List the "requirements." Then, figure out the quickest path to delivering the solution, also known as a "point solution."

This is an expedient but potentially shortsighted way to build your technology. With so many needs to meet, it's easy to understand the temptation to take the fastest path. Technology people are sometimes heralded for quick "hacky" approaches. But technology architecture—designing data, software, interfaces, APIs, networking, and infrastructure—is different. If you build solely to the point solution, you are just building another room in the Winchester Mystery House with no eye for design. And without a vision, there are two very important things you won't be prepared for: things to go wrong and tomorrow.

GET THE *-ITIES* FROM YOUR ARCHITECTURE

Paul Tearnen, a friend and former colleague at Alvarez and Marsal, is one of the best business technology architecture minds I know. He told me that your technology architecture needs to deliver the "-ities." Say what? The suffix *-ity* means "denoting a quality or condition." What are the qualities or conditions—the *-ities*—that the data and technology architectures ideally take into consideration?

- **Scalabil-ity:** The capability to quickly increase or decrease the throughput or capacity of the system.

- **Secur-ity:** Keeping out what you want to keep out; keeping in what you want to keep in. Isn't that security? Security was tackled in Idea 36.

- **Flexibil-ity:** Multipurpose and transformable to different use cases, different geographies, similar needs with variable or conditional processing requirements.

- **Interoperabil-ity:** Integration and interaction with grace with other types of technology, particularly different brands of technology, and external systems. APIs are one way of creating interoperability for data and processes across an enterprise and enterprises.

- **Measureabil-ity:** The instrumentation and monitoring capability of the system, to be able to identify, report, and even predict how well things are running and where challenges or failures might be. This can help both IT operations, as well as business processes dependent on measures, such as tolling or billing.

- **Usabil-ity:** The ease and intuitive interaction between the technology and users. It is the ergonomics and machine-device interface of the technology. Usability also addresses the environmental suitabil-ity of the technology to the operating conditions.

- **Traceabil-ity:** The ability to track, audit, or explain how transactions, decisions, and systems processes have occurred. "Reconciliation" is not sexy, but with Sarbanes-Oxley and other legal requirements, the ability to show how steps happened across the entire enterprise, often from a "cash-to-cash" perspective, the ability to demonstrate that all transactions happened as they should have happened, is the essence of "control." As more automation and machine learning are utilized, creating transparency and demonstrating how decisions are made is an aspect of traceabil-ity.

- **Extensibil-ity:** The essential quality of being able to efficiently meet future business needs with as minimal cost, time, and effort as possible.

- **Reusabil-ity:** An element of extensibility, the quality of using the same technology for multiple purposes. Modularity, object-oriented design, and appropriate abstraction are all approaches to create reusabil-ity.

- **Integr-ity:** In distributed architectures, where data and technology are running over multiple data centers, multiple cloud zones, and wide geographies and locations, the quality of having consistency and trustworthy authenticity, especially with data that has to be correct and have authority. The traditional example of an "atomic transaction" in which either all aspects of a transaction successfully commit to the distributed database or the transaction rolls back is a key now being augmented with the concept of "eventual consistency" in which the valid value for data is eventually made across all distributed versions of the data.

- **Modular-ity:** Creating discrete, well-defined, and separated functions of capabilities in software. A solution typically integrates multiple module services together. An important strategic notion at Amazon is that modular services need to be "self-service"—that is, to use your capability, someone should not need to talk to you to understand, design, test, deploy, or operate your service. This helps not only scale the technology but scale the organization.

- **Qual-ity:** The notion of a system doing what is expected. In technology, key enablers include the ease of being able to test and verify, deploy, manage versions, and effectively deal with software bugs.

- **Stabil-ity:** The ability to deal with new requirements and operating dynamics while not affecting the underlying architecture. Proper abstraction in the architecture design is the key to achieving stability. In the physical environment of computers, networks, and data centers, stabil-ity also is reflected in redundancy, failover, and disaster recovery scenarios.

- **Availabil-ity:** The ability to respond immediately. As the ESPN football analysts often say about athletes and injuries, "the best ability is availability." In retail, if an item is not available, you've lost an order and often lose the customer. In technology, it is no different. Systems must be available and deliver the response times required by the user and business. Near-real-time (NRT) systems in which there is minimal lag are critical architecture notions (neither cheap nor easy) that enable many digital experiences.

HELP ME HELP YOU

Who can forget the classic *Jerry Maguire* scene where the sports agent has a heart-to-heart with his player, Rod Sterling, in the locker room after the game? The agent is pleading with the player to do some things differently, to make it easier for the team to offer an extension to his contract. "Help me help you!" Maguire begs. How often do businesspeople simply turn to their technology team and basically say, "This is your problem, nerds"? If you're going to win in the digital era, being a better business partner and collaborator with your technology team is critical. (And referring to them as "nerds" is probably unhelpful too, in case you actually call them that.)

What's your role as a business partner to your technology team? First, care about these elements, and work to articulate what metrics are needed and how to measure them from a business standpoint. Drill down on the use cases, and specify exactly how it needs to work. Be curious about how these scenarios are supported, and ask a lot of questions on each one. Second, focus on the long term. You must be willing to fund the construction of these underlying qualities and capabilities. And third—and here's where your architecture becomes your strategy—go on the offense.

Understand how the *-ities* will be architected, and understand the trade-offs. Figure out how to use these *-ities* as competitive elements to sell to your customers and differentiate from competition. If you can articulate to the market that you are better than your competition on these qualities and demonstrate why it matters to your customers, then funding the *-ities* can be moved from the "overhead costs" to the "direct costs" column. Direct costs, also known as the "costs of goods sold" (COGS), are costs associated directly with revenue production. The architecture is now becoming the business!

BEZOS'S API MANIFESTO

I was present for a major turning point at Amazon. In 1999, *Barron's* printed its now classic cover story "Amazon.bomb," which predicted that Amazon's stock was going the way of Pets.com and Drugstore.com.[2] But instead of becoming a disaster, Amazon turned the corner from a market confidence standpoint, and it grew to become one of the "Four Horsemen of tech."[3] It wasn't long after the *Barron's* cover story that we began recognizing that Amazon was really two key types of businesses.

First, of course, we were a broad, multicategory e-commerce retailer. At the time, I ran Marketplace, or as we referred to it, the "Merchants @" business. M@ was critical to creating "the everything store." Using the M@ platform, we opened over 14 categories, such as apparel, sporting goods, musical instruments, gourmet, and jewelry.

However, it was around this time that Amazon began seeing itself as a platform company, serving many other companies in addition to being Amazon the retailer. We decided that all systems needed to interoperate, internally and externally, through APIs. These APIs needed to have hardened interfaces, which meant they were well architected, not prone to sudden changes, and were forward compatible. APIs had to have SLAs measuring against a set of performance standards for speed and availabilities. And SLAs had to be fault tolerant—that is, they needed to assume that other dependencies might fail or degrade. Regardless, the APIs had to process gracefully in a situation where other system components where not operating properly.

Like any big change, the technology was difficult, but getting people aware, committed, and all going in the same direction was the big hurdle. In Bezos's classic clear communication style, this memo in 2002 contained the 10 commandments from the top of the mountain.

Steve Yegge, a former Amazon engineer, recalls the memo in this classic blog post:

> His Big Mandate went something along these lines:
>
> 1. All teams will henceforth expose their data and functionality through service interfaces.
>
> 2. Teams must communicate with each other through these interfaces.
>
> 3. There will be no other form of interprocess communication allowed: no direct linking, no direct reads of another team's data store, no shared-memory model, no backdoors whatsoever. The only communication allowed is via service interface calls over the network.
>
> 4. It doesn't matter what technology they use. HTTP, Corba, Pubsub, custom protocols—doesn't matter. Bezos doesn't care.
>
> 5. All service interfaces, without exception, must be designed from the ground up to be externalizable. That is to say, the team must plan and design to be able to expose the interface to developers in the outside world. No exceptions.
>
> 6. Anyone who doesn't do this will be fired.

7. Thank you; have a nice day!

Ha, ha! You 150-odd ex-Amazon folks here will, of course, realize immediately that number 7 was a little joke I threw in, because Bezos most definitely does not give a shit about your day.

Number 6, however, was quite real, so people went to work. Bezos assigned a couple of Chief Bulldogs to oversee the effort and ensure forward progress, headed up by Uber-Chief Bear Bulldog Rick Dalzell. Rick is an ex-Army Ranger, West Point Academy graduate, ex-boxer, ex-Chief Torturer slash CIO at Walmart, and is a big, genial, scary man who used the word "hardened interface" a lot. Rick was a walking, talking hardened interface himself, so, needless to say, everyone made *lots* of forward progress and made sure Rick knew about it.[4]

Through their architecture, Amazon set upon both scaling their internal organization, as well as their business model. Today, Amazon has hundreds of public APIs, everything from product-related APIs to AWS APIs, Echo APIs, and APIs in their fulfillment network through Fulfillment by Amazon.

INVEST MORE IN CUSTOM SOFTWARE

The 1980s through the early 2000s were dominated by the ERP wars. Companies rushed to implement SAP, Oracle, PeopleSoft, or other packaged software solutions that were excellent at standardizing core business processes such as manufacturing, order management, HR, or finance. While helping to scale and drive improvements in processes, these systems did not change the essence of the business model for the companies.

Now as technology and digitizing products, services, and experiences become all important, being thoughtful about building proprietary software is one of the most important decisions made by an enterprise. Don't let the CIO make this decision. Have the CIO participate in the decision. The *Wall Street Journal* notes that "new data suggests that the secret to the success of the Amazons, Googles, and Facebooks of the world—not to mention the Walmarts, CVSes, and UPSes before them—is how much they invest in their own technology. . . . IT spending that goes into hiring developers and creating software owned and used exclusively by a firm is the key competitive advantage.

It's different from our standard understanding of R&D in that this software is used solely by the company and isn't part of products developed for its customers."[5]

Your architecture is composed of many types of technology, but software is where the business logic and customer experience are enabled, and it requires a key set of strategic decisions, particularly about where more development is required.

IT'S NOW THE JOB—PUT IN THE TIME

You're likely not the technical architect, the software developer, or the CTO of the organization. As a business leader, with accountability for driving the business, you need to be curious and become current on these key technology concepts. Everyone needs to raise their technology understanding in becoming digital. Discuss what's important to you with your technology team. Make sure there are metrics and SLAs so you know if you are getting the performance required.

Blur the lines across the organization between "a business discussion" and "a technology discussion," and you will set a course for becoming digital. When you have a discussion, a great place to start is with the questions you ask.

QUESTIONS TO CONSIDER

1. Is your technology and data architecture well documented, and do you understand it?

2. Are you overly reliant on packaged software for your core capabilities? Would custom software in a few select capabilities be a strategic differentiator for you?

3. Does your technology architecture have a plan that aligns with your digital business strategy?

THE QUESTIONS
YOU ASK

Ask Your CIO
These Questions—for
Everyone's Benefit

I never learn anything talking.
I only learn things when I ask questions.
—Lou Holtz

Becoming a digital business and a digital leader places an increased burden on the organization to deliver new capabilities, to capture and use data in new ways, and to collaborate both internally and externally with speed and agility. Getting the best out of your technology, limited budget, and technology team is critical. Making the environment a great place for technology teams to do work is key for recruiting and retaining.

As part of your planning process, think of a new set of questions for your technology leader that will help everyone to think through what's needed to compete and win.

> **idea 40:** Ask your technology leader and leadership team a set of questions that will likely force discussion, change, and commitment well beyond your CIO. Put the CIO in charge of developing the answers and plans, but approach the work as a cross-business collaboration.

WHY QUESTIONS?

A client who is the CIO at a large fashion retailer had previously been a supply chain operating executive at the company for years. Many people wondered if he would be effective at improving the technology function since he was not a career-long IT leader. What I saw over the next few months was the board, executive team, and IT leadership team asking a set of questions that was different from what they usually asked as a way to help enlighten what their strategy and expectations were going to be. These were questions like, "How do we measure efficiency and productivity?" Sometimes there are not satisfactory answers to these questions, but the process of struggling through them results in ideas and considerations.

Here's a set of questions to consider asking your technology leader, which we would ask technology teams at Amazon:

1. What are our key (prioritized) technology capabilities, intellectual property (IP), and data assets? How do we measure their value and health?

2. What are our prioritized technology risks? How do we evaluate the risk? What is the mitigation, acceptance, and response plan for each risk?

3. How do we rank against our peers as a company for technologists to work at? What can we do to improve?

4. What are the key digital and technology-fueled ideas the technology team has for each line of business?

5. What technology capabilities and considerations need to be centralized?

6. What technology capabilities and considerations could be embedded in the business?

7. How do we measure our cyber and technology security risks?

8. What functions do we operate today with IT that we should consider partnering or outsourcing?

9. How do you measure the productivity of our IT organization? Are we getting better?

10. If the business were to double in volume, what IT capabilities are ready to scale and why? What IT capabilities are not ready to scale and why?

11. If data is an asset to our organization, what is the quality of our data (by type), and how do we measure it? Has quality improved?

12. What business functions are we performing manually today that you think we could or should automate?

13. What are the mega-trends in technology that we should take more advantage of in the next five years? What are specific use cases to be considered (machine learning, IoT, robotics, block chain, or others)?

14. Grade each business unit on "being an effective partner to IT." What (specifically) can each one do to improve the partnership?

15. What are the services provided by IT to the business? Are these well defined and measured?

16. What technology should be custom for our business? How are we going to differentiate ourselves in this technology?

17. What technology should be package software for our business? Are we able to easily take advantage of their new features and advantages?

18. What is our technology innovation model? How do we support experimentation with new technologies and capabilities? Through what path are these "formalized" into the "core" business capabilities?

19. What are the current technology opportunities? Are there new technologies that should be on our road map? What problems could they solve? What advantages could they create?

20. How does IT partner with service and software providers? How are these architected into a coherent whole?

HAVE A PLAN

President Dwight Eisenhower said, "The plan is nothing; planning is everything." A written plan is a forcing function for the planning effort. Begin by outlining the questions that should be addressed. Oftentimes, a multilegged journey can help, one that helps you explore questions as you go and helps you reach agreement on the next set of questions.

IT planning is key, and it should entail deep participation, review, and understanding by all business leaders. The opportunity for most businesses is both to improve the technology capability and to be a better partner to the technology team. The preceding types of questions and engagement will help both happen.

QUESTIONS TO CONSIDER

1. How do you measure and evaluate the effectiveness of your technology budget?

2. Is technology planning and strategy primarily owned by your technology group?

3. What's a new set of questions to your leadership team to get more innovation and technology delivered?

THE END OF ARTIFICIAL ARTIFICIAL INTELLIGENCE

Prepare for a Future of Machine Learning

Intelligence is the ability to adapt to change.
—Stephen Hawkings

In the early 2000s, Amazon released the Mechanical Turk, a tool advertised as "artificial artificial intelligence." The Mechanical Turk was built as a platform to outsource small pieces of work, called *human intelligence tasks* (HITs) to people around the world who would do the typically small pieces of work. Since then, it has been used primarily for scaling the kind of work that is difficult for computers to accomplish, such as reviewing the quality of written content or images.

However, AI and machine learning are progressing at a rapid clip—exponentially, if Elon Musk is to be believed.[1] Regardless of its exact evolutionary rate, AI and machine learning can tackle an increasingly wide array of tasks, including those often performed by Mechanical Turk. The potential power and impact is such that Jeff Bezos included a special warning (or encouragement?) in his 2017 letter to shareholders, in which he advised his audience to "embrace external trends." "We're in the middle of an obvious one right now: machine learning and artificial intelligence," he warned. When Bezos takes the time to deliver a specific warning, I'd recommend sitting up and paying attention.

idea 41: Machine learning will be a capability deployed in narrow, targeted manners such as augmenting specific management decisions and creating broad new capabilities and business models—changing dynamics across all industries. Leaders need to prepare themselves and their organizations to take advantage. At a minimum, you need to be curious and learn about machine learning, and you need to actively seek out expertise and stories in your industry. Prepare your organization by creating services, instrumentation, and better decision rules in your key processes.

IT'S CONNECTED

It's not accidental that many of the ideas we've discussed in this book are building toward being able to take advantage of the machine-learning age. Collecting lots of data about your customer experiences, your processes, your environment? Vital. Defining your processes in a deliberate and granular manner, figuring out how to make them services, and "doing the math" and trying to create the rules and formulas for your work and decisions? Great building blocks. Understanding your principles, how you make decisions, and the patterns of your logic? Essential. These types of deliberate engineering and introspection are the bedrock of what algorithms need to automate a process.

Amazon is well situated to take full advantage of these capabilities because they've built these underlying blocks. And they recognize the need, so they start learning and experimenting. "In the early part of this decade, Amazon had yet to significantly tap these advances, but it recognized the need was urgent. This era's most critical competition would be in AI—Google, Facebook, Apple, and Microsoft were betting their companies on it—and Amazon was falling behind. We went out to every [team] leader to basically say, 'How can you use these techniques and embed them into your own businesses?'" said David Limp, Amazon's VP of devices and services.[2]

PRINCIPLES

"Everything happens over and over again," explained Ray Dalio, founder of Bridgewater Associates. "Principles are a way of looking at things so that everything is viewed as 'another one of these,' and when another one of those comes along, how do I deal with that successfully?"

Dalio built a decision-making system by writing down the criteria of every issue he encountered. This system allowed him to characterize issues, develop criteria, and easily identify the signal from the noise. In addition, he could synchronize with others and convert many of these issues to algorithms.[3]

In their *2018 Artificial Intelligence Innovation Report*, the good people at Deloitte characterized the future of AI in executive decision-making as a "partnership,"—one in which humans define the issues and have a final say on the best answer for their business, while AI analyzes terabytes of data to provide a basis for the decision.[4]

Dalio likens the perfect relationship between human and machine to playing chess side-by-side with a computer. "So, you make the move, it makes the move," he said. "You compare your moves, and you think about them, and then you refine them."[5] Needless to say, Dalio continued, it can be difficult to understand cause and effect in a complex, black-box model.

We can leverage his approach to take advantage of machine learning for our core management approaches. Specifically, we can adopt his clarity and meticulous attention to detail regarding thinking through the patterns in our businesses, creating rules to manage them, writing them down so others can use and improve on them, and making computer models from them.

What's the minimum an executive or board should be doing with regard to machine learning? Actively learning, interviewing, and paying attention to how it is affecting the industry and functions your company is in. You should be constantly probing "how and when" to start and find ways to do small pilots. An organization needs to build experience and the capacity to experiment with innovations if it is going to be able to rely on those capabilities later on.

BE A PREPPER

"The outside world can push you into Day 2 if you won't or can't embrace powerful trends quickly," Bezos wrote in Amazon's 2016 letter to shareholders. "If you fight them, you're probably fighting the future. Embrace them and you have a tailwind. These big trends are not that hard to spot (they get talked and written about a lot), but they can be strangely hard for large organizations to embrace. We're in the middle of an obvious one right now: machine learning and artificial intelligence."[6]

Looking back, it's easy to identify the tidal waves of technological progress—the printing press, the electric light, the automobile, the transistor—that drove business and society into entirely new eras. All of these inventions had (mostly) positive impacts on society, but their wholesale social applications and adoptions were not without fear and lessons learned.

In his book *Hit Refresh: The Quest to Rediscover Microsoft's Soul and Imagine a Better Future for Everyone*, Microsoft CEO Satya Nadella wrote, "Today we don't think of aviation as 'artificial flight'—it's simply flight. In the same way, we shouldn't think of technological intelligence as artificial, but rather as intelligence that serves to augment human capabilities and capacities."[7] In the same way as "e-commerce" is becoming just commerce, in the coming decade "artificial intelligence" will become just part of our management intelligence, integrated into everyday processes and everyday decisions.

Management must be deeply curious, not just "paying attention." Figure out how to ride the wave instead of being crushed beneath it. As we will discuss in the next chapter, we must train ourselves and our teams to make good decisions.

QUESTIONS TO CONSIDER

1. Is machine learning affecting your industry?

2. Are you educating yourself on machine learning and thinking through where it might be impactful?

3. Where could you do a small experiment to begin building organizational experience in using machine learning?

Part IV
Approach and
Execution

ONE-WAY OR TWO-WAY DOOR?

Make Better and Faster Decisions

*Wherever you see a successful business,
someone once made a courageous decision.*
—Peter Drucker

How do you make a major life decision? In the summer of 2016, we faced one as a family. We had the opportunity to move to Southern California from Seattle, Washington. At the time, my son AJ was between his sophomore and junior year in high school. He plays water polo, and he saw the potential that having better everyday coaching, competition, and exposure would have for his college prospects, but he did not want to leave his friends or school.

It was a big decision. A simple list of pros and cons was not going to cut it.

> **idea 42:** Train yourself and your team to understand how to make decisions. In most cases, you need to speed up decision-making. Develop a culture in which customer obsession and data lead the debate, but decision-making rights are respected. When a decision is made, announce it and expect everyone to move forward.

THE REGRET MINIMIZATION FRAMEWORK

Instead of the old "pros and cons" approach, I told AJ about how Jeff Bezos decided to leave a lucrative job at the hedge fund D.E. Shaw and move to Seattle and start Amazon in 1994.[1]

Bezos was 26 when he arrived at D.E. Shaw. Despite bouncing around from job to job before joining Shaw, Bezos became vice president in just four years. In this role, he researched business opportunities on the new-fangled Internet, which was rumored to be a potential gold mine in the early 1990s if anyone could just figure out a business plan that didn't seem absurdly risky.

According to *Business Insider*, Bezos created a list of 20 products he could sell online, and he decided books were the most viable option. The problem? D.E. Shaw, his boss, disagreed. He didn't think it would work. When Bezos insisted on leaving, Shaw advised him to think about it for 48 hours before making a final decision. So that's what he did. And faced with what, in hindsight, would amount to a world-changing decision, young Bezos turned to a process he dubbed his "regret minimization framework." Years later, he would explain it in an interview:

> I wanted to project myself forward to age 80 and say, "OK, now I'm looking back on my life. I want to have minimized the number of regrets I have." I knew that when I was 80, I was not going to regret having tried this. I was not going to regret trying to participate in this thing called the Internet that I thought was going to be a really big deal. I knew that if I failed, I wouldn't regret that, but I knew the one thing I might regret is not ever having tried. I knew that that would haunt me every day, and so, when I thought about it that way, it was an incredibly easy decision. And I think that's very good. If you can project yourself out to age 80 and sort of think, "What will I think at that time?" it gets you away from some of the daily pieces of confusion. You know, I left this Wall Street firm in the middle of the year. When you do that, you walk away from your annual bonus. That's the kind of thing that in the short term can confuse you, but if you think about the long term, then you can really make good life decisions that you won't regret later.[2]

It's classic Bezos. Think long term. Forget the thrill of depositing your 1994 Wall Street bonus in your bank account today. How are you going to feel about it in 50 years? Once he established Amazon, Bezos would extrapolate this even further, considering the ramification not just decades, but even centuries and millennia in the future. When it comes to forward thinking, Bezos does not mess around.

Great, you say. This framework may be helpful for some big decisions in life, such as quitting a great job, moving, and launching a risky startup, but how about everyday decisions in business?

WATCH THE DOOR

One of the reasons small organizations can move so much faster than big companies is the speed at which they make decisions. Indeed, decisions are not only made faster but their effects on the business are more impactful. As Amazon has grown by leaps and bounds, Bezos has devoted a great deal of time and energy to ensure that his leaders make good, fast decisions.

"To keep the energy and dynamism of Day 1, you have to somehow make high-quality, high-velocity decisions," Bezos has said. "Easy for startups and very challenging for large organizations. The senior team at Amazon is determined to keep our decision-making velocity high. Speed matters in business— plus a high-velocity decision-making environment is more fun too."[3]

Amazon's leaders are expected to be right, a lot. In fact, it's a core principle. How? They must possess strong judgment, but they must also actively work to disconfirm their beliefs to avoid the pitfall of "confirmation bias." Humans seek out data and points that confirm our initial opinion. (This is why Facebook is so popular. America is so politically polarized, and no one seems able to have a civil argument in public anymore. People expect to have their own opinions reflected back at them.) However, if we actively work to find alternative perspectives and data, we make better decisions. This is not an opinion. It's a fact. Jim Collins will tell you even the most successful of businesses take that first certain step toward decline when a leader is surrounded by yes-men. Hubris sows the seeds of ruin.

Yet how can you make balanced, unbiased, good decisions *fast*? You choose the ones that are reversible. To maintain a high decision-making velocity, you must first consider the implications of the decision. Can the result of the decision be tested and reversed, or is it permanent and, thus, untestable? At Amazon, we used the binary analogy of "one-way versus two-way doors."

"We think about one-way doors and two-way doors. A one-way door is a place with a decision if you walk through, and if you don't like what you see on the other side, you can't get back. You can't get back to the initial state," explained Jeff Wilke, CEO of Worldwide Consumer Business at Amazon. "A two-way door, you walk through and can see what you find, and if you don't like it, you can walk right back through the door and return to the state that you had before. We think those two-way-door decisions are reversible, and we want to encourage employees to make them. Why would we need anything more than the lightest weight approval process for those two-way doors?"[4]

WITH PURPOSE

Underlying these two examples of decision-making frameworks is the core understanding that how you make decisions is a skill and a corporate strategy. Figuring out what can be done quickly—versus the decisions that require more debate and careful discussion—must be a core aspect of your skills and how your business operates. Do it with purpose, and talk about how you make a decision and how that approach could be used in other circumstances. If you practice enough, you'll develop the right tools, experiences, and tempo for your organization. Being digital puts a premium on making faster decisions, so evaluate how to incorporate faster decision-making as part of your digital journey.

Some decisions, however, should not be made fast. Let's discuss a type of decision to not make in haste next.

QUESTIONS TO CONSIDER

1. Is there a good decision-making approach or hygiene in your organization?

2. Is fast decision-making important to compete? Do you have it?

3. Are people thoughtful about what conversations and decisions need to be escalated?

RAISE THE BAR

Avoid the Biggest
Hiring Mistakes

Be quick, but don't hurry.
—John Wooden

When you've been in business for as many years as I have, you've undoubtedly made some mistakes. Looking back, what are the biggest whiffs of my career? That's a tough one, but I think the real answer is hiring. The true cost of a hiring mistake is hard to calculate: lost time, lost culture, lost business, lost opportunity, lost confidence.

If I dig down in search of the root cause of most hiring mistakes, the common denominator is often haste. The organization has a role that needs to be filled yesterday, and the process is rushed. Because of that sense of urgency, the hiring manager compromises and takes a candidate that might solve today's need but does not fit for some other reason or reasons. Inevitably, this hire becomes a liability rather than an asset down the road. How do we avoid that mistake? Create a hiring process that systematically helps avoid it. Amazon's is called "the bar raiser."

> **idea 43:** Create a hiring process that systematically helps avoid the root cause of most hiring mistakes, haste. Ensure that this process is defined, measured, and systematic in its approach. Don't just hire for today's job. Hire for growth and adaptability and an orientation to change.

THE BAR RAISER

The interview process at Amazon is rigorous. I was interviewed by 23 people over two months. Although this isn't the norm, it demonstrates how seriously Amazon takes hiring. There are specific roles and goals for each interview. Detailed notes are taken and shared by each interviewer. Debriefs are timely and mandatory. Consensus decisions are made. It is a process, which means it is defined, measured, and systematic in its approach.

"There is no company that sticks to its process like Amazon does," said Valerie Frederickson, whose Menlo Park, California, human resources consultancy works with Silicon Valley companies, including Facebook and Twitter. "They don't just hire the best of what they see; they're willing to keep looking and looking for the right talent."[1]

The bar raiser is a specially trained person, independent from the hiring team. "Independent" means they are not part of the organization doing the hiring, so they will not be influenced by the hiring team's potentially mistake-producing "urgency." The bar raiser's first goal is to screen the candidate to evaluate if the person is fungible—that is, if he or she is capable of expanding into new roles and new areas of the business. If people can't be useful in many roles, then future flexibility is compromised. Second, the bar raiser raises the bar within the general job classification. Bezos famously put the philosophy this way: Five years after an employee is hired, he said, that employee should think, "I'm glad I got hired when I did, because I wouldn't get hired now."

"You want someone who can adapt to new roles in the company, not just someone who can fill the role that's vacant," said John Vlastelica, who now runs the HR consultancy Recruiting Toolbox and counts Amazon among his former clients. "It can be an expensive process because it takes longer, but think of how expensive it is to hire the wrong person."[2]

The bar raiser participates in the debrief process, hearing everyone's feedback and vote (which can only be yes or no). It's really a partnership between the hiring manager, the bar raiser, and other members of the hiring team. It's a consensus test, but the bar raiser has a clear veto. If everybody else says yes but the bar raiser says no, it's a no.

RAISE THE BAR

It's quite an honor to be named a "bar raiser." The selection is based on the success and retention of the hires you've already made. Yet in having a veto over hiring, the role often puts you in direct opposition to the manager doing the hiring. As an outside voice, your job is be an independent force, free from the pressure of work demands that sometimes lead hiring teams to make hasty or shortsighted decisions.

Gregory Rutty was an Amazon bar raiser who started his career as an editor at a New York book publisher. In a 2016 *Puget Sound Business Journal* interview, he admitted his editing skills didn't seem like a natural fit for the Amazon Books job he initially interviewed for, but he was hired anyway.

"I wasn't your typical Amazon employee," Rutty said. "I didn't even know how to use Excel, but Amazon—above all things—is looking for people who are talented, ambitious, and driven. Relate what you did in a past life to how it might be applicable to a future role."[3]

Amazon's interviewers evaluated Rutty on his adherence to the company's leadership principles, values such as ownership, leadership, a bias for action, and customer obsession. They also rated Rutty's potential to grow within the organization and provide value down the road. Clearly, they hit the mark with Rutty because he became a bar raiser himself.

"It's important to understand what those leadership examples are and to be able to relay your past experiences," Rutty said. "When I think of interviewing in general, the most important things are clear examples that demonstrate who you are as a worker and as an employee. I think a lot of people miss that stuff accidentally."[4]

Even if you are not the bar raiser, your role in the hiring process is vital. At Amazon, it was understood that every successful candidate's career was inextricably linked to our own. And this was, without a doubt, the most effective forcing function for excellence.

SHOW YOUR WORK

To support the rigorous interview process, Amazon built an application called the Matt Round Tool (MRT), named after the engineer Matt Round who wrote it. One of the features of the MRT was that others on the interviewing team could give their fellow team members feedback on their interviewing approach and provide notes to help drive improvement.

Amazon's custom recruiting process forced every interviewer to provide a lengthy, narrative analysis of the candidate and a yes-or-no recommendation. No "maybe" option was available. I often felt that I needed to be a court reporter. I consider myself a summary person, but the process put an emphasis on being able to write really deep reviews on what the conversation covered and how the candidate reacted.

To avoid the subjectivity inherent in most interview processes, Amazon asked very real, problem-solving questions. After all, the best way to maintain an objective perspective is to simply ask a candidate, "How would you solve this problem?"

For example, interviewers might have asked the candidate a classic elevator shaft problem, such as, "How would you optimize the number of floors or stops that an elevator would make, given a set of circumstances, while explaining what the logic would be?" Another would ask, "How would you parse a set of code to count the number of words and the number of letters in a paragraph or document?"[5]

As an interviewer, your notes were expected to be detailed enough to justify your answer. The after-interview questioning could be almost as intense and consuming for the interviewer as it had been for the interviewee. The data was then immediately processed and applied to the next round of interviews. The process was so efficient that the next set of interviewers would often adapt their questions to push the candidates in directions suggested by answers they had provided just an hour or two earlier. As an interviewer, I sometimes forgot to listen to the candidate's answers because I was so busy directing my line of questioning to suit the previous interviewer's data or scribbling madly to record everything that was said. After the interviews were completed, the hiring manager and bar raiser would review the notes and the votes of every interview. If a debrief was required, it was mandatory that everyone attend. And, of course, the bar raiser could veto the hire without question, no matter how the team or hiring manager felt.

It's like anything in life. There's a certain degree of good processing, but taken over a certain line of reasonableness, it can become a ludicrous and absurd parody of the hiring process. There is a line. It is a rigorous process, one that would be considered wildly excessive at almost any other company.

UNWAVERING COMMITMENT

Because standards are so high, hiring can be problematic. What many people don't realize is that Amazon almost went out of business in 2000. There was not enough revenue and way too much cost. The stock price plunged from $100 to $44 to $20 to below $5. The company closed down customer service, and massive layoffs ensued. Over the next few years, it was tremendously difficult to hire the best because Amazon wouldn't pay them competitive market salaries, and the stock options were far from enticing. There was a lot of risk, and we basically expected people to take a pay cut to join us.

Yet the incredible commitment to hiring only the best remained unwavering. One colleague of mine wasn't able to find a suitable hire for over two months, so they just axed the position and told him that, if he hadn't been able to make the hire, then he obviously didn't need the person in the first place.

THE PASSING GRADE IS A

The kiss of death at Amazon was being known as a "solid guy." While this might seem like a perfectly acceptable description at another company, Jeff's perception was different. As far as he was concerned, everyone at Amazon was fortunate to be there. People who didn't excel at their jobs were failing to contribute appropriately, in effect free-riding on the rest of us. As leaders, we were expected to work with laggards like these to improve their performance into the A+ category—or else find some way to incent these people to leave.

As a result, Amazon experienced systematic and significant turnover during my years there. Jeff told us to focus our positive reinforcement on our A+ people; he was comfortable with a high degree of churn below that standard.

This strategy was distinctly underlined by the compensation policy. At Amazon, the majority of stock options went to the A+ employees; the crumbs went to the B and C players. And since the salaries were, relatively speaking, quite low, a vast majority of the compensation came in the form of stock. So being "a solid B" meant a significant falloff in stock options and promotion opportunities. It was all part of Jeff's way of instilling a sense of ownership in the company: our financial fortunes were directly tied to the success of the company.

If you really believe that your people are your company, you must invest the time and effort required to identify and hire only the very best. Does your business have a true process for evaluating new talent? Are your hiring mistakes affecting business performance? What is the root cause of hiring mistakes, and can you create a method that helps avoid that root cause? How will you raise the bar in recruiting talent?

QUESTIONS TO CONSIDER

1. Is interviewing and hiring a rigorous process at your company?

2. Are hiring decisions ever made in haste or with shortsighted perspectives?

3. Do people actually interview candidates in a meaningful manner, or do they just engage in conversations with the applicants?

A NARRATIVE ABOUT NARRATIVES

Ditch the PowerPoint and Gain Clarity

*The single biggest problem in communication is
the illusion that it has taken place.*
—George Bernard Shaw

Amazon Web Services (AWS) is the largest cloud computing technology company in the world. In 2017, it produced an annual revenue run rate of $20.4 billion. To put this into perspective, AWS accounted for all of Amazon's operating income that year. AWS's business growth is on a more than $18 billion annual run rate, growing 42 percent a year.[1] According to Gartner, AWS is bigger than the next 14 cloud providers combined.[2]

While its size and growth are impressive, the number of new products and major feature developments—the pace of innovation—is what really stands out. Year after year, AWS has launched more than 1,100 major new services and features in its global cloud platform, according to CEO Andy Jassy. That has kept AWS the undisputed leader in cloud computing in terms of cloud services, features, and functionality. It far outpaces other technology companies.

How does Amazon manage that degree and intensity of innovation? How do Amazon's leaders decide what to do and what not to do? How do they develop ideas and rationalize them? Much the same way they hire the best people. They use the narrative process to answer these questions and to capture and explain their ideas. While "writing it" seems like a counterintuitive process for creating twenty-first-century innovation, Bezos has proven that sometimes the oldest ideas are the best.

> **idea 44:** Writing ideas and proposals in complete narratives results in better ideas, more clarity on the ideas, and better conversation on the ideas. You will make better decisions about what to do and how to do it. The initiatives will be smaller and less risky. Writing narratives is hard, takes a long time, and is an acquired skill for the organization. High standards and an appreciation for building this capability over time are required.

WHAT IS INNOVATION?

I had an advisor at the Gates Foundation who was a former senior Microsoft technology leader, and he always emphasized that "the only features that matter are the ones that ship." While this statement is a little anachronistic today (obviously no one is shipping software anywhere these days), he was 100 percent correct. Innovations are not ideas; neither are they attempts or prototypes. Innovations consist of new capabilities that are "shipped." In other words, they are capabilities that affect customers and generate new revenue, improve quality, or decrease costs.

Leaders and companies frequently mistake innovation with being creative. While being creative plays a role in innovation, deciding what ideas to pursue is the first, under-the-waterline step toward creating capabilities that affect customers and generate new revenue. Let's call this process "innovation portfolio rationalization," or strategy setting.

The second under-the-waterline step is executing or delivering that capability as quickly, as affordably, as nimbly, but most of all, as predictably as possible.

THE KILLER FEATURE: CLARITY

Michael Porter, Harvard professor of strategy, has stated that "strategy is about making choices, trade-offs; it's about deliberately choosing to be different."[3] By developing clarity and simplicity in what you are doing and not doing, you are improving the ideas, making deliberate decisions, and gaining shared under-standing in the organization. The fundamental mistake leaders make in devel-oping digital strategies is not seeking clarity, especially regarding the customer experience. What will delight the customer? What operational model supports this experience? What data and technology support the operational model? How will we measure?

Achieving clarity can be uncomfortable. It can disrupt. People tend to want to avoid conflict, be collaborative, and basically accept all the ideas and all the wording. This tactic does not demand the best thinking and avoids the sensitive topics in the spirit of "getting along." A well-written narrative, on the other hand, demands rigor on exactly the right wording, compels getting to the heart of risks and sensitive topics that have to be addressed to achieve the goal, and requires straight and simple language to ensure that everyone understands the key points. A well-written narrative and the process of writ-ing it will force teams to get beyond being polite and get to insights.

Amazon Leadership Principle 3 is "Invent and Simplify." Driving toward clarity of thought through a written narrative is a key operational approach to get both invention and simplification. "Almost every meeting which involves making a business decision is driven by a document," says Llew Mason, an Amazon vice president. "One of the great things about a written document is that it drives a lot of clarity in the process."[4] Ah, clarity in thinking. Clarity on what you decide to do. Clarity on how the idea will affect users and the busi-ness. A longtime business partner of mine who worked with me both before and after Amazon has told me many times that what he sees me doing with my clients, which he has seen to be tremendously helpful, is that I'm always trying to simplify and clarify the communication. I learned this at Amazon.

WHAT IS A NARRATIVE?

At Amazon, leaders write narratives for all plans, proposals, services, and in-vestments. PowerPoint is not used (insert applause). Much has been written about how PowerPoint dumbs down an organization. In his 2017 letter to share-holders, Bezos wrote, "We don't do PowerPoint (or any other slide-oriented) presentations at Amazon. We write narratively structured six-page memos," Bezos continues. "We silently read one at the beginning of each meeting in a kind of 'study hall.' Not surprisingly, the quality of these memos varies widely. Some have the clarity of angels singing. They are brilliant and thoughtful and set up the meeting for high-quality discussion. Sometimes they come in at the other end of the spectrum."[5]

Narratives at Amazon are two- or six-page documents written in complete sentences. A narrative must be expressly tailored to the situation based on the topic, the timing in the initiative, and the audience. It must flow in a way that makes sense relative to the topic and audience. It is verboten to dump excessive bullet points or slides into the narrative. Data, charts, and diagrams can be included, but they must be explained in the narrative. Appendix material is also allowed. I believe that the discipline of writing out ideas is at the heart of Amazon's innovation process and can be replicated to the same effect. As explained by Greg Satell:

> At the heart of how Amazon innovates is its six-page memo, which kicks off everything the company does. Executives must write a press release, complete with hypothetical customer reactions to the product launch. That is followed by a series of FAQs, anticipating questions customers, as well as internal stakeholders, might have.
>
> Executives at the company have stressed to me how the process forces you to think things through. You can't gloss over problems or hide behind complexity. You actually have to work things out. All of this happens before the first meeting. It's a level of rigor that few other organizations even attempt, much less are able to achieve.[6]

THE PROCESS OF A NARRATIVE

Why do programs and projects take too long, go over budget, become bloated, and fail to deliver according to expectations? Execution and project management technique can be reasons, but the biggest root cause is failing to accurately define the end state at the beginning. Teams want to launch quickly and start designing, building, and testing. Taking the time to write a narrative will dramatically improve the definition of what needs to be done, plus make it as small and concise as possible, so it can be done faster, cheaper, and with more agility. But writing narratives takes time, so they are done when they are done. It is difficult to predict how long it will take and how much effort will be required. It is completely reasonable to create a deadline. "You have one week to write a narrative" might be appropriate.

Narratives can be written by one person, but it is often a group effort because multiple people and teams contribute to the idea. Forcing people to own the narrative jointly has huge benefits in both getting the best ideas on paper and building shared understandings and relationships through authorship. Part of Amazon's practice on narratives is not to include the author's name or names on the narratives. This sends the signal that the narrative is a community activity.

When the narrative is done, think through the review meetings and decision-making process. Who needs to deeply understand and agree with the narrative before a decision is made? Who are the key decision makers? At Amazon, review meetings tend to be 60 minutes long. They start with 10 to 15 minutes of silence to deeply read or "grok" the proposal and vision. This is followed by a discussion debating the merits, options, appropriate next steps, and decisions.

The process of authoring, reviewing, and deciding must be carefully considered. It must be rigorous. It must take time and effort. It is done when it's done. What do narrative writers do wrong? They don't spend enough time on their writing. As Bezos wrote: "They mistakenly believe a high-standards, six-page memo can be written in one or two days or even a few hours, when really it might take a week or more! . . . The great memos are written and re-written, shared with colleagues who are asked to improve the work, set aside for a couple of days, and then edited again with a fresh mind. . . . The key point here is that you can improve results through the simple act of teaching scope—that a great memo probably should take a week or more."[7]

THE STRUCTURE OF A NARRATIVE

A narrative must be constructed of complete thoughts, complete paragraphs, complete sentences. You may include charts, numbers, and diagrams, but those items must be explained in the narrative. Other than that, there are no rules on structure, and the structure the authors choose will depend on the topic, the timing in the discussion cycle, and the audience.

The first sections of the narrative are typically customer focused. "Who are the customers? What benefits are we bringing them? What problems are we solving for them? Why would this idea delight them?" Sections after that might include what the customer experience would be, dependencies or requirements, metrics to measure success, business case, and key risks.

A SAMPLE NARRATIVE

If you're looking for an example, look no further than this chapter. You've been reading one. Now you, the target audience, hopefully understand the importance of writing ideas out completely and clearly. For your projects, investments, strategies, and executive topics, ditch the PowerPoint presentations, and force teams to put their ideas and plans in writing. Meetings start with 10 to 15 minutes of silence to read the narrative. Phones and computers are left outside. Then debate the merits of the narrative. Don't be afraid either to ask that the narrative be improved or to write a follow-up related narrative.

Make no mistake. Creating narratives takes skill, experience, commitment, and patience. You can't rush great narratives because you can't rush great thinking and communications.

It takes practice. Writing is less an artistic exercise and more a practiced skill. It's less of a spontaneous combustion and more of a methodical construction—like building and rebuilding the perfect birdhouse. Do you have the discipline and commitment to write in plain English your most important ideas and proposals? Other executives and big companies are recognizing how writing as a forcing function to create clarity is key to innovation. JPMorgan Chase, whom I have had a chance to talk to about many of these ideas, is using narratives as one of the ways to try to be literary, more like Amazon. "Mr. Bezos notoriously banned slide presentations to keep Amazon in startup mode as it grew, instead asking employees to craft six-page documents complete with a press release and FAQs. Over roughly the past 18 months, JPMorgan has started a similar practice in its consumer businesses under Gordon Smith, the bank's co-president and co-chief operating officer."[8] Are you able and willing to commit to hard habits like writing narratives to change culture, speed, tempo, and innovation?

Now that we've covered narratives, the next three ideas build on the heart and soul of Amazon's innovation process—continuing to get it down on paper with clarity and simplicity and having rigorous debate as the key core attributes.

QUESTIONS TO CONSIDER

1. Do ideas and plans suffer from incomplete thought?

2. Do projects get bloated with size and unnecessary complexity?

3. Do executives understand and influence the details of a proposal sufficiently to make a well-informed decision?

THE FUTURE
PRESS RELEASE

Define the Future and
Get Teams on Board

The future ain't what it used to be.
—Yogi Berra

When it comes to innovation, there is rarely a straight line from *A* to *B*. Why is that? In general, we usually create only a vague sketch of the goal we're trying to achieve. As a result, we tend to revise the goal as we go, a process that costs time, money, and, sometimes, the project's very success. Or we all have various definitions of the goal.

But what if you could see into the future and accurately visualize your end product before launching a project? Sound good? Well, there's really nothing stopping you. At Amazon, they do it every day. It's an exercise in clarity they call the *future press release*. Not only can it define the future but it can also keep your organizational structure from transforming into a bureaucratic rat's nest (see Idea 13) and empower a leader to drive the initiative across multiple teams.

> **idea 45:** Start important projects or changes with an announcement. Be clear about what the "killer feature" is for the future state capability. Give it to one leader to make this vision happen across the organization. Everyone works for this person to transform this vision into reality.

IMAGINE THE FUTURE

Most innovation and change initiatives take work and true ownership from multiple teams and leaders. While long-form narratives (see Idea 44) are great for developing a deep understanding, sometimes a brief, more impactful approach is necessary to excite and engage a wider range of parties.

Jeff Bezos is famous for requiring teams to create the future press release before launching a new product, undergoing any kind of transformation, or entering a new market. The process of creating a simple, but specific product announcement clarifies the original vision. It acts as a forcing function to thoroughly examine key features, adoption, and your project's likely path to success. Committing to a press release, speculative though it may be, also helps leadership clearly express to important stakeholders the road map to success.

THE RULES FOR THE
FUTURE PRESS RELEASE

The future press release is a great approach to defining clear and lofty goals, requirements, and objectives and to building broad understanding from the start of a program or enterprise change. There are, however, rules to make this approach effective:

> *Rule 1.* The goal must be stated at a future point in time at which success has been achieved and realized. Press releases at launch are good, but a better one is sometime after launch, where true success can be discussed.

> *Rule 2.* Start with the customer. Use the press release to explain why the product is important to customers (or other key stakeholders). How did the customers' experience improve? Why do the customers care? What *delights* customers about this new service? Then discuss other reasons it was important and key goals.

> *Rule 3.* Set an audacious and clear goal. Articulate clear, measurable results you've achieved, including financial, operating, and market share results.

Rule 4. Outline the principles used that led to success. This is the trickiest and most important aspect of the future press release. Identify the hard things accomplished, the important decisions, and the design principles that resulted in success. Discuss the issues that needed to be addressed to achieve success. Getting the "tricky" issues on the table early on helps everyone understand the real nature of the change needed. Don't worry about how to solve these issues yet. You've still got time to figure that out.

THE FORCING FUNCTION

Once you've created a future press release, the project leader needs to be empowered to make these changes happen. Focus on creating a future press release–oriented communication plan that helps that project leader find success across the organization.

Remember, the future press release is a type of forcing function. Once the press release is reviewed and approved, teams should have a very difficult time backing out of the commitments they have made. A leader can refer to parts of the press release and use it to remind and hold teams accountable. It paints a clear vision to galvanize understanding and commitment. It is a contract.

Figure 45.1 is an example of a future press release, dated December 1, 2022. Notice how the lead paragraph clearly states the objective. In this case, "*Consumer Reports* gave Acme Co. its 'Most Admired Home Appliance Brand' award." Once the aspirational goal and time limit are set, the future press release goes on to clarify why the award was presented and illustrates how Acme Co. started by asking a different set of questions and being willing to build and collaborate within an ecosystem of partners, including traditional competitors. It concludes with a series of specific milestones that can be used by the organization as a road map from here to there.

With the long-form narrative (Idea 44), we explored a deeper understanding of an internal project. With the future press release, we've created a definition for success to drive engagement, clarity, and enthusiasm for the project. In 2002, I wrote the future press release for the Amazon Marketplace business. There was one sentence in it that was critical: "A seller, in the middle of the night, can register, list an item, receive an order, and delight a customer as though Amazon the retailer had done it." Pretty simple sentence, but

December 1, 2022

Breaking News: *Consumer Reports* gave Acme Co. its "Most Admired Home Appliance Brand" award.

Palo Alto, December 1, 2022: *Consumer Reports* named Acme Co. the "Most Admired Home Appliance Brand." *Consumer Reports* noted the industry-leading reliability, safety, and connected customer experience as the hallmarks for recognition.

"Acme's appliances go beyond the expected and traditional customer experience. The ability to personalize every aspect of performance, to have predictive maintenance managed for customers, and to optimize the energy and operating costs for the customer all distinguish Acme home appliances," noted Hal Greenberg, CEO of *Consumer Reports.*

In discussing Acme's acceptance of the award, Acme's CEO noted that "in 2018 we started on a journey to reinvent the buying, ownership, and operating experience of appliances. We embraced a different set of questions to drive our strategy and willingness to innovate. These questions opened up opportunities for Acme and for others."

By asking a different set of questions and being willing to build a collaborative ecosystem of partners that includes traditional competitors, everyone ended up winning. Key examples of Acme's improvements include the following:

- Predictive maintenance programs delivered as warranty service that saved 10 percent of the energy used

- Hazardous environment and usage monitoring that saves homeowners on insurance, and most importantly has prevented an estimated 10 home fires this year alone

- Complete voice control and updates both directly to the appliance or through the customer's preferred voice speaker such as Amazon Echo or Google Home

- Appliance sharing programs allowing for an Airbnb type of business opportunity for apartment owners to use their appliance

- Energy Grid optimization intelligence allowing homeowners to save an estimated 20 percent annually through dynamic load management

The biggest innovation is the in-depth data Acme combines with other in-home environment and appliance data to optimize its customers' experience.

"We had to break a lot of traditions both here at Acme as well as in the industry to create this type of innovation."

Creating the home appliance data standards platform was advancement. Acme is now the U.S. market leader in both customer satisfaction and market share.

Acme stock closed the day at record $198, up 25 percent from a year ago.

Figure 45.1 Example of a Future Press Release

it imposed tremendous requirements on both Amazon and our sellers. For example, just to do self-service registration, over 20 different systems had to be integrated. I used this press release as a forcing function to compel all of these teams, none of which reported directly to me, to get this hard work done. We avoided bureaucracy and launched quickly because we were able to act nimbly and avoid our organization structure to focus on an initiative. The future press release, given to one leader in the organization, is one of the methods Amazon uses to get its results.

But what about our users? How do we develop empathy and insights for our customers? Amazon, of course, has thought of that too. I give you, the FAQs.

QUESTIONS TO CONSIDER

1. Do your initiatives start with a definition or vision that can be shared across the organization?

2. Does organizational structure get in the way of achieving cross-functional delivery and success for change initiatives?

3. Are leaders who are accountable for delivering change initiatives given license to nimbly work across the organization?

FAQS

Answer Others' Questions for Your Benefit

Judge a man by his questions
rather than his answers.
—Voltaire

arly in my career, while at a consulting company, I worked on a project for Boeing at a missile factory in Tennessee. We were implementing a shop floor control program in the production area. My colleague was training some of the staff on the new technology we had labored so hard on for months. We were confident the system was perfect. The client team had affectionately nick-named my colleague "Oatmeal" for his wholesome demeanor. Like me, he was a newly minted industrial engineer, and this project was one of our first. As the operator worked to input work order information in the system, he shouted across the room, "Oatmeal! Which is the 'any' key?" The system instructions had instructed the operator, "Hit any key to continue."

I had written that instruction and user interface. This was not the oper-ator's problem. This was my problem. I had not been curious or empathetic enough about the user's perspective to recognize how confusing this instruc-tion potentially was. I had written the document solely from my context and from my orientation, not from my target user's point of view. If I had written a set of frequently asked questions (FAQs), I might have predicted this user confusion.

> **idea 46:** Develop insights and empathy for your user and other in-
> volved parties by writing FAQs. Make these available for anyone in the or-
> ganization or involved in the initiative to both read and contribute to. Do
> this before you start developing and keep it up to date. Make it thorough.
> The only dumb question is the unasked one.

WRITING FAQS AS A WAY TO ANTICIPATE KEY QUESTIONS ABOUT YOUR PRODUCT

Once you've written the narrative and press release, you can forecast some of the questions you're likely to get about your product or business in a list of frequently asked questions (FAQs) document. The purpose of the FAQs is to add more details to the press release and answer other business and execution questions necessary to launch. This can be either a separate document or appended to the end of your future press release.

By proactively writing an FAQs document, you're forcing yourself to think through the key questions about your product and helping to pre-answer the big questions your stakeholders are likely to have.

A good set of FAQs allows for the press release document to stay short and focused on what the customer gets. The FAQs document should include resolutions to issues and answers to questions that come up when you are writing the press release. It should also address questions that arise through the process of socializing the press release. A good FAQs document includes questions that define what the product is good for, how it will be leveraged by the customer, and why it will delight the customer.

Building the FAQs document forces you to put yourself in the role of the customers using the product and consider all the challenges or confusion they might have. It also provides inspiration for designing a fully self-service, confusion-free product.

A SAMPLE SET OF FAQS

One of the companies I've been fortunate to be involved in as an advisor is a startup company called Modjoul (www.modjoul.com). Modjoul makes a sensor-based rugged belt used by workers to help prevent and manage workplace injuries and unsafe behavior. It has eight sensors and collects over 56 metrics.

I encouraged the team at Modjoul to write the following set of FAQs, which they found helped them scale and train their growing team. They have kept FAQs on an intranet, and they continue to add and update them. We started with a question (Q), an answer (A), and a discussion (D). The following questions and answers are a subset of the Modjoul FAQs broken into sections for the worker, the direct supervisor, and the risk manager and the IT, legal, and finance departments. Be prepared.

This is a lengthy set of questions and answers, as it should be. The exercise captures all the different types of questions that might arise so that the team can avoid them or be prepared to answer them. The length of this sample set demonstrates the exhaustive length appropriate for FAQs. We wrote this FAQ document with the purpose of being able to train new sales staff at Modjoul. We improved it by adding a discussion (denoted by D) to many of the questions and answers.

For the Worker

Q1: *How do I wear the belt? (Everything from what side is up, to does the belt go through the belt loops or over them?)*

> **A1:** The Modjoul SmartBelt is worn like a regular belt—through the belt loops of your pants. The side with the on/off switch, charging port, and SOS/alert button is the bottom, and it should not be visible to the user when worn correctly.
>
> **D1:** The questions around the proper wearing of the belt led to our creating quick user guides on the subject. Modjoul had quick user guides on setting up dashboards and connecting to Wi-Fi, but sometimes when designing a product, you get so accustomed to the little things that you forget you have to start with the basics—the simple task of putting the belt on correctly.

Q2: *How do I use the belt?*

> **A2:** The belt is worn like any other belt. It is designed to fit through the belt loops, and it is designed to hold your pants up. The biggest difference is the on/off switch. When wearing the belt, make sure the belt is turned on so it is able to collect data.

D2: That is the simple answer. There have been a lot of lessons learned around this question in attempts to make the user experience as simple as possible.

Q3: *How do I charge the belt?*

A3: Charging the belt is simple. Plug the micro USB cable into a USB wall adapter, then plug the adapter into the wall. The LED next to the charging port will turn blue when the belt is charging.

D3: One item of note for this was the decision to go with industry standard connections. Everyone knows what a micro USB is. It was a simple design choice to stick with the concept of use, to work with what people know and what people are familiar with.

Q4: *What do the different LED colors indicate?*

A4:

Top LED:

Red: Belt is powered on **but** not connected to Wi-Fi.

Green: Belt is powered on **and** connected to Wi-Fi.

Blue: Belt is powered on **and** connected to Wi-Fi **and** connected to GPS.

Bottom LED (applies only while belt is on the charger):

Blue: Belt is charging.

None: Belt is done charging.

D4: Indicators can help clue users into the status of the device, they can help with troubleshooting devices, and they can lead to a lot of questions. I believe that indicators need to be kept simple and serve as a quick check of the device status.

Q5: *What if I wear the belt home?*

A5: No need to worry about it. Turn the belt off, plug it in using any micro USB charger, and remember to bring it into your place of employment the next day.

D5: Honestly, we were happy to hear this question. It reassured us that the belt was something that people could forget about while wearing. One of the goals for any safety device, really any wearable device, is to not be intrusive. In order to help with adoption, form, fit, and function, it should align with what people are used to. This question was an indicator that the belt felt like any other belt, and employees might really forget that they had a workplace wearable on.

Q6: *What types of activities does the belt monitor?*

A6: Human location, movement, and ambient environment. There are eight sensors and a GPS in the belt. These sensor values are processed and placed into one of seven activities, then further broken down into 1 of nearly 50 associated metrics.

D6: In my opinion, the real important takeaway of this question is how many times it gets asked directly or indirectly. People want to know what the belt does and what types of data it gathers. This information is a huge driver of our data models and our new features that are rolled out.

Q7: *What is the end goal?*

A7: The end safety goal is to make the workplace a safer place. People should leave work the same way they came into work. Whether it is using the aggregated data of a group to learn of a process that needs to be improved, using the data to validate the purchase of a new, safer piece of equipment, or using the data from like groups of individuals to identify who is more likely to get injured, the belt is a tool to access data that has never been easily obtainable before.

D7: Transparency and trust also play a role in the answer to this question. It is a common question that we get from the employees. It might be phrased slightly differently, but they are curious about the point of wearing the belt. Sometimes they see and understand the short-term-fix answers (improving bend counts week over week for, example), but sometimes they ask with a larger end goal in mind. For instance, would the company buy vacuum lifts or some other assisted-lifting device to help with bins that need to be packed or unpacked?

Q8: *How long do I need to wear the belt?*

A8: The answer varies by use case, but the general answer is the longer, the better. Wearing the belt as long as possible will provide a solid data set to use as a goal threshold or an improvement number, and employee trend lines can track progress across all the metrics.

D8: We have two types of customers: (1) the organization that wants to use the belt for a few months as a training tool or for process improvement and/or validation and (2) the organization that is in it for the long haul and wants to continuously monitor the safety of its employees.

Q9: *Why does the belt buzz (or vibrate)?*

A9: The belt vibration is a configurable parameter to provide the user with instant feedback of a movement that might be considered risky by his or her organization.

D9: We have had lots of really good feedback about this. We started vibrating the belt only once every five minutes for a bend of over 60 degrees because we didn't want to be "too intrusive." However, the point was raised a few different times, that if we were using it to provide real-time feedback to the employee of an event that should be given attention, the belt should buzz every time. Eventually, the employee will become aware of it and will try to eliminate those movements out of his or her workday.

Q10: *Can we put tools on the belt?*

A10: Yes. The whole right-hand side of the belt is simply just a nylon strap. Anything can be clipped on it or attached to it.

Q11: *How do I know the belt is mine?*

A11: There is a name tag slot on the back of the belt. The employee can also be creative with it if the uniform code allows. We have seen some employees put a piece of colored tape on the buckle as a quick identifier.

D11: This is a point that we are continuously exploring how to improve. We have thought of industry standard sizing color strips sewn into the nylon to help identify which is yours.

Q12: *Do I need to wear the same belt every day?*

A12: Yes. One belt for one person.

D12: Belts can be reassigned to new users, but it is not encouraged on a day-to-day basis. If anything, questions around this have led to better flexibility with managing users and shift schedules. Ultimately, Modjoul believes that if something is tedious or time-consuming to change, the user will get tired of using it. The user experience (belt and its setup and/or configuration) needs to be easy and painless for users.

For the Direct Supervisor

Q16: *How can I view the data?*

    A16: As a supervisor, you have access to the supervisor level dashboard where you can view all your employees and their associated metrics on an aggregate level view.

    D16: There are three different personas through which to view data within an organization. The first is the employee view (an individual view of the data). The second is the supervisor level view (an aggregate level view of the data for a given team). The third is the risk manager level view (an aggregate level view of different supervisors, locations, and roles). Taking this question one step further, I believe there is an element of simplicity that lies within this question as well. Everybody is doing a full-time job. The ability to view the data easily is important.

Q17: *What types of data are collected?*

    A17: See Q6.

Q18: *Can I view the data of my team holistically?*

    A18: Yes. See A16.

    D18: Modjoul thinks one of the greatest benefits of the belts comes when groups of employees are observed at the same time. When we look at groups of employees, we can quickly see the outliers within specific job roles. If the outlier is high compared to the group (bend counts over 60 degrees as an example), they are considered a *pre-loss indicator*. The concept of a pre-loss indicator is that this employee hasn't been injured yet, but if these methods are sustained, this person is more likely to get injured than the rest of the group.

Q19: *Can I export the data out of the dashboard?*

    A19: Yes. Data can be exported to a .csv file from the dashboards, or it is accessible via an API.

    D19: For the technical and programming folk, an API makes sense, but average supervisors aren't going to know what an API even is. Modjoul puts a lot of time and design work into the dashboard user interface (UI) to make sure that it satisfies as many users as we can. Unfortunately, we know that some people will come up with new, one-off requests, so our goal is to make the data available for even the supervisor with very little technical expertise. There is an export button built into the dashboard so that any one of the metrics can be exported to a spreadsheet.

Q20: *Can I print the dashboards that are created online?*

A20: Yes, all the charts and reports in the dashboard can be printed.

D20: This was a great idea that was actually brought to us by a supervisor in one of our customers. The customer already had a safety board in the office where the the company had posted all of its relevant safety information. The ability to print out the reports for the team not only helped with familiarity of the SmartBelt for the users but also led to broader exposure of the device to the larger organization.

Q21: *Any ideas on how to handle employee resistance?*

A21: Ultimately, the answer varies from organization to organization.

D21: My personal opinion is that inclusiveness with the belts within a team can really help build a culture around the product. If everyone is wearing the belt, everyone is on a level playing field. We learned this in one of the ongoing pilot projects with a major airline company. The project started with 2 belts, went to 10, and now has close to 70 across two teams. When everyone on the team is wearing the belt, they all keep an eye on each other and hold each other accountable, but if only a few are wearing the belt, they always ask, "Why are those people not wearing the belt while I have to wear one?" Another way to handle employee resistance is by incorporating the belt into a businesswide safety program and gamifying the data to create a bit of a competition. Modjoul has learned a lot with this, and we have worked these learnings into our "keys to successful pilot" talks.

Q22: *Is the belt the only product that is available?*

A22: Yes, at this time.

For the Risk Manager (VP of Safety)

Q28: *How can this data be turned into actionable insights?*

A28: A few items play into this answer. The first is customizable dashboards and alerts based on the activities that your business is really interested in looking at. The second is active engagement between supervisor and employee to really understand the data and what that person is doing. The third is that the belt will give the user real-time haptic feedback on a configurable metric.

D28: This is a relatively uncommon question to get directly right now, but we believe it is very important. I think we will encounter it more as we move from the 10-25 belt pilot, or proof of concept, into the larger orders. The belt needs to drive change and be used as a tool to drive safety improvements. With all the different metrics to look at, a company needs to start small, and honestly, it just needs to start somewhere, when looking at the data. Too much data can be overwhelming. Using actively engaged supervisors, safety professionals, ergonomists, and haptic feedback on the belt itself allows the users to be alerted of an at-risk movement and allows the supervisors to get involved with the business to better understand their risk and make changes. This question is always something that we try to keep in the back of our minds while creating dashboards and building out the UI. It is easy to spot issues, but we can take that data one step further and try to pinpoint issues, or we can use it as a starting point for eventually getting us to be able to take corrective actions.

Q29: *Can the information be used for pre-loss and post-loss use cases?*

A29: Yes, it can be used for both. A *pre-loss use case* would be similar to the example used in D18. A *post-loss use case* would be a return-to-work situation when the employee wears the belt to validate or prove that he or she is following the doctor's orders.

For the IT Group

Q32: *How does the device work?*

A32: Coming from an IT person, this question is more about how the device sends data. The short and simple answer is that it communicates via Wi-Fi. The longer answer involves storing data on the storage device (SD) card when the device is out of Wi-Fi range and uploading bulk data after shift times are complete.

D32: On 10-20 belt rollouts, this has not been a big issue yet. However, these discussions with IT groups have already been really valuable with helping design the next generation to make sure our product can work with a large variety of Wi-Fi standards and networks. The lesson for Modjoul on this has been that we "squeaked by" with the Wi-Fi capabilities that we have now, but our feedback from our customers around this topic has pushed us to really focus on connectivity next time around.

Q33: *How is the data sent to the cloud?*

A33: Through the industry standard encrypted MQTT port (8883).

D33: The part of the answer that the IT guys really want to hear is that the data is encrypted while in transit, and at rest. It helps using industry standard protocols because it builds trust when it's a reputable protocol.

Q34: *Is the data encrypted in transit and at rest?*

A34: Yes.

D34: There isn't a ton to discuss about data encryption. Our customers just want to make sure that when it is being sent and stored, it is encrypted.

Q35: *What kind of encryption is used?*

A35: A variety of encryption methods are used throughout the various stages the data passes through.

Q36: *Where is the data stored?*

A36: In the Virginia AWS facility.

D36: The interesting lesson Modjoul learned here was that some of our customers have rules against storing data internationally.

Q37: *How are the devices onboarded to connect to the network?*

A37: There are a few ways the device can be onboarded. For initial setup, the two methods are either through the web dashboard setup process or through coding in the firmware. After the initial setup is done, Wi-Fi credentials can be sent directly to the belt from the dashboard.

D37: This is a continuous learning and improvement process for us. With one belt, we can afford to take a few minutes to get it configured. Working with over a thousand belts, however, we can't afford to take that long. Speed of configuration and ease of use on configuration are two areas we always are trying to improve.

Q38: *Can passwords be changed on a specified schedule?*
  A38: Passwords can be changed when desired.

Q39: *What are the security functions surrounding user credentials?*
  A39: Users get locked out after five attempts of logging in.
  D39: Security is the name of the game nowadays for these IT guys, and concerns range from how we encrypt data to how we make sure users are who they say they are. As a company, we just need to understand that and try our best to protect our customers' data.

For Legal

Q41: *Who owns the data?*
  A41: The data is co-owned between the customer and Modjoul.
  D41: Data ownership is a hot topic in any business. Everyone wants to own the data. As a company, we use the data to help with our data models. More data will lead to better models.

For Finance

Q42: *What kind of data is collected?*
  A42: See A6.

Q43: *How much does the belt cost?*
  A43: $500 (*subject to change).

Q44: *Do you have a pay-as-you-go model?*
  A44: Yes, $20 per belt per month.
  D44: We have been making good progress with this model. Most of our companies want to just get their toes wet a bit before jumping into a full commitment. The subscription model lets us get some cash flowing

in, without requesting too much of a financial commitment from the customer to us.

Q45: *What is included in the price?*
A45: The belt hardware, IoT infrastructure, data models, and all dashboards.

Phew. As you can see in the example, predicting questions posed by various users and stakeholders can be a long, arduous, and surprisingly expansive exercise. When we did this, we found many ideas to improve the product or clarify its operation. However, by committing to a thorough examination of the end user's entire point of view, you can prevent your own version of the "any key." And, as you will discover in the next chapter, there is another exercise that allows you to drill even deeper: writing the user manual.

QUESTIONS TO CONSIDER

1. Do you have a project or situation that FAQs document might clarify and inform?

2. Have you had projects where different perspectives were not considered that created issues?

3. Where do projects or initiatives typically go wrong for you? How could writing FAQs help?

WRITE THE USER MANUAL

Start with the Customer and Work Backward

Simplicity is the ultimate sophistication.
—Leonardo da Vinci

If you build product, the ultimate power play is not having to include user instructions. The capability or product is so obvious and well designed to the needs of the user that instructions are superfluous. I think about the unboxing experience of an Apple product. The ultimate in sophistication. Elon Musk has said, "Any product that needs a manual to work is broken." The product should be so intuitive it doesn't need a user manual. That is power.

We should all strive to deliver products and services so obvious, ergonomic, and intuitive that no user manual is needed. Ironically, a great way to achieve this is to write the user manual at the outset of the product's design and understand the user journey before you begin development.

> idea 47: If you can't explain how your product or service or capability will be used, you aren't ready to build it. By developing personas, user journeys, and user manuals before building, you will gain insights to make your product better for its users. You will make smarter trade-offs and judgments throughout its development.

PERSONAS AND JOURNEY MAPS

User-focused design is a mentality and approach that puts the user smack dab at the center of requirements and product development. "Well, how else would you do it?" you might ask. The common approach is making the concept or specific technology the driving force and then attaching a market and user definition later. I'm not an expert on any of these, and the goal is not to argue for one over the other, but if "easy" is a goal, starting with the user is likely the best path to get there.

Part of the user-focused design tool kit is the development of personas and journey maps. A *persona* is a deep articulation, as rich and as broad as possible, of the target customer of your potential product or service or business. You want to know this person inside and out when you are done. The *journey map* uses the persona to develop insights into the events, questions, and activities going on in the person's life before, during, and after the involvement of your service.

Developing customer personas and mapping those customers' current journeys are terrific ways to document specific unmet needs and identify key friction points your future customers are experiencing right now. Following the path from start to your desired outcome can help you identify details and priorities that might otherwise be dealt with at too high a level or skipped over entirely.

It's hard work to craft strong customer personas and journeys. It's likely you'll need a few iterations before you really nail them. (I often need to start over more than once before I gain any real insights.) The biggest mistake you can make on these is to build them for show rather than for function. Don't worry about the beauty of these deliverables at this point. Do worry about getting insights, talking to customers, and validating your findings with others who can bring ideas and challenges to your work.

USER MANUALS

Developing a preliminary user manual for your service can be a powerful tool early on in a project. We used this at Amazon when developing products or APIs.

Your user manual should address at least two key customer segments: the *end user* of the device or service, and if you are developing a technical product or service, the *programmer developing on your platform*:

- **The end user of the device or service:** Who is the customer who will be installing, using, adjusting, and getting feedback from your product? Outline what the unpacking directions will be, what the installation process will be, how updates will happen, what the data privacy terms will be, how to use and read the device, and how to connect it. Think through all the major steps the users of the product will need to take, and include them in a close-to-real-life user manual. Forcing you or your team to keep these steps simple will lead to great product ideas, user experiences, and technology designs.

- **The programmer developing on your platform:** If you are developing a technical product or service that developers will be using, perhaps an IoT product, it includes an API allowing developers to access, deploy, integrate, and extend your product. You will also want to build a user manual for the developer. Write the interface for the API, what events will be supported, and the data to be sent and received. Give sample code snippets, and outline key operational topics such as how testing occurs and how operational status and updates are facilitated. You'll also want to use this exercise to outline key business and use terms. Are there charges involved?

Obviously, this can be extended to other key roles—for example, the salesperson or agent who represents your company or the service person who conducts maintenance and repair.

ALL HAT, NO CATTLE

It's easy to announce, "We are focused on the customer" or even, "We want to be the most customer-centric company of all time!" That's all well and good, but unless you're willing to put in the hard work, spend crazy amounts of what may feel like "unproductive time" writing narratives, future press releases, FAQs, and user manuals for products that don't exist, you're just another cowboy moseying around the digital prairie who's all hat, no cattle. It's becoming increasingly apparent that people can say anything they want, regardless of the truth, in America these days. However, eventually, you have to produce.

John Wooden, the legendary UCLA basketball coach, is credited with saying, "The true test of a man's character is what he does when no one is watching." You need to ask yourself these questions: "Am I truly willing to start with the customer and work backward? Am I willing to be customer obsessed? Am I willing to do the hard work when no one else is watching?" The only person who can answer these questions is you. However, the answer will be crystal clear to everyone, especially your customers, down the road. Don't forget that.

QUESTIONS TO CONSIDER

1. Do personas and journey maps play an important part in building customer insights and obsession?

2. Is your product or service so simple that no user manual is needed?

3. Are there any aspects of your leadership practices in which you are "all hat and no cattle"?

YOU ARE WHAT
YOU EAT

Create Change Via the
Executive Team Reading List

You can't out-train a bad diet.

—Anonymous

I'm in my fifties, but I still eat like a teenager. Although I love to exercise, I am a bon bon–snarfing dietary degenerate. Cookies and candy are my downfall.

The mind operates under similar principles. Although you may have outlined a set of exercises for your brain, you may not be conscious of what your brain is fed. Well-balanced mental nutrition is of the utmost importance, and minimizing "sweets" like ubiquitous Internet clickbait is necessary to keep your brain fighting trim.

"As if we aren't busy enough," you mutter. "Now this guy's going to recommend a book club for my executive team?" Yup. As I've mentioned throughout this book, a strategic road map to true transformation includes creating new habits for yourself and your organization. Creating new habits is partially about how you work with your direct team. Every executive can pay lip service

idea 48: Live the leadership objective of lifelong learning, which helps your team create new habits to compete differently. Be it a book club, a reading list, or a lecture series, create change by upgrading the quality of the content you consume. Share the content with others on your team.

to the idea that lifelong learning is essential, yet how many of us shortchange this belief? Improving the content you digest to drive organization change is a great complement to all the other tools for competing in the digital era.

I'll refer to this as a "reading list," but it includes podcasts. There are many ways to formulate the group activity: meet once a week to discuss; have someone write an "implications" memo from a book; have the author come talk to the team; or just share the content.

AMAZON'S S-TEAM BOOK CLUB

When I was at Amazon, the S-team (of which I was not a member) was reading many different books. The broader organization would often "take the hint" and also read the books. In Brad Stone's excellent book *The Everything Store*, the appendix is a list of books that were part of Jeff Bezos's reading list. I've included only two of these books on my list (*The Goal: A Process of Ongoing Improvement* and *The Mythical Man-Month*).

Books

- *The Goal: A Process of Ongoing Improvement* by Eliyahu Goldratt and Jeff Cox (1984)
  The Goal is the essential book on the theory of constraints and getting to root-cause understandings. Stylistically, it has influenced me in telling personal stories to deliver business recommendations. If I could only write something as impactful as *The Goal* . . .

- *The Mythical Man-Month* by Frederick Brooks (1975)
  Brooks outlines the complexity of large software development projects, and the principles are applicable to other large projects. *The Mythical Man-Month* will influence your perspective on small teams and creating services in your business.

- *The Master Algorithm: How the Quest for the Ultimate Learning Machine Will Remake Our World* by Pedro Domingos (2015)
  "Pedro Domingos demystifies machine learning and shows how wondrous and exciting the future will be."   —Walter Isaacson

- *Hit Refresh: The Quest to Rediscover Microsoft's Soul and Imagine a Better Future for Everyone* by Satya Nadella and Greg Shaw (2017)
  This is a story about both leadership and company transformation.

- *The Lean Startup* by Eric Ries (2011)
  Ries blends together many key elements of continuous improvement, hypothesis testing, and metrics that matter.

- *Zero to One* by Peter Thiel (2014)
  "An extended polemic against stagnation, convention, and uninspired thinking. What Thiel is after is the revitalization of imagination and invention writ large."   —*The New Republic*

Podcasts

- *a16z Podcast*
  Ignoring some of the intellectual snobbery that goes on, the Andreessen and Horowitz team creates great conversations with founders and other experts.

- *Internet History Podcast*
  The host, Brian McCullough, does fantastic preparation and talks to guests who have shaped the Internet. You can learn a lot about business models, innovation, and history through this podcast. Really great interviews and lessons.

- *Recode Decode*
  Kara Swisher gets great guests and talks about many of the challenges of innovation and Silicon Valley.

- *IoT-Inc. Business Show*
  Bruce Sinclair, the author of *IoT Inc.*, has great guests discussing many of the technical and practical aspects of IoT. Sinclair does an excellent job diving down to key points of costs, value, and other practical aspects.

- *ETL*
  The *ETL* (Entrepreneurial Thought Leaders) is a Stanford live-presentation format podcast that has company founders come and talk to an audience.

WHAT'S YOUR DIET?

Big wave surfer and waterman extraordinaire Laird Hamilton once wrote, "Potato chips in = potato chips out. That's the rule." In other words, improve the input to fuel the output. Sharing with others and creating a group exercise just magnifies the impact. Yes, it takes time and commitment. We all agree that lifelong learning and the development of leaders in our company are essential. Here's a fun, cheap, and impactful way to do it. Now where are those Pringles?

QUESTIONS TO CONSIDER

1. Would improving the content you and your team reads be impactful?

2. Would you have more impact if you discussed the content together?

3. How do you insert new and perhaps contrarian thinking into your management team?

FINANCE FOR FOOLS

Free Cash Flow, Accounting, and Change

Life is like accounting. Everything must be balanced.
—Anonymous

Amazon's annual letters to shareholders are always instructional. Jeff Bezos has used these letters as a superb megaphone for his views on what it takes to innovate. The 2014 letter was one of the more sanguine. It addressed accounting and the fact that free cash flow would be the financial measure for which Amazon optimized.

"Our ultimate financial measure, and the one we most want to drive over the long term, is free cash flow per share," Bezos wrote. "Why not focus first and foremost, as many do, on earnings, earnings per share, or earnings growth? The simple answer is that earnings don't directly translate into cash flows, and shares are worth only the present value of their future cash flows, not the present value of their future earnings."[1]

As Amazon's Leadership Principle 2 espouses, leaders "think long term and don't sacrifice long-term value for short-term results. They act on behalf of the entire company, beyond just their own team." Be smart and strategic about gaining alignment between the business you want to be versus how your P&L and accounting are defined.

> **idea 49:** Accounting, like metrics, can often be manipulated. Be smart about how you leverage your accounting as you drive change in your organization. Often, your internal P&L can be a change inhibitor.

THE BASICS OF FREE CASH FLOW

Writer and former Wall Street analyst Henry Blodget responded to Bezos's letter in an April 14, 2013, *Business Insider* article that contrasted his long view with the myopic focus on the bottom line that characterizes most companies today:

> This obsession with short-term profits has helped produce the unhealthy and destabilizing situation that now afflicts the U.S. economy: The profit margins of America's corporations are now higher than they ever have been in history, while the employee wages paid by America's corporations are the lowest they have ever been in history. Meanwhile, a smaller percentage of America's adults are working than at any time since the late 1970s.[2]

Amazon has never put short-term profits ahead of long-term investment and value creation, a strategy many believe has the potential to boost the entire American economy. Sometimes overlooked is the fact that maintaining low margins and deliberately eschewing short-term profits is a brilliant strategy in the tumultuous age of the Internet. Not only do low prices drive customer loyalty but they also discourage competition. If you want to jump into the fray against Amazon, you can't just match them on value—you must significantly beat them. Easier said than done. Bezos has left very little room to huddle beneath Amazon's price umbrella, leaving most competitors out in the soaking rain.

"We've done price elasticity studies," Bezos once said. "And the answer is always that we should raise prices. We don't do that because we believe—and we have to take this as an article of faith—that by keeping our prices very, very low, we earn trust with customers over time, and that actually does maximize free cash flow over the long term."[3]

The key phrase in this comment is "free cash flow" (FCF). Bezos returned to the subject in a January 3, 2013, *Harvard Business Review* interview: "Percentage margins are not one of the things we are seeking to optimize. It's the absolute dollar free cash flow per share that you want to maximize. If you can do that by lowering margins, we would do that. Free cash flow, that's something investors can spend."

The move toward free cash flow as the primary financial measure at Amazon began in earnest when Warren Jenson became CFO in October 1999. The finance organization moved away from a percentage-margin focus to a cash-margin focus. Bezos loves to guffaw loudly and toss out the axiom, "Percentages don't pay the light bill—cash does!" He then follows up with the question, "Do you want to be a $200 million company with a 20 percent margin or a $10 billion company with a 5 percent margin? I know which one I want to be!"[4] Again, the guffaw.

As explained in his 2004 letter to stockholders, Bezos likes the FCF model because it provides a more accurate view of actual cash generated through Amazon's operations (primarily retail sales) that is truly free to use to do a number of things.[5] In Amazon's model, capital expenditures are subtracted from gross cash flow. This means that the cash is available to grow the business by adding new categories, creating new businesses, scaling through technology, or paying down debt. Of course, that extra cash could also be given back to stockholders in the form of dividends (never really considered) or given back to shareholders via stock repurchases (maybe someday—no, not really).

Bezos believed then, as he does now, that without constant innovation, a company will stagnate. And the primary ingredient for investment in innovation is FCF. This philosophy and the need to practice it successfully drove the creation of other capabilities, such as Amazon's robust, extremely accurate *unit economics model*. This tool allows merchants, finance analysts, and optimization modelers (known at Amazon as quant-heads) to understand how different buying decisions, process flows, fulfillment paths, and demand scenarios would affect a product's contribution profit. This, in turn, gives Amazon the ability to understand how changes in these variables would affect FCF. Very few retailers have this in-depth financial view of their products, which thus makes decision-making and building processes that optimize the economics difficult. Amazon uses this knowledge to do things like determine the number of warehouses it needs and where they should be placed, quickly assess and respond to vendor offers, accurately measure inventory margin health, calculate to the penny the cost of holding a unit of inventory over a specified time period, and much more.

While Amazon's short-term investors may grouse that Amazon should be "making more money," Bezos continues to build one of the most dominant, enduring, and valuable enterprises in the world. Meanwhile, other Internet-boom companies have bitten the dust, mostly because they put too much emphasis on short-term profitability and failed to invest enough in long-term value creation.

Bezos has explained it this way: "Take a long-term view, and the interests of customers and shareholders align."[6] That's the philosophy that has made Amazon so successful.

NOT DYING

As retailers hustle to counteract the "Amazon effect," they are building ways to leverage their store presence to create new shopping and service scenarios using Internet, mobile, and in-store assets. Often referred to as "omnichannel," the key scenarios are "order online, pick up in store," "buy online, return to store," and "buy in store, delivered to home."

An ex-Amazon leader who is now the chief digital officer at a large retailer recently told me he wanted to launch a small, regional pilot that allowed customers to order groceries online and then pull through a pickup lane at the store. Perfect for a busy parent! Guess what stopped the pilot from proceeding? Accounting, metrics, and siloed thinking. The store managers and regional leaders refused to risk the negative impact to their P&L, as their bonuses and ratings were tied to this. The difficulty of convincing big enterprises is a recurring challenge. If you don't want to suffer Bezos's "Darwinian death," you can't let your internal P&L be the enemy. You have too many other real constraints to deal with. I worked for Tom Elsenbrook at Alvarez and Marsal for many years, and he would always quip, "Show me your organizational P&L, and I'll show you where the dysfunction starts." Amen.

How does Amazon avoid this? Imagine you are the owner of the Amazon Prime P&L. If you were to load all the transportation costs, content costs, and advertising costs onto the Prime P&L, you would probably have a horrible P&L. Yet Amazon recognizes the strategic importance of Prime. Consequently, they're not concerned with optimizing the Prime P&L. Instead, they are focused on optimizing the long-term free cash flow of Amazon, the enterprise. How do they know this is the right tack?

That brings us to the final word.

QUESTIONS TO CONSIDER

1. Does your accounting or P&L structure ever lead to poor or suboptimized thinking?

2. Have incentives or internal politics tied to accounting ever created additional hurdles in innovating?

3. How could different approaches to finance help you innovate better?

THE LAST WORD ON BECOMING DIGITAL

Trust

Continue to learn with humility, not hubris.
Hubris is boring.
—Jimmy Iovine

For three straight years, the Harris Poll's annual corporate reputation survey ranked Amazon number one. Amazon has been named to the "masters" group in Gartner's Supply Chain survey, joining Apple and P&G. The Drucker Institute named Amazon the number one corporation in their Management Top 250 measuring 37 metrics. And Amazon tops the ACSI Internet Retail category for customer satisfaction for the eighth year in a row. That is what you call being on a roll. And I haven't even mentioned Amazon's stock price.

In contrast, Facebook's Mark Zuckerberg testified before Congress in the aftermath of the Cambridge Analytica scandal. He answered questions from politicians regarding his organization's lack of governance and its apparent inability to prevent bad actors from hijacking the platform. It was uncomfortable to watch. The poor guy was squirming. But it's hard to feel sorry for him. I'm not certain if it was hubris or naivete that landed Zuckerberg in the hot seat. Maybe a combination of both. I do know he made an unforgivable mistake: he undervalued the trust of his customers. And it has tarnished his brand. Badly.

When I was at Amazon, there was nothing more sacred than building and keeping customer trust. The first leadership principle notes, "Leaders . . . earn and keep customer trust." We understood intrinsically that customer trust was

> **idea 50:** Beware hubris and optimistic assumptions regarding business. Your brand is your promise to your customers. Make sure you know it, make it (your promise to your customers) core to everything you do. With integrated smart and digital products, you can create, keep, and measure trust with your customers.

the brand and the enterprise. Here's the rub. The final word. The bottom line. You are never done inventing the customer experience, which includes keeping your brand promise to your customers.

WHAT IS TRUST?

When I was at Amazon, we talked about "customer promise" as the essence of customer trust. "Promise" meant the right item would arrive in the right condition at the right address at the right time. As we started launching and scaling the Marketplace business, in which independent sellers outside of the Amazon fulfillment network were responsible for shipping items to customers, we felt that "promise" applied there as well as to Amazon retail orders. The customers didn't care (nor should they be required to care) whether they were buying from Amazon the retailer or from a third-party seller via Amazon.

Yes, we could have just trusted our sellers to do the right thing, but we applied the mindset of "trust, but verify." We forced the sellers to manage all communication to the customer through us, so we could understand the issues. We obliged sellers to send shipment notifications to us, and we tracked when packages were shipped and when they were delivered through the transportation providers. We tracked the number of complaints, refunds because of item issues, and out-of-stock situations.

In other words, all the components of "promise." It made selling at Amazon an intricate choreography of transactions, a far more complex process than selling at eBay. As a result, it slowed down the adoption of the Amazon Marketplace among sellers because we demanded more from them. Finally, we extended the Amazon A-to-Z guarantee to all orders. Initially, this policy extension garnered fierce internal resistance because of the financial and procedural implications in managing tens of thousands of sellers. But it was key.

DOWNFALL OF SUCCESSFUL
COMPANIES: THE ABCS

After I left Amazon in late 2005, I became a managing director at Alvarez and Marsal, a consulting and advisor firm based in New York. Alvarez and Marsal is the premier restructuring firm. It excels at helping clients through challenging periods in a business cycle. Of course, we also retained very healthy clients who were not in crisis. I particularly enjoyed working with restructuring clients and private equity clients because they were usually humble, striving for change, and not holding onto the past. These companies and leadership teams were typically truly committed to change, willing to embrace the pain and work to make a future, and eager to let go of past traditions.

Conversely, the most difficult clients were the large, successful companies. They typically resisted efforts to create lasting change and increase enterprise value. That's because they often suffered from what Warren Buffett calls "the ABCs of business decay—arrogance, bureaucracy, and complacency."[1] One warning sign of the ABCs is when company results become more important than keeping customer trust. The brand erodes when short-term financial results are prioritized over doing the right thing—that is, implementing controls in the business to protect the customer.

Take the massive Equifax data breach of 2017. The company's leaders' poor response and lack of accountability are one of several recent examples of big companies without governance. "Capping a week of incompetence, failures, and general shady behavior in responding to its massive data breach, Equifax has confirmed that attackers entered its system in mid-May through a web-application vulnerability that had a patch available in March. In other words, the credit-reporting giant had more than two months to take precautions that would have defended the personal data of 143 million people from being exposed. It didn't," stated *WIRED* magazine.[2] Furthermore, the company took six weeks to notify the public about the situation. It was a master class in how to lose customer trust.

WHAT'S YOUR PROMISE?

What do you promise to customers? What does your brand stand for? High reliability? Low cost? Current style? Durability? Personalized service? Design?

There are many potential brand elements, but you should be able to outline and prioritize yours. This is your customer promise. But don't stop. Find ways to create systems and approaches to measure and manage. Actively interrogate the risks that could most affect customers, prepare for these, and find ways to actively monitor them. This often takes real innovation and might end up producing other benefits!

Great brands, great companies, and great civilizations are lost when greed and complacency infect leadership. I know. In 1999, I was a young partner at Arthur Andersen. Fortunately, I left a year before the Enron situation materialized. Our promise to clients was "think straight, talk straight," which implied that our advice and services would not be self-serving. Arthur Andersen lost control of that promise. The digital era offers more challenges, but more approaches and tools to manage them.

And now, what you've been waiting for—the ½ idea.

QUESTIONS TO CONSIDER

1. Are there signs of ABCs in your company?

2. What does your brand stand for?

3. What is the customer promise you make? Do you actively measure it?

PRINCIPLES ARE NOT A POSTER

The Pursuit of Speed, Agility, and Digital Leadership

I think it's important to reason from first principles rather than by analogy. The normal way we conduct our lives is we reason by analogy. [With analogy] we are doing this because it's like something else that was done, or it is like what other people are doing. [With first principles] you boil things down to the most fundamental truths . . . and then reason up from there.
—Elon Musk

Like any industry, the management consulting industry has a marketing machine devoted to constantly generating interest and demand. The term "digital transformation" is one of those concepts conceived and perpetuated by this machine. Conceptually, it is meant to insinuate that any company should be able to become the digital version of itself with the proper assessment and implementation.

Yet, as I've worked with executives to create digital strategies and cultures over the past 10 years, I've become convinced that competing and winning in the digital era is as much about creating personal change in executives and their beliefs, habits, and priorities as it is about the overall strategy. But guess what? Most don't really want to challenge their assumptions of the business, change their operating model, or make personal changes. They are "all hat and no cattle."

277

> **idea 50½:** The only correct path to digital transformation is the one that you and your team connect with and commit to and the one that yields results. Lasting change requires equal parts personal commitment and organizational change. What are you willing to change and do differently to become a leader in the digital era? Building a set of first principles on how you will differentiate your company, how you will work together, and what you will prioritize can be vital to insights and engaging your team.

THE 10-YEAR AMAZON FORECAST

You can be certain Amazon is running financial, logistics, headcount, and infrastructure scenarios to 2029. Of course, we don't have access to those. At the likely risk of being highly inaccurate or even flat-out wrong, let's look forward 10 years at what Amazon might be.

Amazon's 2018 financial result was roughly $240 billion in revenue, and has been growing between 20 percent and 40 percent for years. If, for the next 10 years, Amazon grows at a rate of 20 percent, Amazon's revenue will be roughly $1.5 trillion in 2029 Given the breadth of Amazon's businesses, its penchant for expanding into new ones, and its ability to ride global market trends such as e-commerce, I would argue this estimate might even be low. Wow!

What projections do I have beyond astronomical financial growth? Here are a few more peeks into the future.

In some ways, Amazon is becoming an infrastructure company. Much of what you will see in the next 10 years concerns building and optimizing infrastructure to make retail delivery easier or to make computing power more local through AWS. By 2029, Amazon will operate a large, last-mile carrier fleet, which will deliver a sizable chunk (although not a majority) of its packages to customers. Many of these trucks will be autonomous driving trucks manned by a sole runner. Sustainable power generation and use will be an increased area of innovation for Amazon. By 2029, Amazon will generate all the power needed for AWS and for their completely electric-power truck fleet, which will also be primarily autonomous. In addition, Amazon will have greatly expanded its blimp and drone operations. As a result, I expect 50 percent of all Amazon fleet deliveries to be done by either an autonomous truck or by a drone.

On-demand and adaptable manufacturing will be a capability and a business (manufacturing-as-a-business) at Amazon. What's the best way to give the customers exactly what they want? Let them configure and choose exactly what they want. What's the best way to minimize inventory, returned inventory, and transportation costs? Manufacture a custom item close to the customers. Like many of Amazon's most profitable businesses, this is a platform engaging in on-demand manufacturing both for Amazon and for others, taking the momentum of the "maker movement" and unleashing the creativity of hundreds of thousands of designers and makers for unique products such as eyeglasses, apparel, and devices. Perhaps it will be called "Manufacturing By Amazon" (MBA). I'm predicting that Amazon will be the largest apparel manufacturer and retailer in the world.

Alexa will be a major operating system in 2029, running a Windows-like 75 percent of all voice interfaces in all industries. Alexa will not only be a force in the home but also in business settings as voice becomes a powerful interface.

Food and grocery will be a big business as well for Amazon. By 2029, the company will have revolutionized agriculture by developing high-tech growing farms in major urban areas, and those farms will achieve 100 times more effective food production than the current model.

Amazon will own or brand a 5G cellular network, and part of the Prime proposition will be a peerless, always-on 5G data plan for Prime members. This will largely reshape the current wireless carrier picture given that 70 percent of all U.S. households will be Prime members, and a majority will utilize Amazon 5G cellular service. And the most profitable Amazon business in 2029? Advertising. Amazon Advertising is a powerful competitor to Google, and it runs digital and next-generation in-store advertising at all Amazon properties and beyond Amazon properties.

Amazon will be a major player in healthcare reform, but it will still be early in the industry transformation. Amazon will have "just-walk-in clinics" leveraging the next-generation capabilities that will allow their employees to receive on-demand and primarily remote doctors' appointments. Amazon will be selling generic pharmaceuticals, and it will have launched a Prime Health healthcare insurance plan for Prime members.

In 2029, Bezos will be just Amazon's chairman. He will have stepped away from the CEO position to focus his time and fortune on Blue Origin, which will be setting up its first permanent space colonies. Amazon will be fighting a European-led effort to force the breakup of Amazon into three separate companies—Consumer (retail), AWS, and Logistics. Amazon will have come up with a novel approach—actually splitting the company into over 15 companies, independent but managed under one stock and transparent operating agreement. This fragmentation will help avoid the dreaded ABCs.

In 2029, HQ4 will be in the process of being set up in Brazil, and Amazon will have 700,000 worldwide employees, which is not so different from today's 500,000. Why is that? Since fulfillment center automation will have become so widespread, Amazon's employee growth rate will have slowed. In addition, Amazon will have reinvented many management techniques, including an Echo-based management assistant that participates in all management meetings for immediate recall and validation of facts and trends and for capturing decisions and commitments made by team members.

Amazon will change a lot in the next 10 years. Growth, new businesses that they are not in today. The largest company in the world. So, what will not change about Amazon? The principles of leadership will continue to define their expectations for all Amazon employees. The 50 ideas in this book will be constant, and they will remain at the center of Amazon's core culture: metrics, operational excellence, thinking big but betting small, and of course, customer obsession. In 2029, they will still believe it is Day 1, and they will prioritize long-term optimization over short-term results, invent and simplify, create accountability and avoid bureaucracy. They will also still have ridiculously high standards for employees and will be viewed as a demanding, but great place to work.

PERSONAL HABITS

It's not just that new habits are hard to create. It's that old habits are hard to break. I've tried to give up desserts this year. So far, I've been reasonably successful, but at the end of the year, will this new habit be ingrained, or will I degenerate into the same old dessert-addicted adult who eats like a teenager?

Many of Amazon's ideas in this book require personal commitment. You need to become the chief product officer. You need to spend time designing the right metrics. You need to spend time writing and editing narratives. Will you commit to doing these things? The best way to catalyze this type of change is to focus on the group habits of you and your direct leadership team. Commit to them for at least a year. See what works for you.

Creating change in organizations takes tremendous effort and is often high risk. Even calling the process an "initiative" sends the message that it's a temporary state. People with entrenched attitudes know they can outlast the commitment to change, and they will simply bide their time until everyone loses focus and submits to organizational entropy. Part of the leadership challenge is being sincere—actually believing and practicing the behaviors you are espousing. Nothing is as toxic as a poser. If you say it, you must also live it.

Amazon's leadership principles work because they are authentically Amazon. Although they borrowed many ideas from others, they spent years hammering out and practicing the leadership principles before they were codified. When I was at Amazon, the principles were not even written down. However, we practiced them every day, at all levels in the organization. At some point along the way, the leadership team did commit pen to paper. I can imagine the intensity of the debates that spawned those sentences. Today, Amazon continues to internally question and refine those principles. It is a given that they will need to evolve. After all, it's still Day 1.

Even smart leaders naturally want to snap their fingers and announce, "From now on, this is how we will operate." It is a completely understandable pitfall. While dramatic, the classic "change by declaration" approach doesn't work. Organizational transformation is not magic. It is not spontaneous. It is not easy.

The 50 ideas in this book are authentic beliefs, strategies, and techniques used at Amazon to build and manage the dynamic business we all admire, if not fear, today. But that does not mean they are all the right ideas for you. Be thoughtful, be deliberate, be authentic, and be patient in creating the changes in your business, and in yourself, to compete in the digital era.

GIVE ME THE ½ IDEA!

You've patiently read the book (maybe you skipped ahead!), wondering, What is the "half idea"? Amazon's leadership principles and how the company's leaders operationalize them, how they drive accountability, build world-class operations, and systematically solve problems to drive innovation and come up with big ideas for new businesses—these are the 50 ideas you are now equipped with.

The "half idea" is the following question, which only you can answer: *How will you build the traits of the truly digital business and culture to ensure Amazon-like results, to become the best digitally enabled business you can be and not become roadkill on the side of the digital disruption highway?*

What's the second half to this idea? Your answer to this question. Take it from here!

NOTES

INTRODUCTION

1. Charlie Rose, "Amazon's Jeff Bezos Looks to the Future," *60 Minutes*, December 1, 2013.
2. CB Information Services, "Amazon's 'Beehive,' Drone-Carrying Trains Reinforce Focus on Logistics Tech," *CB Insights*, August 3, 2017, https://www.cbinsights.com/research /amazon-warehouse-patent/.

IDEA 1

1. Beth Billington, "Housing Inventory Reaches Record Low, but Brokers Expect Spring Bounce," *NWREporter*, March 7, 2017, https://www.bethbillington.com/housing -inventory-reaches-record-low-brokers-expect-spring-bounce/.
2. Seth Fiegerman, "Amazon Now Has More Than 500,000 Employees," *CNN Business*, October 26, 2017, https://money.cnn.com/2017/10/26/technology/business/amazon -earnings/index.html.
3. Todd Bishop, "Amazon Soars to More Than 341K Employees—Adding More Than 110K People in a Single Year," *GeekWire*, February 2, 2017, https://www.geekwire.com /2017/amazon-soars-340k-employees-adding-110k-people-single-year/.
4. Amazon, "Amazon's Urban Campus," *Amazon dayone blog*, https://www.amazon.com/p /feature/4kc8ovgnyf996yn.
5. Steven Levy, "Jeff Bezos Owns the Web in More Ways Than You Think," *WIRED*, November 13, 2011, https://www.wired.com/2011/11/ff_bezos/.

IDEA 2

1. JP Mangalindan, "Jeff Bezos's Mission: Compelling Small Publishers to Think Big," *Fortune*, June 29, 2010.

IDEA 3

1. Jeff Bezos, "2016 Letter to Shareholders," *Amazon dayone blog*, April 17, 2017, https:// blog.aboutamazon.com/company-news/2016-letter-to-shareholders.

2. Amazon Leadership Principles, https://www.amazon.jobs/en/principles.
3. Jeff Bezos, "Day One Fund," Twitter, September 13, 2018, https://twitter.com/JeffBezos /status/1040253796293795842/photo/1?ref_src=twsrc%5Etfw%7Ctwcamp%5Etwe etembed%7Ctwterm%5E1040253796293795842&ref_url=https%3A%2F%2Fwww .businessinsider.com%2Fjeff-bezos-launches-2-billion-bezos-day-one-fund-for -homeless-2018-9.

IDEA 4

1. Anna Mazarakis and Alyson Shontell, "Former Apple CEO John Sculley Is Working on a Startup That He Thinks Could Be Bigger Than Apple," *Business Insider,* https://www .businessinsider.com/john-sculley-interview-healthcare-pepsi-apple-steve-jobs -2017-8.
2. Chris Davis, Alex Kazaks, and Alfonso Pulido, "Why Your Company Needs a Chief Customer Officer," *Forbes,* October 12, 2016.

IDEA 5

1. Jodi Kantor and David Streitfeld, "Inside Amazon: Wrestling Big Ideas in a Bruising Workplace," *New York Times,* August 15, 2015, https://www.nytimes.com/2015 /08/16/technology/inside-amazon-wrestling-big-ideas-in-a-bruising-workplace .html.
2. Drake Baer, "Jeff Bezos to Social Cohesion: Drop Dead," *Fast Company,* October 17, 2013, https://www.fastcompany.com/3020101/jeff-bezos-to-social-cohesion-drop -dead.

IDEA 6

1. Jocko Willink, "Extreme Ownership," TedxUniversityofNevada, February 18, 2017, https://singjupost.com/jocko-willink-on-extreme-ownership-at-tedxuniversityof nevada-transcript/.
2. Jay Yarrow, "Steve Jobs on the Difference Between a Vice President and a Janitor," *Business Insider,* May 7, 2011, https://www.businessinsider.com/steve-jobs-on-the -difference-between-a-vice-president-and-a-janitor-2011-5.
3. Matt Rosoff, "Jeff Bezos 'Makes Ordinary Control Freaks Look Like Stoned Hippies,' Says Former Engineer," *Business Insider,* October 12, 2011, https://www.business insider.com/jeff-bezos-makes-ordinary-control-freaks-look-like-stoned-hippies -says-former-engineer-2011-10.
4. Total square footage of Amazon's fulfillment capacity in the United States as of November 2017, by type of facility (in million square feet). *Source:* Statista, "Amazon: Statistics & Facts," https://www.statista.com/topics/846/amazon/.
5. Year-on-year growth of Amazon web services revenues from first quarter 2014 to fourth quarter 2017. *Source:* Statista, "Amazon: Statistics & Facts," https://www .statista.com/topics/846/amazon/.
6. Amazon, "Amazon Compute Service-Level Agreement," https://aws.amazon.com /ec2/sla/.

IDEA 7

1. Adam Lashinsky, "Amazon's Jeff Bezos: The Ultimate Disrupter," *Fortune*, December 3, 2012.
2. *W. Edwards Deming Institute Blog*, https://blog.deming.org/w-edwards-deming -quotes/large-list-of-quotes-by-w-edwards-deming/.

IDEA 8

1. "FYIFV," *Wikipedia*, https://en.wikipedia.org/wiki/FYIFV.
2. Jodi Kantor and David Streitfeld, "Inside Amazon: Wrestling Big Ideas in a Bruising Workplace," *New York Times*, August 15, 2015, https://www.nytimes.com/2015 /08/16/technology/inside-amazon-wrestling-big-ideas-in-a-bruising-workplace .html.
3. Ibid.
4. Ian McGugan, "How Buffett Believes Berkshire Can Avoid the ABCs of Business Decay," *Globe and Mail*, March 6, 2015, https://www.theglobeandmail.com/globe-investor /investment-ideas/how-buffett-believes-berkshire-can-avoid-business-decay/article 23342395/.

IDEA 9

1. Todd Bishop, "Amazon Go Is Finally a Go: Sensor-Infused Store Opens to the Public Monday, with No Checkout Lines," *GeekWire*, January 21, 2018.

IDEA 10

1. Ayse Birsel, "Why Elon Musk Spends 80 Percent of His Time on This 1 Activity," *Inc.*, July 21, 2017, https://www.inc.com/ayse-birsel/why-elon-musk-spends-80-percent -of-his-time-on-thi.html.
2. Ibid.

IDEA 11

1. Neal Ungerleider, "Free Shipping Is a Lie," *Fast Company*, November 2016.
2. Chris Matyszczyk, "Apple Exec Mocks Google Home and Amazon Echo," *CNET*, May 6, 2017.
3. Eugene Kim, "FedEx: Amazon Would Have to Spend 'Tens of Billions' to Compete with Us," *Business Insider*, March 16, 2016.
4. Jonathan Garber, "Foot Locker: We Aren't Afraid of Being Amazon'd," *Business Insider*, August 18, 2017.
5. Berkeley Lovelace, Jr., "Saks President on Artificial Intelligence: 'We Don't Need A.I. in Our Stores. We Have I,'" *CNBC*, January 12, 2018.
6. Jim Finkle, "What on Earth Is 'Cloud Computing'?" *Reuters*, September 25, 2008.
7. Staff, "Mark Hurd Says He Doesn't Worry 'So Much' About Amazon Web Services," *CNBC*, October 2, 2017.
8. Shira Ovide, "How Amazon's Bottomless Appetite Became Corporate America's Nightmare," *Bloomberg*, March 14, 2018, https://www.bloomberg.com/graphics

/2018-amazon-industry-displacement/?fbclid=IwAR3TX4ASdtzh3zlcT5NT-t_vJt87 QcXGkrVx01AJbMI7ex4iAvQ_NN9LIKM.

9. Max Nisen, "Jeff Bezos: 'Inventing and Pioneering Involves a Willingness to Be Misunderstood,'" *Business Insider*, January 7, 2013, https://www.businessinsider.com /bezos-pioneering-requires-being-misunderstood-2013-1.

10. Alan Deutschman, "Inside the Mind of Jeff Bezos," *Fast Company*, August 1, 2004 https://www.fastcompany.com/50106/inside-mind-jeff-bezos-5.

11. Ibid.

12. John Cook, "Jeff Bezos on Innovation: Amazon 'Willing to Be Misunderstood for Long Periods of Time,'" *GeekWire*, June 7, 2011, https://www.geekwire.com/2011 /amazons-bezos-innovation/.

IDEA 12

1. Kimberly Reuter, private interview with the author, 2015.

IDEA 13

1. Jeff Bezos, "2016 Letter to Shareholders," Amazon.com.

2. Mel Conway, "Conway's Law," Melconway.com, http://www.melconway.com/Home /Conways_Law.html.

3. Nigel Bevan, "Usability Issues in Web Site Design," April 1998, https://www.researchgate .net/publication/2428005_Usability_Issues_in_Web_Site_Design.

IDEA 14

1. *Quora*, "Does Amazon Give Any Award to Employees for Sending Patents?" answered May 29, 2015, https://www.quora.com/Does-Amazon-give-any-award-to -employees-for-sending-patents.

2. Jeff Bezos, "2013 Letter to Shareholders," Amazon.com, April 10, 2014.

3. Ibid.

4. Ibid.

5. Day One Staff, "Change for the Better: Why We Focus on Kaizen," *Amazon dayone blog*, Amazon.com, https://www.amazon.com/p/feature/7vgnru22nddw5jn.

6. Bruno Frey and Susanne Neckermann, "And the Winner Is . . .? The Motivating Power of Employee Awards," *Journal of Socio-Economics*, vol. 46, October 2013, pp. 66–77.

7. George Anders, "Inside Amazon's Idea Machine," *Forbes*, April 23, 2012.

8. Laura Stevens, "Jeff Wilke: The Amazon Chief Who Obsesses Over Consumers," *Wall Street Journal*, October 11, 2017.

IDEA 15

1. "Bezos on Innovation," *Bloomberg Businessweek*, April 16, 2008, https://www.bloomberg.com/news/articles/2008-04-16/bezos-on-innovation.

2. JP Mangalindan, "Amazon's Core? Frugality," *Fortune*, March 26, 2012, http://fortune.com/2012/03/26/amazons-core-frugality/.

3. Jeff Bezos, "1997 Letter to Shareholders," Amazon.com.

IDEA 16

1. Seth Clevenger, "Travelocity Founder Terry Jones Says Companies Must Innovate or Face Disruption," *Transport Topics*, January 24, 2018.
2. Maxwell Wessel, "Why Big Companies Can't Innovate," *Harvard Business Review*, September 27, 2012, https://hbr.org/2012/09/why-big-companies-cant-innovate.
3. Taylor Soper, "Amazon's Secrets of Invention: Jeff Bezos Explains How to Build an Innovative Team," *GeekWire*, May 17, 2016, https://www.geekwire.com/2016/amazons -secrets-invention-jeff-bezos-explains-build-innovative-team/.

IDEA 17

1. Jeff Bezos, "2015 Letter to Shareholders," Amazon.com.
2. *Interview: Amazon CEO Jeff Bezos*, YouTube video, 52:53, from *Business Insider's Ignition* 2014. Posted by *Business Insider*, December 15, 2014.
3. Ibid.
4. Bill Snyder, "Marc Andreessen: 'I'm Biased Toward People Who Never Give Up,'" *Inc.*, June 30, 2014, https://www.inc.com/bill-snyder/marc-andreesen-why-failure -is-overrated.html.

IDEA 18

1. Christian Sarkar, "The Four Horsemen: An Interview with Scott Galloway," *Marketing Journal*, October 20, 2017.
2. Jeff Bezos, "2011 Letter to Shareholders," Amazon.com.

IDEA 19

1. Warren Buffett. "1979 Letter to Shareholders," Berkshire Hathaway, http://www .berkshirehathaway.com/letters/1979.html.
2. Benedict Evans, "The Amazon Machine," December 12, 2017, www.ben-evans.com /benedictevans/2017/12/12/the-amazon-machine.

IDEA 20

1. Benedict Evans, "The Amazon Machine," December 12, 2017, www.ben-evans.com /benedictevans/2017/12/12/the-amazon-machine.
2. Ibid.
3. Ibid.

IDEA 21

1. Andrea James, "Amazon's Jeff Bezos on Kindle, Advertising, and Being Green," *Seattle-PI*, May 28, 2009.
2. Adam Lashinsky, "The Evolution of Jeff Bezos," *Forbes*, March 24, 2016.
3. Amazon, "Leadership Principles," *Amazon Jobs*, https://www.amazon.jobs/en /principles.
4. Bill Chappell and Laurel Wamsley, "Amazon Sets $15 Minimum Wage for U.S. Employees, Including Temps," *NPR*, October 2, 2018, https://www.npr.org/2018/10/02 /653597466/amazon-sets-15-minimum-wage-for-u-s-employees-including-temps.
5. Pete Pachal, "How Kodak Squandered Every Single Digital Opportunity It Had," *Mashable*, January 20, 2012.

IDEA 22

1. Marc Wulfraat, "Amazon Global Fulfillment Center Network," *MWPVL International*, August 2016, http://www.mwpvl.com/html/amazon_com.html.

IDEA 23

1. Jim Collins, "Best Beats First," *Inc.*, August 2000.

IDEA 25

1. Jim Collins, *Good to Great: Why Some Companies Make the Leap . . . and Others Don't*, HarperCollins, New York, 2001.
2. Jeff Bezos, "2014 Letter to Shareholders," Amazon.com.
3. Ibid.
4. Jeff Bezos, "2016 Letter to Shareholders," Amazon.com.
5. John Cook, "Jeff Bezos on Innovation," *GeekWire*, June 7, 2011.

IDEA 26

1. Spencer Soper, "Amazon Will Consider Opening up to 3,000 Cashierless Stores by 2021," September 19, 2018, https://www.bloomberg.com/news/articles/2018-09-19/amazon-is-said-to-plan-up-to-3-000-cashierless-stores-by-2021.

IDEA 27

1. "The Visa," *Seinfeld*, season 4, episode 15.
2. Amazon Press Center, "Wanted: Hundreds of Entrepreneurs to Start Businesses Delivering Amazon Packages," press release, June 28, 2018, https://press.aboutamazon.com/news-releases/news-release-details/wanted-hundreds-entrepreneurs-start-businesses-delivering-amazon.
3. Jeff Bezos, "2014 Letter to Shareholders," Amazon.com.
4. C. K. Prahalad and Gary Hamel, "The Core Competence of the Corporation," *Harvard Business Review*, May-June 1990, https://hbr.org/1990/05/the-core-competence-of-the-corporation.

IDEA 28

1. Adam Lashinsky, "Amazon's Jeff Bezos: The Ultimate Disrupter," *Fortune*, November 16, 2012, http://fortune.com/2012/11/16/amazons-jeff-bezos-the-ultimate-disrupter/.
2. Orit Gadiesh and James L. Gilbert, "How to Map Your Industry's Profit Pool," *Harvard Business Review*, May-June 1998.
3. "The Boring Company," https://www.boringcompany.com/faq/.

IDEA 29

1. Emily Glazier, Liz Hoffman, and Laura Stevens, "Next up for Amazon: Checking Accounts," *Wall Street Journal.* April 29, 2018.
2. Brian Deagon, "Amazon Price Target Hike Based on Savings from New Airline Fleet," *Investor's Business Daily*, June 16, 2016.

3. Orit Gadiesh and James L. Gilbert, "How to Map Your Industry's Profit Pool," *Harvard Business Review*, May-June 1998.

4. Alison Griswold, "A Dot-Com Era Deal with Amazon Marked the Beginning of the End for Toys R Us," *Quartz*, https://qz.com/1080389/a-dot-com-era-deal-with-amazon-marked-the-beginning-of-the-end-for-toys-r-us/.

5. Brian Deagon, "Amazon's Booming Apparel Business in Position to Pass Macy's, TJX," *Investor's Business Daily*, December 5, 2017.

IDEA 30

1. Peyton Whitely, "Computer Pioneer's Death Probed: Kildall Called Possible Victim of Homicide," *Seattle Times*, July 16, 1994.

2. Gary Kildall, *Computer Connections*, available at http://www.computerhistory.org/atchm/in-his-own-words-gary-kildall/.

3. Amazon, "AWS IoT Greengrass," Aws.Amazon.com, https://aws.amazon.com/greengrass.

4. Derrick Jayson, "Remember When Yahoo Turned Down $1 Million to Buy Google?" *Benzinga*, July 25, 2016.

IDEA 32

1. Jeff Bezos, "2017 Letter to Shareholders," Amazon.com.

IDEA 35

1. Amazon, *Introducing Amazon Go and the World's Most Advanced Shopping Technology*, YouTube video, December 5, 2016, https://www.youtube.com/watch?v=NrmMk1Myrxc&t=11s.

2. Nick Wingfield, "Inside Amazon Go: A Store of the Future," *New York Times*, January 21, 2018, https://www.nytimes.com/2018/01/21/technology/inside-amazon-go-a-store-of-the-future.html.

3. Ibid.

4. Elisabeth Leamy, "The Danger of Giving Your Child 'Smart Toys,'" *Washington Post*, September 29, 2017.

IDEA 36

1. "Secure by Design," *Wikipedia*, https://en.wikipedia.org/wiki/Secure_by_design.

2. House Committee on Commerce, Science and Transportation, "A 'Kill Chain' Analysis of the 2013 Target Data Breach," March 26, 2014.

3. Rick Dakin, "Target Kill Chain Analysis," *Coalfire* blog, May 7, 2014, https://www.coalfire.com/The-Coalfire-Blog/May-2014/Target-Kill-Chain-Analysis.

IDEA 37.

1. Samir Lakhani, "Things I Liked About Amazon," *Medium*, August 27, 2017.

IDEA 38

1. Nick Wingfield, "As Amazon Pushes Forward with Robots, Workers Find New Roles," *New York Times*, September 10, 2017.
2. Ibid.
3. Ibid.

IDEA 39

1. "Winchester Mystery House," *Wikipedia*, https://en.wikipedia.org/wiki/Winchester_Mystery_House.
2. Jacqueline Doherty, "Amazon.bomb," *Barron's*, May 31, 1999.
3. Christian Sarkar, "The Four Horsemen: An Interview with Scott Galloway," *Marketing Journal*, October 20, 2017.
4. Steve Yegge, "Stevey's Google Platforms Rant," October 12, 2011, https://plus.google.com/+RipRowan/posts/eVeouesvaVX.
5. Christopher Mims, "Why Do the Biggest Companies Keep Getting Bigger? It's How They Spend on Tech," *Wall Street Journal*, July 26, 2018, https://www.wsj.com/articles/why-do-the-biggest-companies-keep-getting-bigger-its-how-they-spend-on-tech-1532610001.

IDEA 41

1. James Cook, "Elon Musk: You Have No Idea How Close We Are to Killer Robots," *Business Insider*, November 7, 2014.
2. Steven Levy, "Inside Amazon's Artificial Intelligence Flywheel," *WIRED*, February 1, 2018, https://www.wired.com/story/amazon-artificial-intelligence-flywheel/.
3. Ray Dalio, Alex Rampell, and Sonal Chokshi, "Principles and Algorithms for Work and Life," *a16z Podcast*, April 21, 2018, https://a16z.com/2018/04/21/principles-dalio/.
4. Deloitte, *Artificial Intelligence Innovation Report 2018*, https://www2.deloitte.com/content/dam/Deloitte/ie/Documents/aboutdeloitte/ie-Artificial-Intelligence-Report-Deloitte.pdf.
5. Richard Feloni, "The World's Largest Hedge Fund Is Developing an Automated 'Coach' That Acts Like a Personal GPS for Decision-Making," *Business Insider*, September 25, 2017.
6. Jeff Bezos, "2016 Letter to Shareholders," *Amazon dayone blog*, April 17, 2017, https://blog.aboutamazon.com/company-news/2016-letter-to-shareholders.
7. Satya Nadella, and Greg Shaw, *Hit Refresh: The Quest to Rediscover Microsoft's Soul and Imagine a Better Future for Everyone*, Harper Business, New York, 2017, p. 210.

IDEA 42

1. Emmie Martin, "Jeff Bezos Hasn't Always Had the Golden Touch: Here's What the Amazon of Founder Was Doing in His 20s," *CNBC Make It*, August 2, 2017.
2. Jeff Bezos, *Regret Minimization Framework*, YouTube video, uploaded December 20, 2008, https://www.youtube.com/watch?v=jwG_qR6XmDQ.

3. Jeff Bezos, "2016 Letter to Shareholders," *Amazon dayone blog*, https://blog.about amazon.com/working-at-amazon/2016-letter-to-shareholders.

4. John Cook, "The Peculiar Traits of Great Amazon Leaders: Frugal, Innovative and Body Odor That Doesn't Smell Like Perfume," *GeekWire*, May 13, 2015.

IDEA 43

1. Greg Bensinger, "Amazon's Current Employees Raise the Bar for New Hires," *Wall Street Journal*, January 7, 2014.

2. Ibid.

3. Ashley Stewart, "Former Amazon 'Bar Raiser' Offers Insight into Hiring Process: What Job Seekers, Companies Can Learn," *Puget Sound Business Journal*, October 27, 2016.

4. Ibid.

5. Doug Tsuruoka, "Ex-Amazon Exec Details Company's Tough Hiring Policy," *Investor's Business Daily*, February 10, 2014.

IDEA 44

1. John Furrier, "How Andy Jassy Plans to Keep Amazon Web Services on Top of the Cloud," *Forbes*, November 27, 2017.

2. Gartner, "Magic Quadrant for Cloud Infrastructure as a Service, Worldwide," May 23, 2018.

3. "Michael Porter," *Wikiquote*, https://en.wikiquote.org/wiki/Michael_Porter.

4. Amazon, "What Is Amazon's Writing Culture?" LinkedIn article, no date, https://www.linkedin.com/feed/update/urn:li:activity:6423244366495776768.

5. Jeff Bezos, "2017 Letter to Shareholders," Amazon.com.

6. Greg Satell, "How IBM, Google and Amazon Innovate Differently," *Inc.*, October 14, 2018, https://www.inc.com/greg-satell/how-ibm-google-amazon-innovate-differently.html.

7. Jeff Bezos, "2017 Letter to Shareholders."

8. Emily Glazer, Laura Stevens, and AnnaMaria Andriotis, "Jeff Bezos and Jamie Dimon: Best of Frenemies," *Wall Street Journal*, January 5, 2019, https://www.wsj.com/articles/jeff-bezos-and-jamie-dimon-best-of-frenemies-11546664451.

IDEA 49

1. Jeff Bezos, "2004 Letter to Shareholders," Amazon.com, April 13, 2004, https://www.sec.gov/Archives/edgar/data/1018724/000119312505070440/dex991.htm.

2. Henry Blodget, "Amazon's Letter to Shareholders Should Inspire Every Company in America," *Business Insider*, April 14, 2013.

3. Morgan Housel, "The 20 Smartest Things Jeff Bezos Has Ever Said," *Motley Fool*, September 9, 2013.

4. HBR IdeaCast, "Jeff Bezos on Leading for the Long-Term at Amazon," *HBR Blog Network*, January 3, 2013.

5. Jeff Bezos, "2004 Letter to Shareholders," Amazon.com, April 13, 2004.
6. Jeff Bezos, "2012 Letter to Shareholders," Amazon.com, April 12, 2012.

IDEA 50

1. Ian McGugan, "How Buffett Believes Berkshire Can Avoid the ABCs of Business Decay," *Globe and Mail*, March 6, 2015, updated May 12, 2018, https://www.theglobe andmail.com/globe-investor/investment-ideas/how-buffett-believes-berkshire-can -avoid-business-decay/article23342395/.
2. Lily Hay Newman, "Equifax Officially Has No Excuse," *WIRED*, September 14, 2017.

INDEX

ABOUT THE AUTHOR

John Rossman was an executive at Amazon, where he launched and scaled the Marketplace business, which now accounts for more than 50 percent of all units sold at Amazon.com. He also led the enterprise services business, with responsibilities for Target.com, the NBA, Toys R Us, and other top brands.

He now heads Rossman Partners, a niche business advisory firm that helps clients succeed and thrive in the digital era. Rossman has worked with the Gates Foundation, Microsoft, Nordstrom, T-Mobile, Walmart, and many others, and he serves as a board advisor to several executive teams. He is highly sought after for expert commentary regarding Amazon by global news media, such as the *New York Times*, CNBC, and Bloomberg, among others.

For more information, visit think-like-amazon.com